PRESENT CONDUCT AND FUTURE DELINQUENCY

First Report of the Cambridge Study in Delinquent Development

by

D. J. West

HEINEMANN

LONDON

Heinemann Educational Books Ltd
LONDON EDINBURGH MELBOURNE TORONTO
AUCKLAND SINGAPORE JOHANNESBURG
HONG KONG NAIROBI IBADAN

SBN 435 82936 X

© D. J. West 1969

First published 1969

Publisher's note: This series is continuous with the Cambridge Studies in Criminology, Volumes I to XIX, published by Macmillan & Co, London

Published by
Heinemann Educational Books Ltd
48 Charles Street, London W1X 8AH

Printed in Great Britain by
Morrison and Gibb Ltd, London and Edinburgh

Table of Contents

	Page
Foreword *by Leon Radzinowicz*	vii
Preface	x

I. The Theme of the Inquiry   1
1. *The Problem Defined* · 2. *Advantages and Difficulties of a Prospective Study* · 3. *Selecting Topics of Importance* · 4. *Sources of Information* · 5. *Recording Information from Home Interviews*

II. A Grey Outlook   15
1. *The Background of the Study:* (a) *The Neighbourhood under Survey*, (b) *Socio-economic Status of the Study Sample*, (c) *Family Size*, (d) *Neighbourhood Characteristics*, (e) *The Housing Problem*, (f) *Stability and Tradition*, (g) *Summing up the Background* · 2. *The Boys in their Schools:* (a) *Characteristics of the Schools*, (b) *The Boys' Intelligence and Attainment*, (c) *The Boys' Physical Growth*, (d) *A Glimpse of Commencing Delinquency*

III. Assessing Conduct and Personality at Age Eight   38
1. *Teachers' Ratings of Conduct in School* · 2. *Conduct Disorder Rated by P.S.Ws* · 3. *A Combined Assessment of Boys' Conduct* · 4. *Assessments of Neurotic Tendency:* (a) *Psychological Testing*, (b) *Interview Reports of Nervous Disturbance in Boys* · 5. *Psychomotor Performance:* (a) *The Porteus Mazes*, (b) *The Gibson Spiral Maze*, (c) *The Tapping Test*, (d) *The Body Sway Test*, (e) *Combined Psychomotor Scores* · 6. *Popularity among Classmates* · 7. *Summing up the Picture at Age Eight* · 8. *Identifying Boys at Special Risk of Delinquency*

IV. Assessing Adversities of Home Background   60
1. *Broken Homes, Separations and Child Neglect* · 2. *Working Mothers* · 3. *Financial Hardship and Social Handicap* · 4. *Parental Disharmony* · 5. *Parental Mis-*

v

management and its Relation to Poor Conduct in Boys: (a) *Six items of Parental Behaviour,* (b) *Relationships between Upbringing and Conduct at different Social Levels* · 6. *Parental Attitude and Quality of Discipline* · 7. *Parental Attitude and Discipline in relation to Boys' Conduct* · 8. *Parental Attitudes to Child-Rearing as revealed by Questionnaire Responses* · 9. *Physical and Mental Health of Parents:* (a) *P.S.Ws' Assessments,* (b) *A Questionnaire Assessment of Neuroticism in Mothers* · 10. *Parental Health and Temperament and Sons' Behaviour* · 11. *Summing up the Effects of Home Background*

V. **Some Special Criminogenic Factors**   99
1. *Criminality in the Family:* (a) *The Incidence of Criminal Convictions,* (b) *The Significance of Criminal Convictions* · 2. *Dullness, Retardation and Misconduct:* (a) *Duller Boys are more Trouble-prone,* (b) *Differential Effects according to Social and Intellectual Level* · 3. *Conduct Incongruous with Background* · 4. *Brain Damage and Subsequent Misconduct:* (a) *The Background of the Theory,* (b) *The Present Investigation,* (c) *The Present Findings*

VI. **An Over-View of the Factors in Interaction**   116

VII. **Pitfalls of Interpretation**   124
1. *Differences between Raters* · 2. *The Dangers of Contaminated Measures* · 3. *Negative Halo* · 4. *Absence or Unreliability of Information in Particular Segments of the Sample*

VIII. **A Tentative Summing up and Some Suggestions for Further Study**   135
1. *The Incidence of Personal and Social Problems* · 2. *Reliability of Social Assessments* · 3. *The Concomitants of Early Misconduct*

Appendices   150

List of References   199

Index   205

Foreword

by Leon Radzinowicz

This research is in the great tradition of explorations of the springs of delinquency. Although on a smaller scale, it will ultimately claim a place alongside such classics as the works of Robins, the Gluecks and the McCords. All too little of the sort has been attempted in England.

It has been a complex undertaking. Normal groups of schoolboys are being followed through from the age of eight to that of sixteen, by which time the delinquent minority amongst them should have revealed themselves and their characteristics should have become apparent. They and their families are being repeatedly assessed by a variety of means. The purpose has been not only to identify the factors associated with delinquency, either at the time or later, but to discover how they rank in importance.

Dr West takes up a whole range of the generalizations so common in discussions of delinquency. He explores rigorously both popular and scientific 'explanations', bringing them down to earth and examining them in a technically sophisticated way. Yet he never loses sight of the fact that he is dealing with reality, with the wholeness of human life which does not lend itself to division. What he finds is a complex of personal inadequacies and external handicaps, reinforcing each other. Of special interest in a study primarily concerned with the individual characteristics which distinguish juvenile delinquents, is the demonstration of the extent to which troublesome boys, together with many other family problems, are concentrated amongst the very poorest. It may be that the next stage of the inquiry will go some way to answering the question of whether these problems spring from poverty or whether poverty itself merely reflects an underlying individual inadequacy. But, as Dr West says, rather than trying to answer the conundrum 'which comes first?' it may be more useful to ask at what point to break into the vicious circle.

Much past research on delinquency has been confined to such easily accessible groups as young offenders in institutions. A study of the incidence of factors like broken homes, backwardness and parental criminality within a normal group provides a more realistic starting-point for judging the significance of these factors among delinquent minorities. But both in choosing to start with a normal group of boys and in working with them, their families and their schools in the open, Dr West and his team have faced formidable complications. Some of the difficulties have been less than might have been anticipated. The boys themselves, and in most cases the parents, have proved highly co-operative. Amongst other things it has been possible to see fathers, so often omitted from this type of study.

Where difficulties have arisen they have been turned to good account: they are described with a frankness and detail which should be of value to all concerned in carrying out or interpreting social surveys on such topics. The facts that the study has lasted over a considerable period, that tests and assessments have been made at intervals and by different people, that a large number of factors have been considered: all these have contributed to a critical approach. Dr West points out, for example, that it is much more difficult than is generally acknowledged to obtain reliable assessments of the backgrounds of potential delinquents, and he points out why. The study reveals the lack of tests of personality and behaviour adequately standardized on a British population, and it attempts to find means of supplying some. It emphasises the need to translate inventories into language that can be understood by poorer working-class families. It explores the significance of inadequate response, or of failure to respond at all.

Much of this is relevant not only to research but to social policy and social planning. Dr West found that many of the boys whose behaviour and problems might have warranted special supervision or attention were not receiving it, and it was not necessarily the worst cases who got financial help. The situation calls not only for legislation but for more resources and better understanding of where and how they should be used. On this, too, his findings so far may provide pointers.

It must be remembered, however, that 'the end is not yet'. This book is no more than a preliminary study, dealing only with the first stages of the research and with the characteristics and behaviour of the boys only in the first two or three years. The full significance of the findings will not become apparent until the project is completed and it can be seen how far characteristics and patterns of behaviour remain constant, whether the factors most strongly associated with very early delinquency are the same as those linked with delinquency in adolescence. It may be that it would be profitable to trace the links even into adult life.

In spite of the complex and sometimes technical nature of his subject, Dr West writes simply, clearly and directly. His book makes fascinating reading and should have an appeal far beyond specialist circles.

I would like to more than echo Dr West's thanks. He has had a team of devoted collaborators. He has been most fortunate in the Reviewing and Consultative Committee, whose Chairman, Dr J. W. B. Douglas, has been our wise counsellor throughout. And we are all indebted to the schools and local authorities, who have ungrudgingly smoothed the way in an enterprise that has depended upon the co-operation of so many.

An important stage in an imaginative venture, which began seven years ago, has now come to an end. It is good to know that much material has already been gathered for the second volume of what I hope will come to be known as the Cambridge Study in Delinquent Development.

Institute of Criminology,
University of Cambridge.
February, 1969.

Past and Present Members of the Consultative and Advisory Committee

J. W. B. Douglas, B.A., B.Sc., B.M., B.Ch. (Chairman), *Director, Medical Research Council Unit, London School of Economics*; J. B. Howard, *formerly Home Office Children's Department*; the late Lady Hilda Lewis, M.D., F.R.C.P.; T. S. Lodge, C.B.E., *Home Office Research Unit*; D. H. Morrell, *Home Office Children's Department*; Professor J. N. Morris, D.Sc., D.P.H., F.R.C.P., *Social Medicine Research Unit, London Hospital*; R. L. Morrison, M.A., Ed.B., *formerly Institute of Criminology*; Miss J. J. Nunn, C.B.E., *formerly Home Office Children's Department*; Professor L. Radzinowicz, *Director, Institute of Criminology*; Peter D. Scott, M.A., M.D., D.P.M., *Institute of Psychiatry, University of London*; Professor J. Tizard, M.A., B.Litt., Ph.D., *Institute of Education, University of London*.

Past and Present Research Officers responsible for the Project

Joan Deales, A.A.P.S.W.; Joan Court, A.A.P.S.W., S.R.N., M.S.W. (Smith); P. J. Didcot, B.A., Dip.Crim.; Susan Ellis, B.A.; Janet Finney, B.Sc., A.I.M.S.W.; H. B. Gibson, B.Sc., Dip.Psych., Ph.D.; Gwen Gundry; Ruth Hanson, B.A.; Hilary King, B.A., A.I.M.S.W.; T. Knox, M.A.; Eve Road, A.A.P.S.W.; Ruth Williams, B.A.; D. J. West, M.D., Ph.D., D.P.M.

Author's Preface

In so far as he instigated the inquiry, and the account is written in his words, this book has a single author; but as the list of research officers and consultants reveals, in reality it is the product of the labour and thought of a whole team. From the beginning of the Study Dr H. B. Gibson has been responsible for the design of the psychological methods of inquiry and for the analysis of the entire data. Joan Court, Eve Road, and at a later stage Joan Beales, were the three psychiatric social workers who carried out the original interviews with parents. Dr C. L. E. H. Sharp, Schools Medical Officer at Bedford, was the person who first suggested, back in 1960, that the Institute of Criminology should sponsor a long-term study of normal young children with the ultimate object of identifying the characteristics of the minority who become delinquent in later years. Professor Radzinowicz at once foresaw, correctly, that the research workers embarking upon such a project would be grey-haired before it was finished, but nevertheless he lent his support. The Home Office has provided the necessary finance, and Mr T. S. Lodge, Director of the Home Office Research Unit, and his colleagues have given much-needed advice and encouragement. Happily these indispensable supports continue, and it is hoped that the completion of the project, and the sequel to this preliminary report, will not be too long delayed.

So many social agencies have contributed to the research by supplying information, providing facilities, or allowing access to records, that it is impossible to mention them all. The citations in the text must be read as sincere and grateful acknowledgement. In the preparation of the text, the author is particularly indebted to Gwen Gundry, who has loyally worked through a succession of drafts, and to Dr Roger Hood, of the Institute of Criminology, who read the manuscript and made most helpful criticisms. Finally, a special word of thanks to Dr J. W. B. Douglas, Chairman of the Advisory Committee, who has been a most willing and knowledgeable adviser and friend, and to his colleagues on the Committee, who have been very ready with all kinds of help.

The boys and their families deserve a separate note of thanks. Without their quite remarkably persistent, though unrewarded, participation there would have been no research to report.

List of Tables

I. The Theme of the Inquiry

Appendix

I A (1)	Percentage Frequencies of Teachers' use of Behavioural Categories	151

II. A Grey Outlook

II (1)	Socio-Economic Status in the Study Sample Compared with the National Census	18
II (2)	Distribution of Scores on Attainment and Intelligence Tests in Terms of Percentile Rank	30
II (3)	Distribution of Heights and Weights of Boys in Terms of Percentile Rank	33

Appendices

II A (1)	Constitution of Sample by Age and School attended when admitted to the Study	157
II B (1)	Percentage of Families of Specified Size	160
II B (2)	Socio-Economic Class by Number of Children in Family	160
II C (1)	Reading Ability at Age 14½ compared with a National Sample	161
II D (1)	Socio-Economic Class by Height/Weight Ratio	162
II D (2)	Boys' Conduct (combined P.S.Ws' and Teachers' Ratings) against Body Build	162

III. Assessing Conduct and Personality at Age Eight

III (1)	Boys' Conduct (Combined Ratings) against Level of Family Income	44
III (2)	Conduct against Personality Inventory Rating	45
III (3)	Teachers' Ratings of Boys' Conduct against P.S.Ws' Ratings of Nervous Disturbance in Boys	47
III (4)	Psychomotor Performance (Combined score of four tests) against Boys' Conduct (Combined Ratings of P.S.Ws and Teachers)	51

III (5)	Boys' Conduct against Boys' Popularity among Peers	53
III (6)	Behaviour Difficulties in Boys (at about age 12) reported to social workers against the Acting-out Classification	56
III (7)	Relationships of Boys Classed as 'Acting-out' to other Variables	57

Appendices

III A (1)	Derivation of the Combined Scale of Boys' Conduct	165
III C (1)	P.S.Ws' Nervous Disturbance Ratings against Parents Interviewed Separately	168
III C (2)	Incidence of Nervous Boys against P.S.Ws' Impression of Mothers' Intelligence	169
III C (3)	P.S.Ws' Ratings of Nervous Disturbance in Boys against Boys' Reading Ability	169
III C (4)	Incidence of Severe Nervous Disturbance of Boys in relation to some Background Variables	170

IV. Assessing Adversities of Home Background

IV (1)	Boys' Conduct against Various Home Adversities	63
IV (2)	Teachers' Rating of Boys' Conduct against Working Mothers	66
IV (3)	Social Handicap against Boys' Conduct (Combined Ratings of P.S.Ws and Teachers)	69
IV (4)	Inter-correlations between six assessments of Parental Child-Rearing Behaviour and Teachers' Ratings of Poor Conduct at School	75
IV (5)	Boys' Conduct against Rating 'Physical Neglect' by Income Level	76
IV (6)	Maternal Attitude and Discipline related to three degrees of Social Handicap	83
IV (7)	Paternal Attitude and Discipline related to three degrees of Social Handicap	84
IV (8)	Boys' Conduct against Maternal Attitude	85
IV (9)	Inventory Ratings of Parental Attitude against Teachers' Rating of Boys' Conduct	88
IV (10)	Inter-correlations between six assessments of Parents' Mental and Physical Health	92
IV (11)	Association between Parental Health and Social Handicap	92

Appendices

IV A (1)	Correlations between P.S.Ws' Ratings of Boy Physically Neglected with certain other Variables of Adversity	172
IV B (1)	Association between Parental Child-Rearing Methods and Inadequate Income	173
IV D (1)	Acting Out Tendency in Boys related to Parental Attitude and Discipline at three Levels of Family Income	177
IV E (1)	Numbers of completed Parental Attitude Inventories against Socio-Educational Status of Mother	182
IV E (2)	Questionnaire Scores of Maternal Authoritarianism against P.S.W. Ratings of Maternal Discipline	182
IV E (3)	Questionnaire Scores of Maternal Over-concern and Under-concern against P.S.W. Ratings of Maternal Attitude, Quality of Discipline and Vigilance	182
IV E (4)	Questionnaire Scores of Fathers' Authoritarianism against P.S.W. Ratings of Fathers' Discipline	183
IV F (1)	Mothers' Neuroticism, according to Health Questionnaire Scores, against Mothers' Nervous Tendency according to P.S.Ws' Ratings	186
IV F (2)	P.S.Ws' Ratings of Nervous Disturbance in Boys against P.S.Ws' Ratings of Nervousness in Mothers	188
IV F (3)	P.S.Ws' Ratings of Nervous Disturbance in Boys against Health Questionnaire Scores of Neuroticism in Mothers	188
IV F (4)	Neuroticism of Mother, assessed by Health Questionnaire Scores against Boy's Conduct, on the Ratings of P.S.Ws and Teachers combined	189

V. Some Special Criminogenic Factors

V (1)	Numbers of Boys with one or more Relative Convicted	100
V (2)	Verbal Comprehension against Boys' Conduct	103
V (3)	Various Parental Attributes in Groups of Early Delinquents and Matching Non-Delinquents	106

Appendices

V A (1)	Variation in Proportion of Boys with a Convicted Father according to Father's Date of Birth	190
V C (1)	Confinement Abnormality in Hospital Births against Teachers' Ratings of Conduct	192

V C (2) Social Circumstances, Birth Order and Abnormality
          of Confinement in Hospital Births   193

VI. An Over-View of the Factors in Interaction

Appendices

VI A (1) Inter-correlational Matrix of Thirty-seven Major
          Variables   196
VI A (2) Loadings of the Thirty-seven Major Variables on
          the two Principal Components of the Correlational
          Matrix   198

VII. Pitfalls of Interpretation

VII (1) Associations between having a Convicted Father
         and certain Objective Variables   127
VII (2) Associations between having a Convicted Father and
         other Variables   128

List of Figures

II. A Grey Outlook

II (1) Diagram of Study Neighbourhood sub-divided into Wards, showing population densities and positions of Primary Schools — 16

IV. Assessing Adversities of Home Background

IV (1) Relationship between Boys' Conduct (combined ratings) and Parents' Marriage at three Levels of Social Handicap — 71

Appendices

IV C (1) Relationships between Parental Vigilance and Mean Reading Quotient of Boys in three sub-samples of Different Income Level — 174
IV C (2) Relationships between Parental Interest in Education and Mean Reading Quotients in Boys, in three sub-samples of Different Income Level — 175
IV C (3) Parents Uninterested in Boy's Education against Boy's Conduct at three Levels of Income — 176
IV F (1) Mothers' Neuroticism, according to Health Questionnaire Scores against 'Mother has had Psychiatric Treatment' — 187

V. Some Special Criminogenic Factors

Appendices

V B (1) Boys' Intelligence Below Average (i.e. Matrices I.Q. <100. N=193) against Combined Ratings of Conduct at three Levels of Social Handicap — 191
V C (1) Percentage of Abnormal Births among Boys born in Hospital — 194

VI. An Over-view of the Factors in Interaction

VI (1) Schematic Illustration of Three Variables in Relation to each other and to the First Principal Component — 118

VI (2) Loadings of the items of the Correlational Analysis on two Principal Components 120

VII. Pitfalls of Interpretation

VII (1) Schematic Representation of some possible Interactions of various Sources of Information in Relation to assessments of Boys and Parents 130

I
The Theme of the Inquiry

1. *The Problem Defined*

This book describes the first stage of a long-term study of the onset and development of juvenile delinquency and behaviour problems among normal schoolboys in a densely populated, working-class, urban district. Four hundred and eleven boys were recruited[1] during their fourth year at school, when they were 8 to 9 years of age. The boys' progress is being followed up to school leaving age or later. The purpose of the research is to trace the influence of community, family and individual factors, as seen at this early age, upon personality, performance and social adjustment in later years.

In spite of the great number of published reports and the enormous public interest in the matter the problem of juvenile delinquency remains one on which experts differ sharply. The most glaring division occurs between those who regard juvenile misbehaviour as a sign of personal maladjustment, and those who see it as a normal and natural response to contemporary social circumstances. The former theorists tend to look for defects either in the individual delinquent himself (as in the theory that much restlessness and misconduct results from sub-clinical brain damage) or in the individual home (as in the theory that inadequate maternal care in the earliest formative years leads to permanent distortion of character). The social theorists, on the other hand, point to extraneous influences, such as the burgeoning of the penal bureaucracy with its urge to apply labels, controls and statistics to naughty boys, or the effect of increased leisure in affording time for mischief, or the special opportunities and temptations to steal in a newly affluent, money-mad society. The truth cannot lie in either one or other, but rather in various combinations and interactions of both personal and social influences; but the question of the relative importance of these contributory elements provides scope for controversy, and hence for investigation.

The present research was designed not so much to explore new factors, as to assess the rival claims of such commonly cited influences as economic hardship, poor discipline or inadequate mothering. The aim was to collect information on a large number of items, all of them said to have relevance to the development of juvenile delinquency, and to see, in the event, which items, or which combinations of items, would prove to be the clearest determinants of future delinquency. The design of the Study precluded consideration of social influences that have become universal, such as television. In order to have some basis of assessment the factors under scrutiny had to be such as to weigh more heavily on some boys than on others.

Modern researchers favour the use of a rigorous system of inquiry in which hypotheses are set forth at the outset, and the whole effort is concentrated upon answering questions formulated in advance, no other questions being admissible. Any one of an infinite number of possible effects of chance might otherwise be falsely interpreted, after the event, as evidence for some causal relationship that nobody had thought of before. For example, an unexpected juxtaposition of bad behaviour and blue eyes in a sample of children might lead the unwary into claiming evidence for the existence of some hereditary factor, manifest in both eye colour and bad behaviour. Unless previous inquiry had suggested such a connection sufficiently strongly for this to have been incorporated as an hypothesis for testing, the observation has little scientific value, except as a lead for further research.

This methodological precaution has particular relevance to surveys which cannot be easily replicated. On the other hand, too slavish a following of the rule curtails freedom to search for the unexpected. In a research such as this, built around the availability of a sample that has cost a great deal of money and effort to assemble, it is desirable to collect information on as many points as possible while the opportunity presents, without having too close a regard for specific hypotheses. For example, we included measures of height and weight among the data collected about the boys, justified, perhaps, by the argument that other workers had already found relationships between physique and delinquency, and so provided some testable predictions. However, the real reason for the inclusion of these and many other measures was not so much to confirm an already known association as to see how these particular measures stood in relation to other variables also known to have a connection with delinquency. In other words, by collecting data on many different points one has the opportunity to observe patterns of relationships between groups of variables that would not otherwise be known or predictable. This is especially important in delinquency research, where clusters of adverse factors, rather than any one acting in isolation, appear to be the true determinants of bad behaviour. It also has the advantage of enabling one to allow for intervening variables in the interpretation of statistical associations. Thus one can ask such questions as how far the known association between large families and high incidence of delinquency is due to number of siblings, low income, overcrowded homes, or parental neglect. Unless one has information about all these simultaneously, one could not begin to answer such a question. Hence the value of collecting a wide range of data.

The principle of formulating hypotheses in advance has not been lost sight of altogether. The selection of points of inquiry, such as the parents' methods of discipline, the presence of criminality in older members of the family, and the boys' behaviour in class, were naturally determined by current hypotheses as to the background factors most relevant to the genesis of juvenile delinquency. We did not in fact formulate detailed predictions as to the relative importance of these factors, or the way they might interact to produce particularly potent combinations. It was thought better, in the first instance, simply to examine and describe what was observed, while the children were young. The associations which emerged, particularly the connections between background factors and bad behaviour at this age, could then be used for making predictions as to what is likely to be of importance in the long run. These predictions will be tested with reference to the boys' actual development, as recorded in the later stage of the research. This report is concerned with the first round of data collection, obtained for the most part when the boys were around 9 years of age. These data have been frozen (in the form of closed case folders and completed entries on punch cards) so that they cannot be altered or affected by subsequent observations,[2] and can therefore be used legitimately for testing predictions.

2. *Advantages and Difficulties of a Prospective Study*

The long-term prospective survey of a normal population (in this instance following a group of boys over a period of eight years of development from childhood to adolescence) has a number of theoretical advantages over the more usual kinds of research, but it also involves some serious practical problems, one of which is that it will not be finished for several years. This book recounts what has so far been done, and describes what is intended in future, but the real fruits of the work are yet to come. Some indications of what may be expected can be described, and certain by-products of the main effort have already yielded results, but the main focus of interest of this first progress report must be the story of the beginnings of a plan of research, the methods used, and the difficulties so far encountered. A frank description of this kind has value for those who need to know what research in this field involves, and may also be of help to those whose chief interest lies in evaluating the conclusions of research surveys.

Many theorists argue that juvenile offences are governed less by accidental temptations of the moment than by a temperamental predisposition to anti-social behaviour which is determined either by hereditary factors or by psychological experiences during infancy and early childhood. If they are right, it should be possible, by examining young children who have not yet reached the age for Court appearances, to identify the potential offenders, and to specify what are the characteristics of the youngster with a special liability to delinquency in their future careers.

Most of the evidence on which the psychological theories of delinquency rest falls short of this ideal. Usually, deductions are made from retrospective studies in which the histories of established delinquents are contrasted with those of a control group of individuals of similar age but free from convictions. Such studies have a number of intrinsic weaknesses. In the first place, it is not very easy to know to what extent the aggressive attitudes and other personality disturbances found among established delinquents may be the consequence of being caught, punished and labelled social pariahs. In the second place, the attitudes of parents and others are naturally changed by appearances in Court, and they may consequently call to mind difficulties and disturbances in a child's past which would have been passed over and forgotten had he not got into trouble. Certain commonly held presumptions about the causes of delinquency (for instance that early separation of mother and child has a deleterious effect upon subsequent behaviour) may be supported by false evidence if the mothers of delinquents are prone to remember and dwell upon such events more than the mothers of non-delinquents.

Another difficulty about the use of contrasting groups of established delinquents and confirmed non-delinquents is that one may be comparing two extremes. For purposes of prevention, especially, the borderline cases who might go one way or the other at slight provocation have a special interest. Yet another difficulty concerns the way juvenile offenders become official delinquents. Every stage of the process, from an offence being noticed, to the offender being apprehended, cautioned or finally brought to court, convicted and committed to an institution, may come about that much more readily if it is common knowledge that the boy involved is from a bad home and might be better off away from it. Thus, by a process of selection that tends to produce spurious confirmation of one's preconceptions, bad homes and other factors credited by contemporary theory with a causal role, may be over-represented among official delinquents for reasons that have little to do with the real causes of juvenile misbehaviour.

The present project was undertaken because it was thought that a particularly good way to secure valid evidence about the origins of delinquency would be by means of a long-term study in which a sample of normal children could be examined while young and their subsequent careers—delinquent or otherwise—followed through in some detail. At the end of the follow-up period the data about the children and their families, collected in earlier years, could then be related to actual outcome at adolescence. Provided the information was properly recorded in the first instance, there would be no opportunity for knowledge of subsequent delinquency to bias the assessments of the children. The time span covered by a research of this nature is generally too long for any single individual to assume responsibility for carrying it through from first to last, but in this instance continuity was assured by the inclusion of the study in the research programme of the Institute of Criminology.

The usual research method of comparing groups of delinquents with control groups matched for such factors as education and social class certainly highlights contrasts that might otherwise be missed, but it has the result of masking the effect of the interaction between factors which occurs in a natural setting. By taking an unselected group of normal children, and studying the whole range of natural variation one has the chance to assess more realistically the relative importance of various background factors in the genesis of delinquency as they operate together in real life. Furthermore, by investigating on these lines, one finds out the actual incidence in a particular segment of the community of the different kinds of personal and social handicap which are believed to favour delinquency. Still more important, it becomes possible to view delinquent developments in proper perspective, as one among a number of possible forms of social maladjustment, and perhaps to elucidate what makes individuals subjected to similar adversities show different forms of maladjustment.

Practical considerations ruled out the ideal method of starting with a sample of babies. As a compromise, the study began with children of 8 to 9 years of age. Since the method involved taking an unselected group, the sample had to be large enough for the delinquent minority to be of sufficient size to compare meaningfully with the non-delinquent majority. For this reason, it was decided to study boys only, and to draw the sample from a working-class urban area, so that the proportion of delinquents would be substantial. A choice had to be made between a study based solely upon social records and group tests, in which case thousands of boys could have been included, or a study of a more personal kind, which could include interviews and home visits. The latter course was chosen, which meant that the size of the sample had to be limited to about four hundred boys.

These practical decisions had far-reaching consequences upon the character of the inquiry, and it must be admitted that not all of them were anticipated. The selection of a working-class neighbourhood with a substantial slum element determined the kind of social problems encountered. A survey in a middle class residential area would undoubtedly have presented a different range of behaviour originating in different ways. The limited number of boys in the sample precluded inquiry into influences confined to very small minorities (such as belonging to a coloured race, or having a serious physical handicap), but at the same time the number was too large to permit either the carrying out or the reporting of protracted case studies, such as would be required for a psycho-analytic approach. In effect, the level of the social background inquiry was essentially similar to what one might expect of an experienced probation officer assessing a home for the purpose of advising the juvenile court, or an experienced social worker doing the same task for a child guidance clinic.

Since the work began, many other practical considerations have arisen which have had effects upon the course of the inquiry. The focus of concern of those engaged upon the project has shifted from one pressing problem to another as the work has progressed through successive stages. During the stage of planning, the chief preoccupation was with working out a compromise between the ideal requirements for research, and practical propositions that would not be prohibitively long-term and expensive to execute. After the plan had been agreed upon by the Institute of Criminology, and received the support of the Home Office, then came the phase of negotiation with local authorities for facilities to put it into operation. At this stage concern centred on the delays and curtailments due to restrictions imposed on the methods of recruiting the sample, and on the scope of the inquiry in which the children were allowed to participate. Then came the time when the main anxiety was the incompleteness of the sample, due to the high proportion of families who failed to respond to requests for interviews. Later, questions of interviewer bias in the collection and recording of information about the families took up more time than anything else. When the first batch of data had finally been coded and transferred to punch cards, and so became available for scrutiny, attention transferred to the problem of putting it into a form suitable for computer analyses. When, after the usual snags and delays, thousands of cross tabulations and correlations finally emerged, the major difficulty became that of deciphering their significance and relating them back to the real-life situation. No doubt, as the research continues, different problems will come into sharper focus. For instance, at one moment, proposed changes in the law governing juvenile courts threatened to alter the system of recording juvenile offences, and thus to deprive the research of the chief source of information about delinquency. Readers of reports on completed projects are usually shielded from these shifts of concern, which weigh heavily upon the workers while they struggle to fulfil a research design. It is worth emphasizing, however, that especially in long-term research of this kind, investigators have an imperfect control over the march of events. The initial design and the final execution are inevitably separated by many unforeseen contingencies which force the workers to make the best compromise they can between the needs of the research plan and the practical difficulties or limitations encountered.

If the end is achieved, this survey will be virtually unique of its kind, at least in England. Of previous long-term surveys of offenders, perhaps the best known are two Boston projects, the Gluecks' (1950) survey of the careers of 500 delinquents and non-delinquents, and the McCords' (1959) follow-up of boys from the Cambridge-Somerville Youth Project. More recently, Lee Robins (1966) of St Louis, Missouri, has published the results of a survey of 500 persons originally seen thirty years previously at a child guidance clinic on account of deviant behaviour. At the time of writing, an important English study is in progress under the direction of Dr J. W. B. Douglas, in which a national sample of children, all born in the same week, are being followed up and their juvenile delinquency records traced (1964). However, our own Study is probably the first to combine the following features: delinquency as the focus of interest; use of a cohort of unselected, normal children; and observations (including interviews) repeated over a substantial span of time. In previous long-term studies, either the sample was artificially weighted with delinquents or potential delinquents (as in the Gluecks' and the McCords' surveys) or if, as in Douglas' work, a normal sample was under scrutiny, data have been limited to official records and reports from agencies, without benefit of direct observation of individuals.

3. *Selecting Topics of Importance*

The main consideration in selecting items for investigation was the importance and relevance assigned to them in contemporary criminological literature. Many topics of potential interest had to be ignored, however, because the time and labour available was limited, because some questions could not be asked of parents without causing offence, and because the limited expressive capacity of children of this age, and the education authorities' veto on personal questions, severely restricted the information obtainable from the boys themselves.

Basic social information, such as the household membership, the parents' financial circumstances, occupations and educational background, the family's accommodation and style of living, and the incidence of criminal convictions among parents and older siblings, was a first essential, and great efforts were made to obtain such data on every case. Where interviews were refused by parents, the necessary information was usually available at social agencies. Attempts to assess more personal aspects of the boys' home backgrounds depended upon extended and repeated interviews with the co-operating parents. The topics of inquiry included the mental and physical health of each parent, their attitudes to the boy (normal and loving or disturbed in one way or another) their system of discipline, their consistency or otherwise, their attitudes to child rearing, and their relations towards each other. Topics concerning the boys themselves included their present conduct in class and at home (as reported by teachers and parents), their intelligence and educational attainment, their performance on tests of 'personality', their nervous symptoms, if present, and any history of physical difficulties at birth which might have led to brain damage.

During this first stage the scope of the inquiry was made as wide as possible, in order to include a range of presumptively criminogenic factors representing biological, social and psychological influences. Since any one of these topics might be thought more than enough for one modest research team to handle, it will be clear that to cover such a wide field the investigators had to use the most economical methods possible, and at times to resort to some rather rough-and-ready impressionistic judgements. The details of the methods used, and the checks on their reliability, are described in subsequent chapters.

The results of this first phase of the Study will become fully meaningful only when the boys' future progress and delinquent careers become known. Meantime they can be looked at from two points of view. First, the incidence of, and inter-relationships between, various supposedly criminogenic factors, as seen in a normal population, have considerable intrinsic interest. One wants to know, for example, how common are such adversities as missing fathers, rejecting mothers and criminal relatives, and whether these are features widespread among a working-class neighbourhood or whether they are for the most part limited to the roughest and poorest segments of the community. One wants to know whether the notorious problem families, with a high concentration of adverse factors, are really exceptional or merely the peak of some largely submerged iceberg. The data so far collected goes a long way towards answering this kind of question.

The second way of looking at the data is to consider the boys' present behaviour disturbances in relation to all the factors that have been investigated. An attempt has been made, by combining information from several sources, to identify those boys whose behaviour at the age of 9 suggests a considerable risk of their becoming more seriously deviant or delinquent in later years. The background characteristics of these 'acting-out' boys, as we have called them, may be expected to provide some indication of the determinants of future delinquency. With this outline of the main guide lines of the research explained, the more detailed descriptions which follow may fall better into place.

4. *Sources of Information*

The boys themselves were examined by means of psychological tests, their conduct was assessed from teachers' reports, their personal histories and circumstances were inquired into by psychiatric social workers, who visited their homes and consulted social agencies, and their parents' attitudes and personalities were assessed by interviews and questionnaires.

Tests and questionnaires rather than interview examinations were used with the boys because this approach was more natural in the school setting, more acceptable to the education authorities, and, at this age, probably more productive. In addition to standard tests of intelligence and verbal attainments, the measures used with the boys included a personality questionnaire illustrated by pictures, tests of psychomotor habits, which were intended to give some indication of personality traits relevant to delinquency, and a sociometric test of popularity among schoolmates. All of these were administered personally by Dr H. B. Gibson, the chief psychologist of the research team, helped by an assistant when group tests were carried out. The individual tests were given by the psychologist in the medical room, or some other convenient location, at the schools, taking the boys out of their classes one by one. The first battery of individual tests, carried out mostly during 1962 and 1963, and normally given to the boy during his second year at the junior primary school, generally took about fifty minutes.

A second round of repeated and extended tests was carried out during the years 1964 and 1965, when the boys were aged 11, shortly before leaving their primary schools. These will be referred to in passing, but as the results have not yet been fully analysed they will not be dealt with in this report. Among other things, these repeat tests provide useful information about the constancy over time of the particular measures used, as well as revealing important changes in the performance of particular individuals. The third and final phase of inquiry in the schools, which includes more ambitious personality assessments, as well as some interview material, and a confidential questionnaire on delinquent activities, is being carried out as the boys become eligible to leave school, and should be completed about the time this book appears.

Previous research has identified many individual characteristics that seem to have relevance to potential delinquency, but the choice of measures to apply to boys in this Study was restricted by the need to limit inquiry to what could be collected by the psychologist in the course of one individual and one group session, and to concentrate on variables which would be adequately assessed by appropriate instruments and techniques. No great difficulty arose in choosing the measures of intelligence and attainment, since well-tried and reliable tests of cognitive functions are readily available, but in the area of personality measurement psychologists have not yet developed such firmly based or generally accepted techniques. Some schools of psychology criticize as useless or actively misleading such techniques as the Rorschach Tests (Jensen 1964), upon which other schools of clinical and developmental psychology have founded a large part of their studies. Careful scrutiny of technical journals reveals that many published tests which, superficially, appear promising and suitable, are neither so generally applicable nor so unequivocal in their results as the publishers' catalogues suggest. The fact that fruitful results have come from a questionnaire given to 10-year-old boys in America, for instance, is no guarantee that the responses to the same questionnaire by 8-year-old English schoolboys will prove meaningful. Even when psychologists are agreed on the validity of a technique, there may still be sharp divergence on how to assess results (Meehl, 1965). In carefully conducted research it is often found that no previously established test will cope adequately with the particular problems to hand, and so *ad hoc* measures have to be developed by the investigators. With these considerations in mind, the measures used for this Study, were, as far as possible, ones which could be justified on common-sense grounds, without invoking esoteric psychological theory, ones which had been previously standardized on comparable populations, and ones which were simple, practical and swift in administration. Where none suitable could be found ready-made, the psychologist adapted techniques from previous researches.

The opinions of teachers about the classroom behaviour and performance of each boy were obtained on a rating form (reproduced in Appendix I (A) which was modelled, by kind permission of Dr J. W. B. Douglas, on that used in the national survey, but with items referring to home circumstances. This form ended with an open question where teachers could record any comments about the boy they wished.

The outside agencies used for obtaining information about the boys and their families included several that were concerned with delinquency, namely the local offices of the Children's Department, where court appearances of children resident in the area were recorded, the two nearest offices of the probation service, both of which dealt with persons living in the neighbourhood covered by the study, and the Criminal Record Office at Scotland Yard. The schools medical service permitted a perusal of their files on the boys, which were kept in the schools themselves, and recorded any abnormalities discovered at routine examinations. Local representatives of the Child Care Committee, the Family Service Unit, and the N.S.P.C.C., as well as health visitors, housing officers, hospital almoners, and the doctors at psychiatric and child guidance clinics, all gave helpful information from time to time about particular families under their care. In addition, medical records of the boys' births, and in many cases hospital records of in-patient treatments, were also made available. These were the chief sources, although on occasions other agencies, such as the National Assistance Board (as it was then), the local police, and the Youth Employment Officers, gave some help. Concerning confidential records, each agency had its own traditions and rules, and negotiations about using them were sometimes delicate and protracted. Throughout the Study, personal contacts between our own professional workers and those of other agencies often proved more rewarding than approaches on an official level.

The bulk of the data on family background and upbringing was obtained by interviewing parents in their own homes. In explaining the purpose of the research, the interviewers went into more detail with some parents than others, depending on the interest shown or the questions asked. In general, parents were told that this was a study of child upbringing and development, and that anonymous information was being sought which could be of help to children and parents in the future. No special emphasis was placed upon delinquency problems, and the Institute of Criminology was not mentioned for fear of arousing anxiety, but in the course of time many parents came to realize or to assume that the interviewers were particularly interested in delinquency. The range of topics covered was very wide, and included many intimate family matters. Except in a few cases in which some rather hard-up mothers received small sums in cash to compensate them for giving up time to interviews, no special rewards were held out for co-operation, although the research plan envisaged visiting the homes over a period of six years. This social background inquiry was more complicated than the administering of standard tests to a captive audience of schoolboys, and called for great tact and perseverance.

5. *Recording Information from Home Interviews*

It was decided to employ psychiatric social workers[3] to conduct the home interviews, since their experience and training would be of help in establishing and maintaining the necessary rapport with parents, in eliciting information on sensitive topics, in detecting and circumventing defensive and evasive responses, and in identifying signs of disturbance in family relationships. Three women P.S.Ws, all long experienced, carried out this part of the inquiry. Two of them (referred to as A and B) worked full-time throughout the first stage of the study, from its inception in June 1961, to the completion of the coding and punching of the data in November 1964. The third P.S.W. (C) was enlisted for a limited period, from October 1962 to May 1964, because the task proved more than two persons could complete in the time.

In order that the P.S.Ws might work in the way to which they were accustomed, and elicit the maximum of co-operation, they were given a schedule of topics to be covered, but no fixed rules were laid down about the manner in which the information was to be sought, or the order in which topics were to be dealt with. Interviews were thus completely free and unstructured, and conducted in an informal, conversational style, with every opportunity to change the tone according to the interviewee's level of intelligence, co-operativeness and mood. Although a few written notes were sometimes taken during interviews, the P.S.Ws relied on dictating their impressions on to a portable tape recorder as soon as possible after a visit. Each P.S.W. had her own group of families to deal with, so that each family was always seen by the same worker, except in one or two cases of very reluctant parents, when a change of visitor was made in the hope of improving co-operation.

No stipulation could be made about which members of the family might be present at any given interview, but every effort was made to have at least one of the interviews with the mother apart from her husband, and preferably without older children within earshot. Mother was the primary informant, but fathers were also interviewed whenever they could be got to agree, and in fact, of the total sample of 411 boys, a father was interviewed in 70·8 per cent of cases, although in nearly a half of these cases the father was not seen except in mother's presence. At first no systematic record was kept of who was present at interviews, but analysis of 350 follow-up interviews conducted after November 1964 revealed that mother or father were seen on their own, in the absence of spouse, children or any other person, in only 40 per cent of cases.

Some doubts were felt at first about the advisability of trying to include interviews with fathers, especially in view of the large number of visits outside of normal working hours that this entailed, and the impossibility of getting to see them all. Sometimes mothers were unwilling for their husbands to be approached, saying they were unsympathetic to the Study, or much too busy, and it was impossible to get beyond this without risking total loss of co-operation. Some mothers must have exaggerated, for in a few cases supposedly antagonistic fathers, who happened to be at home when a P.S.W. called, proved willing informants.

The P.S.Ws did not consider their interviews with fathers very important in connection with early development, or with the handling of young children. On the whole, mothers were the more knowledgeable and forthcoming on these topics, fathers tending to play down anything unusual or difficult, and to assume that their children were all right unless forced to admit otherwise. On the other hand, on questions of marital history, or on matters concerning the background of the parents themselves, fathers often gave information that changed considerably the P.S.Ws' assessments. The few fathers who happened to have been interviewed first, before their wives, were particularly informative, possibly because they were not inhibited by the thought that they might be contradicting what the P.S.W. had already been told.

Three to four interviews, each one lasting about an hour, were usually needed to complete the case record forms, but the number and duration varied somewhat according to the intelligence and co-operativeness of the informant. Sometimes the more delicate topics were postponed to later interviews when confidence was better established. Sometimes later interviews elicited information that changed or contradicted earlier impressions. Appointments were generally made in advance, but were often cancelled or not kept, and in some cases a great many abortive calls were made before a satisfactory interview was obtained. When the case record form had been more or less completed, which was usually during the first year of contact with a family, subsequent visits were reduced to approximately once a year. These later visits served to maintain contact, to observe changes that had occurred in the family (especially on items already noted on the case record forms), and in some instances to allow the P.S.Ws to make revisions to their initial impressions. After November 1964 a new continuation schedule was introduced for systematic recording of on-going changes in home circumstances. This was designed to be more suitable for immediate coding and analysis than the first case record forms, but this belongs to the second stage of the Study, and is outside the scope of the present report.

The findings from all interviews as well as from inquiries from social agencies concerning a particular family were entered on the same record form under the appropriate headings. The P.S.Ws were asked to distinguish information derived from outside sources by using coloured ink, and dating the entry. Each page of the case record form had a line running down the middle, with the space to the right reserved for P.S.Ws' comments, or quotations from the mother's actual remarks. To the left of this line was printed the item or topic to be asked about, usually followed by a series of rating numbers or adjectives, one of which had to be ringed as being the most appropriate. An accompanying duplicated guide set out definitions of the ratings, and general instructions for filling in the case record form. (Some further details and an example extract are given in Appendix I (B).)

The definitions used for these interview ratings were mostly taken over, with slight modifications, from previous studies. The two main sources of definitions were studies by McCord and McCord (1959) and by Macfarlane (1954). The case record form as a whole was built up in consultation with the two P.S.Ws who were working on the project at the start. As a result of actual experience of interviewing some of the parents of the pilot group during the summer of 1961, the form was extensively revised. Thereafter, the P.S.Ws frequently discussed with each other their methods of rating, in an effort to maintain consistent standards. In addition, minor modifications and extensions of the definitions, as well as rulings about how to rate problematical cases, were made after discussions at the weekly meetings of the research staff.

NOTES

[1] Details of the recruitment of the sample are given on p. 15 and in Appendix II (A).

[2] The only exceptions to this rule were occasional corrections of clerical errors or alterations necessitated by additional information on strictly factual matters, such as dates of birth or criminal convictions.

[3] Subsequently referred to as P.S.Ws.

II

A Grey Outlook

1. *The Background of the Study*

(a) *The Neighbourhood under Survey.* In order to appreciate the nature of the social background, and how the Study sample stands in relation to the country as a whole, one must know something of the character of the neighbourhood where the boys were living. The research workers obtained an office in a local community centre. This was an old-established charitable organization, dating back to the last century, when welfare work often took the form of missions to the labouring classes. The building housed a variety of voluntary organizations for welfare work, but the present project was run quite independently of the other activities at the centre. It was thought that the presence there of a team of social investigators would seem natural to the local people, and would not attract unwanted publicity.

The boys in the Study were taken from six junior primary schools, all within a mile radius of the office headquarters. They were not selected in any way, they included *all* boys of a specified age who were attending the schools in question when the Study began. In order to sample the total day-school population, twelve boys from a nearby school for the educationally subnormal were included.

Since it was too large a task to survey all cases in one year, admission to the Study took place over a two-year period during the academic years 1961/2 and 1962/3. Thus, the sample was made up of two successive classroom generations, the older group (231 boys), born 1952/3, called the first age cohort, and the younger group (157 boys), born 1953/4, called the second age cohort. In addition, a small pilot group of 23 boys, born 1951/2, was admitted to the Study a little in advance of the two main cohorts. More precise particulars of the selection and recruitment of the sample are given in Appendix II (A).

The six schools involved in the Study (five local authority schools and one state-supported Church of England school[1]) served about two-fifths of the children of primary school age in the immediate vicinity, and seemed quite typical of primary schools in the area.

There were no private fee-paying schools anywhere nearby, and since parents in this district practically never sent their children to schools elsewhere, the Study sample can be taken as representative of boys of this generation and neighbourhood.

FIG. II (1)

Diagram of Study Neighbourhood, Subdivided into Wards, showing population densities in persons per acre in 1961, and also the positions of the six Primary Schools (a) to (f)

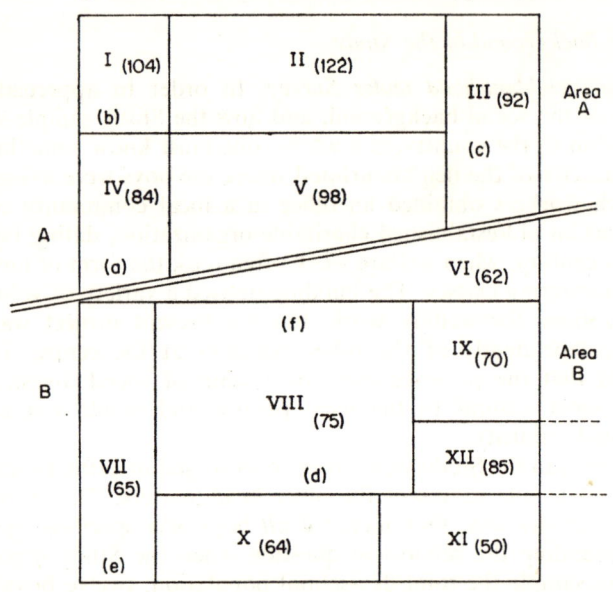

```
                I (104)         II (122)
                                            III (92)    Area
                (b)                                      A
                                            (c)
                IV (84)         V (98)
        A
                (a)                         VI (62)
                                (f)
                                            IX (70)     Area
        B                                                B
                                VIII
                                    (75)
                VII                         XII (85)
                (65)            (d)
                (e)             X (64)      XI (50)
```

The catchment areas of the six primary schools spread over a roughly rectangular shaped area, measuring 1¾ miles long, on a North-South axis, by 1½ miles across. This Study neighbourhood incorporated, roughly speaking, eleven census wards and part of a twelfth. Fig. II (1) shows the twelve wards with their high densities of population, which ranged from 50 to 122 persons per acre in the year 1961. The Figure shows the six primary schools, labelled a to f. The Study neighbourhood was distributed between two larger administrative areas, A and B.[2] Since these larger areas were not homogeneous in character, their published statistics provided only a rough guide to the characteristics of the Study neighbourhood. As a whole, area A was more like the immediate neighbourhood, whereas area B included within its boundaries a more spaciously set out middle-class residential district. In 1961, the population density of Area A was 76·3 persons per acre, similar to the situation in the

Study neighbourhood, while that of B was only 39·1. In 1961, 53 per cent of all dwellings in Area A lacked a fixed bath. In Area B the figure was 34 per cent. When the Study began, 51 per cent (N=402)[3] of the boys were living in homes without a bathroom.

(b) *Socio-economic Status of the Study Sample.* Every available statistic of occupation, income, housing, educational achievement or family composition reflected the predominantly working-class character of the neighbourhood. One indication of the social class of a neighbourhood is the proportion of registered electors eligible for jury service, since to qualify one must be a householder in premises exceeding a specified rateable value, or else own real estate. In the twelve wards of the study neighbourhood in the year 1961, the percentage of eligible electors ranged from 2·7 to 10·1 with an average of 6·1. By contrast, a predominantly middle-class ward in Area B had 16·9 per cent eligible for jury service.

Each boy in the Study was allocated a position on the Registrar General's scale of socio-economic status according to his father's occupation, or in the absence of a father, according to that of the family breadwinner. So as to include all cases, temporarily unemployed persons, and those retired or recently deceased, were classified on their last known employment, and fathers in H.M. Forces were classified on the nearest civilian equivalent. The allocations were made by an independent assistant, and were based upon the descriptions of fathers' occupations recorded by psychiatric social workers from interviews with the parents. Where the parents refused to be interviewed, the information was obtained from records of various social agencies. The results are set out in Table II (1). No cases whatsoever fell into Class I, which is reserved for the highest professional groups, such as company directors and barristers. The proportion in the lowest Class V, the unskilled manual workers, was over two and a half times the national average, whereas the proportion in Class II, the semi-professional grades, was only about two-fifths the national average. The largest proportion of the sample, 49·2 per cent, fell into the manual division of Class III, which contains skilled workers, such as lorry drivers.

Family income proved rather more difficult to categorize than the nature of father's employment. The psychiatric social workers who interviewed the boys' parents found many of them rather sensitive and unreliable on the topic of family income, and many mothers were either vague or genuinely ignorant of their husband's total earnings. The case record forms included spaces for recording father's earnings, mother's earnings, contributions from other members of the household, mother's housekeeping allowance, amounts of family allowances and national assistance, as well as regular financial commitments, such as rent or any special payments. The presence or absence of specified items of household equipment was noted by the P.S.Ws by ticking them off on a printed list. These included: car, refrigerator, television, telephone, washing machine, carpets, plentiful toys and cocktail cabinet (a local status symbol). Of course this information was not so reliable in regard to the less co-operative families, who showed the visitors as little of their homes as possible.

TABLE II (1)

Socio-Economic Status in the Study Sample Compared with the National Census

Registrar General's Class	England and Wales. (1) 1961 Census	Study Sample (2) (N=411)
I	4·4%	—
II	17·3%	6·3%
III	54·4%	56·7%
IV	18·2%	21·2%
V	5·7%	15·8%
TOTAL	100%	100%

(1) Based on 1961 Census figures for married males of classifiable occupation aged 35 to 44 years.
Occupational Tables, London, 1966, H.M.S.O., Table 20.
(2) Based upon last known occupation of family breadwinner, usually the father.

Putting together information gleaned from all sources, the P.S.Ws made an impressionistic rating of each family's financial situation as 'inadequate', 'adequate' or 'comfortable'. In general, families with a total income of £15 per week or less for two adults and four children were rated as 'inadequate', and those believed to have £20 or more net to spend each week were classed as financially 'comfortable'. Where the information volunteered by parents was insufficient, or obviously unreliable, P.S.Ws judged the situation as best they could, taking into account general appearances, style of living and the sparsity or affluence of visible possessions.

On this rating, 22·8 per cent of boys came from families struggling on inadequate incomes, and 21·3 per cent· from financially 'comfortable' homes (N=395). Although occupational grade of father correlated positively with the family income rating (r=·31, N=395), the two did not necessarily coincide.[4] One important reason for the incomplete correspondence between family income and father's occupational grade was the contribution made by other working members of the families. Since employment was to be found fairly easily nearby, many older siblings were able to hold jobs and contribute to the finances without leaving home. In 22·9 per cent of the sample the mothers said they had a full-time job outside the home, and in a further 33·6 per cent of the sample (N = 384) mothers said they worked part time, that is anything less than six hours daily. Incidentally, the better class mothers more often went out to work. In Classes II and III non-manual, twice as many mothers as in Classes IV and V said they worked full time.

(c) *Family Size.* As is usual among working-class communities, compared with the national average, a significantly larger proportion of the boys in this Study came from large families. For the purpose of consistent statistical comparisons, family size was defined as the number of children in the family when the Study commenced.[5] Since it was the socially operative family as much as the biological family that was of interest, half-siblings and step-siblings were also included. The net effect of this method of counting will have been to underestimate slightly the number of children since at least sixty of the mothers gave birth to one or more babies subsequently. Despite this underestimate, it is clear that, compared with a national sample, the Study sample had a deficit of small-sized families of one or two children, and an excess of families of seven or more children. Even so, two-thirds of the families[6] were of moderate size, with two to four children. As is always the case, it was the boys belonging to the lowest socio-economic classes who most often came from big families. (For details see Appendix II (B).)

(d) *Neighbourhood Characteristics.* One might have expected the character of the Study neighbourhood to be reflected in unfavourable health and welfare statistics, at least from Area A, but in point of fact the incidence of illegitimate births, of deaths of infants in the first year of life, and of deaths from respiratory tuberculosis, and the proportion of the population in receipt of national assistance, were not substantially different from that of the total surrounding conurbation. A survey of the incidence of alcoholism in the area indicated that this problem was no greater here than in most big towns. All this rather tended to confirm the impression of the neighbourhood as an area of drabness and relative social deprivation rather than one so poor as to lead to widespread physical disease or malnutrition.

The neighbourhood was, in fact, a crowded urban district, heavily built up with both dwellings and commercial undertakings. A noisy arterial road, lined with shops, and used by long-distance lorries as well as local buses and cars, ran the length of the area, while parallel to this a viaduct carrying a main railway cut across the residential side roads, and nearby a canal brought raw materials for local industry. Increasingly, some of the residential streets, which once formed playgrounds for the young, were being given over to one-way traffic systems in an effort to relieve the chronic congestion on the main roads. Open spaces suitable for childrens' playgrounds were scarce, and many local children had either to walk some way across busy roads to reach them, or else to remain in the streets near their homes playing among an ever increasing clutter of parked vehicles.

Life in the locality seemed rather drab. Tiny street-corner shops supplying the immediate vicinity with basic needs were plentiful, as were the larger shops, mostly branches of chain stores, that were strung along the main roads. But everywhere only a limited range of goods was stocked, and among household durables the shoddy designs and tasteless displays contrasted markedly with the shop windows of the more affluent areas of the town. The dress of the people in the streets was also noticeably poorer than in the better neighbourhoods of the town; with the younger women's dress rather loud, and the older women rather shabby, and with a few walking out in pinafores, hair curlers or folded-down stockings. Among adolescents, the prevailing fashions wore a clumsy, water-down look in comparison with the more exotic elegance of the coffee bars in the town centre. Windows tended to be decked in clashing arrays of elaborate drapes, without regard to the neighbours adjacent. Just outside the periphery of the Study neighbourhood several hostels run by the National Assistance Board, the Salvation Army and other charitable organizations, provided something over 2,000 beds for men, which were occupied mostly by vagrants. These tramp-like characters, some of them chronic alcoholics, could be seen wandering about the streets during the day, causing anxiety to some of the mothers in the Study, who spoke of fearing their children might be molested.

Social amenities in the Study area were limited. There were no theatres or sports stadium, but three cinemas still functioned, and the popular gambling entertainment 'Bingo' was well catered for. Numerous public houses continued to attract many clients, although visits were mostly confined to week-ends, the availability of television at home having probably reduced the patronage of the bars. The area was well served with churches and Sunday Schools of various denominations, but only a small minority attended regularly.

Restaurants and cafés frequented by local work people were also plentiful, but unsuitable for anyone squeamish about the smell of frying or particular about their cooking. Youth clubs with uniformed groups attached to them were run by local churches, but these facilities were unevenly distributed about the area, and some clubs made stipulations about denominational affiliations or general deportment which effectively excluded many youngsters.

Proximity to the business area of the town, with its many offices, and the presence nearby of various manufacturing and processing centres, meant that for residents of the Study area, of all ages and both sexes, a variety of employments was available, and no fit person, whether skilled or not, had much difficulty finding a job. The occupations of our boys' fathers were varied, the commonest types being transport and communications 19 per cent, engineering 12 per cent, services 11 per cent, and labourers 12 per cent. The first group included many who worked in the docks, or on long-distance lorry driving, as well as on local buses and deliveries. The engineers were mostly engaged on metal work, printing, and general light engineering, trades which were well established within and in the vicinity of the Study area. Printing was an industry especially common in the locality, and its employees, many of whom were engaged on night shifts, enjoyed a high level of wages for the district, as well as a degree of prestige which encouraged young recruits. Dock work, on the other hand, was held in rather poor esteem. The service workers included many office caretakers, while the labourers were a rather mixed group, engaged on factory work, building sites and with the local authority cleansing department.

Employment for women, though plentiful, was less varied, and mostly consisted of office cleaning, as the pay was thought reasonable and the hours fitted in with family responsibilities. Many women performed a split shift, early morning and late evening, sometimes for different employers. This gave rise to another traditional feature of the area, an army of Mrs Mops, commuting towards the business centre each morning before the white collar workers were awake, and filling the buses with their noisy laughter and raucous humour.

(e) *The Housing Problem.* The Study neighbourhood had been developed in Victorian times, and many terraced rows of damp and dilapidated workers' cottages, typical of that era, with outside W.Cs and no baths, were still under occupation. Here and there, some relics of a more dignified age in the form of small squares surrounded by Georgian houses, survived, although in a poor state of preservation. Still more depressing were the barrack-like tenement blocks, built in the earlier part of this century, generally surrounding an asphalted compound, with stone stairways leading to communal balconies along which the inhabitants must pass their neighbours' windows to reach their own quarters. In these unimaginative constructions, poor sound-proofing, a high noise level due to the proximity of large numbers of children with inadequate space to play, insufficient lighting and ventilation, and no proper system of maintaining the communal stairways free from rubbish, all contributed to the general unpleasantness.

Throughout the period of this Study the neighbourhood has been undergoing a slow transformation, due to massive slum clearance and reconstruction programmes on the part of the local authorities. In this crowded terrain towering blocks, built on the constricted sites of old slum property recently demolished, naturally took precedence over the traditional villas and gardens of former days, but some variety was achieved by placing a number of small blocks of maisonettes, and a few bungalows for the elderly, among the sky scrapers. These developments produced an area of stark contrasts in which, within a single street, begrimed and crumbling terraces were to be found alongside new estates, where the buildings had been carefully designed as to landscape, and provided with attractive modern facings. The inevitable waste lands, produced by boarded up shells of houses awaiting demolition, or flattened areas of temporary devastation, where bonfires were made from the ancient woodwork, attracted the local children, but added another dismal note to the physical environment.

In spite of all the new building, housing was still the most visible and pressing social problem in the Study neighbourhood, as indeed it is in so many of the old parts of English industrial towns. Owner-occupation was practically non-existent. Most of the older property belonged either to private landlords or had been acquired by the public authorities with a view to demolition. All the new dwellings were owned by the public authorities. At the time of first contact about one-fifth of the boys were living in dwellings so dilapidated they could be called slums, and a total of one-third were in accommodation considered unsatisfactory by the Study interviewers. The criteria of unsatisfactoriness were quite severe, to the extent that the families were seriously harassed by discomfort. The mere absence of a bath, or squalid conditions due to a family's own neglect, were not in themselves sufficient indication, although overcrowding was counted as unsatisfactory if two persons of opposite sex, over the age of 12, other than cohabiting couples, were compelled to share a bedroom.

The situation was steadily improving during the course of the Study. In the first three years, nearly a quarter of the boys moved to better housing provided by the local authority. During this time only ten families bought their own home, moving to some other district for the purpose. Most families considered owner-occupation beyond their reach because of the high price of houses and mortgages and the building societies' requirements about the income and employment of borrowers.

While all of the new housing developments included basic modern amenities far superior to the standards of the old houses, some of them also incorporated the latest types of floor heating, wall surfaces and built-in kitchen and bedroom units. The rents charged for these comparatively luxurious apartments were beyond the means of many families, who were forced to opt for the more modest versions. More serious was the plight of the poorer families with large numbers of children who could not possibly pay the rent for even a modest apartment of the requisite size. In effect, as has been pointed out recently by a number of social commentators, the housing system had failed to provide for the families whose needs were greatest. Compelled to search for the cheapest possible, inevitably they gravitated to the slum streets of old condemned houses, where they stayed on to the last possible moment. In some of these homes dampness, structural deterioration, and overcrowding rendered futile all attempts to keep the interior in good order. An example of the kind was the following:

Case 113
The boy was living in an old house in a back street that had been requisitioned by the local authority. The house was occupied by ten children and four adults, the boy's parents, a maternal grandfather, who was a retired rag-and-bone man, and a maternal uncle. There was no bathroom and only a very small kitchen with a leaking roof, cluttered with buckets to catch the water when it rained. Walls everywhere were peeling and crumbling. The mother was a competent person who managed as best she could. She went out to do a cleaning job to earn an extra £2 a week. Her chief complaint was having to wash the children in relays at the kitchen sink. Father was in regular work, and the total family income was adequate to cover food and clothing, but not to cope with higher rent.

Squalid housing did not always coincide with poverty in other respects. Virtually every household, however poor, had its television set. Many badly housed families spent much time and effort trying to improve their facilities with the addition of new furniture, washing machines, refrigerators and household gadgets. In fact, the dilapidated outside appearance of a dwelling was no sure indication of the state of affairs within. The side streets in the area, including those classed as slums, were cluttered with cars. More than a quarter of the boys in the Study enjoyed the use of a family car.

Although most people's ambition was for a new flat in a smart modern block not everyone was content once having got it. Here, as in many modern housing developments the design of some of the new blocks gave cause for discontent. The almost universal absence of garages, the noise and lack of privacy, the need to restrict children on account of lack of space, the difficulty of supervising young children playing outside when parents are in a flat far above street level, and the prohibition of family pets, all gave rise to complaints. One family actually exchanged a modern flat for an old house with the joys of its own back yard, even though they knew it was due for slum clearance demolition in two years' time.

(f) *Stability and Tradition.* Local housing developments, and the relative ease with which employment was to be found within easy reach combined to discourage migration, and incidentally to facilitate the research. Six years after the Study began, nearly half of the boys had changed their address, but three-quarters of the sample were still in the immediate neighbourhood, and all but fourteen were still in the surrounding conurbation or close to it. Only three had departed overseas.

Although the neighbourhood seemed dreary by middle-class standards, it was a traditional English working-class community, and in no way a ghetto area, or at least no more so than any other large conglomeration of 'council' property. Many families had no wish to move away. Although small West Indian and Cypriot minorities had taken up residence in recent years, there had been no great influx of foreign immigrants in the immediate vicinity and no racial disturbances. Only 2·7 per cent of the boys in the Study were visibly negro or part-negro, and these were mostly of Jamaican origin. The great majority, 86·4 per cent, were both white in racial appearance and were being reared by parents who were themselves born and reared in the United Kingdom. The remaining 11·0 per cent was made up of boys with one or more parents of Irish, British Commonwealth or Continental European origins, plus a few Cypriots. Most of the boys and their parents said they belonged to the Church of England, but these included a great many of purely nominal religion. Only two boys were on record as Jews, another two were Muslims, a few belonged to the Greek Orthodox Church. Surprisingly few belonged to the English Non-Conformist sects. One-fifth[7] of the boys had one or both parents professing affiliation to the Roman Catholic Church, although they were not necessarily attenders. These were mostly of Irish stock.

Customs typical of an old-established working-class district persisted. Some streets, notably those populated by large families at the lower end of the social scale, kept up a close knit community life in which residents knew each other by name, and even if not always on 'dropping in' terms with their neighbours, they would certainly know a lot about each other's affairs. A common sight in these streets was groups of housewives sitting on their doorsteps chatting with neighbours when the weather permitted. Both adults and children sometimes missed the sociability of their street when they moved to a block of flats. A traditional street market of open stalls or barrows, busy six days a week, operated within the Study area, and the 'trip down the lane' in search of bargains and gossip was a regular feature of the local housewife's life. The ancient rag-and-bone trade still flourished, and close to the Study office, underneath some railway arches, pony carts dumped their loads of rags, tyres and scrap metal. Another working-class tradition noticeable in the neighbourhood was the lavish funeral cortege with some four or five cars following a hearse decorated with elaborate floral wreaths in forms such as an empty chair, the deceased's initial, or the simple word 'Dad'. Many friends and neighbours participated on these occasions, and the cost of these displays was sometimes outrageously disproportionate to the family income.

(g) *Summing up the Background.* The general characteristics of the Study neighbourhood can be compared with other working-class English cultures described by sociologists, but only on an impressionistic basis, since we did not set out to collect the kind of data necessary for systematic sociological analysis. Josephine Klein (1965), contrasts traditional working-class life with the recently modified working-class culture that has arisen as an accompaniment of improvement in housing and in the general standard of living. The situation in this Study neighbourhood appeared to be a mixture of these traditional and modern versions. Possibly because of a certain lag behind the national trend, some streets within the neighbourhood were still very like the old rough slum pattern described by Marie Paneth (1944) in *Branch Street*, (Paddington) or by Sprott (1954) in 'Dyke Street, Radby'. However, most of the families in this Study resembled the solid, ordinarily respectable working-class type which made up the bulk of the Radby population. Like the inhabitants of Bethnal Green described by Young and Willmott (1957), many families had been born and bred nearby, were content with the area and its ways, and had no great desire to move or to change. On the other hand, those with a more modern and more socially aspiring outlook, as typified in

Zweig's study (1961), made up a significant proportion of the families in the present study. Of the three types, 'roughs', 'ordinary respectables', and 'aspiring', only the first are characteristically associated with an accepting and uncondemnatory attitude towards thieves.

As the stress of immediate physical want, or the threat of it, has lifted from the working-class in England, it seems attitudes have tended to become less defensive, less clannish, less hostile towards middle-class aspirants. The Study neighbourhood was no exception to this general trend. Although the people were refreshingly friendly and open, for the most part, a respect for privacy, and a discouragement of indiscriminate popping in and out by neighbours, was also characteristic.

Family life, at least in the ordinary respectable and the aspiring grades of the local community, reflected very clearly the trend towards a family and child centred existence which Klein and others have identified as one of the most notable changes in the working class. Parents in the Study sample frequently recalled childhood experiences of poverty, and of parental drunkenness and quarrelling; whereas in their own marriages these features seemed much less frequent. The fathers in the Study usually took an interest in their children, helping them and playing with them, and as husbands it seemed they were more prepared than previous generations to treat their wives as partners, spending their leisure time together and making joint decisions.

One may perhaps sum up the position by describing the area as a traditional English working-class neighbourhood in the process of slow physical and cultural change. Typical slum families still exist in considerable numbers, with all the signs of social deprivation and cultural alienation, but alongside them are living more ambitious and effective families enjoying the material benefits and changed outlook of the new affluence. It remains to be seen how far the diversity within these working-class backgrounds will be reflected in the behaviour and personalities of the boys in the Study.

2. *The Boys in their Schools*

(a) *Characteristics of the Schools.* As has been remarked before, the six primary schools in the Study were not, on the whole, noticeably different from the general run of schools in the area; but each one had its own particular characteristics. The two local authority schools (D and E) which belonged to administrative area B were rather larger, with a total of 182 and 151 boys respectively, than the three schools in area A, which had 116, 137 and 116 boys respectively.

This trend followed a general tendency for the schools in area A to be smaller than those of area B. Statistics for the year 1961, supplied by the Education Authority, showed that, among the six schools in the Study, the percentages of children from overcrowded homes, and the percentages whose fathers were in unskilled or semi-skilled occupations, were much the same as in other schools in the neighbourhood.

All of the schools in the Study were co-educational, with varying proportions of boys and girls in each class. The number of boys in the classes ranged from six to twenty-six with a median of nineteen. On reaching the age for transfer to secondary schools, only 10·5 per cent of the boys in the Study entered grammar schools, which is greatly below the national average, but the comparison is unimportant since the area of the Study was particularly well provided with comprehensive schools, some of which had advanced streams of equivalent standard to grammar schools.

The delinquency rates of the Study schools were compared with those of all the junior primary schools in areas A and B. This was based upon a search at the local offices of the Children's Department of the records covering June 1960 to December 1962; the names, ages and school attended by each boy found guilty being noted. The incidence of convictions of boys under 11 was low, even though at that time the age of criminal responsibility had not yet been raised from 8 to 10. Consequently, the comparisons were based on small numbers, but there was no indication that the delinquency rate of the Study schools differed significantly from that of the general run of schools in the areas.[8]

Apart from the group of boys attending an E.S.N. school, two-thirds of whom belonged to the lowest socio-economic classes (i.e. manual IV or V), the class distribution of boys was much the same in all six schools. Again, apart from the E.S.N. boys, three-quarters of whom were unsatisfactorily housed, the proportion in bad housing was much the same in all six schools. The only exception was School D, which was surrounded by new blocks of flats, and had only 17 per cent badly housed, compared with 33 per cent in the total sample.

The six schools may have been dealing with similar groups of boys; but their methods varied. For instance, they operated different policies concerning the allocation of boys of similar age to different classes on grounds of scholastic performance. At D school, for instance, the children were divided on academic grounds into A, B and C streams by the age of 8, and the C stream children were noticeably noisy and backward and more difficult to test, and they became more so as they grew older. This school was run with stricter, more formal and more overtly punitive discipline than most. The headmaster was generally reluctant to reply to letters or to grant more than minimal facilities for the Study. At C school, the headmaster was kindly and paternalistic, and against the policy of placing young children in separate streams. He prided himself on knowing the community around the school, and did all he could to get the parents to co-operate in the Study. At A school, the atmosphere was in pronounced contrast to that at D school. The headmaster was unconventional in outlook, and easy going in discipline. He afforded plenty of scope to the less academic boys by drawing them into practical tasks, and it was quite usual to find one or two children playing around in his office, or coming to and fro on small errands, while he was at work. The school was justly well known for arts and crafts, and while this Study was in progress they produced an impressive exhibition. The headmaster was helpful and encouraging towards the research workers. E school had premises which were rather superior compared with the others. The head was elderly, but energetic and individualistic, and took a keen interest in the childrens' home circumstances; but he had antagonized a number of parents by his patronizing manner, and was criticized for not providing sports facilities or special tuition for backward readers.

B school, in contrast, was run by a young, cheerful, extraverted headmaster who was popular among parents and encouraged sporting activities particularly. The children there were not noticeably streamed until after the age of 9. The Church of England School F was the smallest. Up to mid-1964, it occupied poor and largely basement premises. It catered for children in the immediate vicinity, which was a rather poor section of the neighbourhood. No strict streaming was in force. The headmaster was very willing to help the research workers. The E.S.N. school, which was situated in rather grim surroundings a little outside the neighbourhood of the rest of the schools, drew children from a wide catchment area. The head was again most co-operative, and in this instance very familiar with the pupils' family circumstances and problems.

So far as could be demonstrated in this research, the contrasting regimes at these schools had not resulted in any marked effect upon their pupils. Apart from the E.S.N. school, which obviously had a very selected population, there were no striking or significant differences in attainment or behaviour at the age of 8 to 9 between the groups of boys attending the six primary schools.[9] At the age of 11 when the boys were tested once more, shortly before their transfer to secondary school, there was still no significant difference in educational level between the six primary schools (according to the boys' performance on the Mill Hill Vocabulary Scale) and at age 13 there was likewise no significant difference in incidence of reported delinquent behaviour (see p. 34 ff.) between the boys who had attended different primary schools. The absence of any striking variation attributable to the experience at different primary schools may perhaps be due to the predominantly working-class character of the Study sample. In his national survey, J. W. B. Douglas (1964, p. 105 and Table XIII (b)) found that between the ages of 8 and 11 years children at primary schools with a good academic record pulled ahead in their performance on scholastic tests more rapidly than those attending less favoured schools. However, the beneficial influence of better primary schools was substantial only in the case of children from middle-class homes, and was minimal in the case of children from the lower classes, which may explain why, in the present Study, differences attributable to the influence of the primary schools were not more noticeable.

(b) *The Boys' Intelligence and Attainment.* Every boy was given Raven's (1956) Progressive Matrices Test, generally given as a group test with the whole class participating, but in some instances administered individually. This is a well-known test of non-verbal intelligence, a quality believed to be relatively independent of educational experience. The test consists of five sets of printed problems, each set having twelve items. The problems are all presented graphically, without any written instruction, so that once the person administering the test has explained what is required the testee can carry on without further guidance. In each case he has to choose from between six or eight printed alternatives the one which completes correctly a pattern or sequence shown on the top half of the page. The test is therefore applicable to both illiterate and literate children, and it is well adapted for group administration.

The problems are of widely varying difficulty, such that the earlier ones are soluble even by children of subnormal intelligence, while a few of the later ones are usually solved only by adults of superior intelligence. Although children of 8 years of age are expected to solve no more than about 40 per cent of the problems, the test is so arranged that most children will continue to work contentedly recording possible answers to problems beyond their range. This feature ensures that all the children are kept occupied long enough to allow the slower children to complete all the problems they are likely to be able to solve without being distracted by those who finish quickly. The wide range of problems has the further advantage that it has enabled the test to be repeated with the same children at a later age, so that the individual boy's improvement or deterioration in relation to his peers can be observed.

The present sample yielded a distribution of scores very close to that of normal population of the same age range. (See Table II (2)). In respect to non-verbal intelligence, at least, the boys in the Study were not particularly retarded.

Most of the boys were given the Sentence Reading Test 1 of the National Foundation of Educational Research (Watts, 1958). This is a well standardized test, designed for administering to groups, and scores for the normal population are available down to the age of 7½. None of our boys were below 8 years of age at the time the test was given.

In contrast to the results of the Matrices Test, the Sentence Reading scores were on average well below expectation for the normal population. In fact, a large number of boys could not manage it at all, and in several trials with the C streams the psychologist confirmed the teachers' assurance that it was quite beyond these pupils' capacities. The results of this and other cognitive tests are displayed in Table II (2) in terms of percentile ranks. Thus, where the population standard is up to the 5th, and the sentence reading scores are up to the 38th, this means that 38 per cent of the sample scored as badly as the worst 5 per cent of the normal population.

TABLE II (2)

Distribution of Scores on Attainment and Intelligence Tests in Terms of Percentile Rank

Population Standard	5th	10th	25th	50th	75th	90th	95th	100th
Progressive Matrices N=411	5·1	7·8	20·9	47·0	70·3	87·6	95·1	100
Sentence Reading N=377	38·5	45·9	60·2	78·3	91·5	97·4	99·5	100
Mechanical Reading N=403	7·4	39·0	60·8	75·4	86·6	94·3	97·0	100
Word Comprehension N=397	2·0	11·1	38·0	68·5	90·4	97·5	99·2	100

The Mechanical Reading Test, which was given individually to nearly every boy, was a measure of ability to read words correctly, but did not involve verbal comprehension. It was thus more a test of ability to read than of capacity for understanding. The test was standardized at the age of 8 and 11 years on the children of Dr J. W. B. Douglas' National Survey. Since our boys' ages at the time of testing fell between these two levels, it was necessary to extrapolate the norms for our purpose.[10]

The scores on this test were better than on Sentence Reading, but still the sample was considerably retarded, 60·8 per cent performing as poorly as the worst quarter of the normal population. The 7·4 per cent of boys who fell into the lowest percentile category on this test was made up of non-readers and those who could only make out a few words like 'cat' and 'egg'. If the equivalent of the lowest 10 per cent of the normal population is regarded as very backward in reading, then 39·0 per cent of our boys, nearly four times the national average, fell into this category.

The Word Comprehension Test, a companion to the Mechanical Reading Test, and coming from the same source, was also administered individually to almost every boy. In this test, the words, which are printed in ascending order of difficulty, were spoken aloud to the boys, who were asked to explain the meaning, and the definitions they gave were scored against standard criteria. The test thus measured comprehension independently of reading ability, and was thus rather closer to a measure of verbal intelligence. The lower verbal comprehension of the boys in our sample reflects the limited verbal level of the families from which they came. The contrast was greater at the upper end of the scale; only 9·6 per cent of our boys were comparable with the top 25 per cent of the normal population. (The scores of the small Cypriot minority are not included in the figures concerning verbal comprehension, as they were at a special disadvantage on this test.)

In brief, the present sample, as is typical of working-class groups, were not retarded in non-verbal intelligence, but they were somewhat lower on verbal intelligence, and were considerably retarded in reading, which is more dependent upon educational experience. These results were not really surprising. At this age boys lag behind girls in educational attainment, and lower class boys perform relatively badly. Since the Study sample was both all male and also over-weighted at the lower social level educational performance would be expected to be below average. In her sample of 11,000 7-year-olds Kellmer Pringle (1966, p. 28) found that 30·9 per cent. of boys, compared with only 17·2 per cent of girls, were classed by their teachers as poor readers or non-readers. In her survey, good readers were less than half as frequent at the lower social levels (Registrar General's groups IV and V) than at the higher social levels (Groups I or II).

The retardation of many of the boys in this Study proved transient. Unlike the findings of national surveys, in which retarded groups tend to become still more retarded in comparison with their peers as age increases, most of the backward readers in this Study tended to catch up later. A count made after the older boys (128 in total) had reached 14 years of age, and been given the Neale Analysis of

Reading Ability, showed that, considering the type of school attended by most of the Study sample, there were almost as many boys up to or above average in reading as in a national sample. (See Appendix II (C).) The reasons for this result are not known; but presumably they have something to do with the nature of the sample. Many of these boys, while retarded according to national norms, were little different from many others at their schools, and therefore did not suffer from being identified and segregated among officially backward groups.

One further test of intelligence remains to be described, namely the Porteus (1959) Mazes. This was included, for one reason, because it was a test of non-verbal intelligence individually administered, and it was thought advisable to have this as a check upon those boys who might not do so well in a group situation on account of excessive distractability. Another reason was that the same test provided a measure of 'personality' related to delinquent tendency. (This aspect is discussed in the following chapter.)

The Porteus Mazes, which have been in use since 1914, are specially attractive to children. They consist of a series of printed mazes, presented in ascending order of difficulty, and the subject is asked to trace a continuous pencil line from the centre to the exit without turning into any blind alleys. There are rather complex rules for administering and scoring this test.

As a group, the study sample gave scores on this test considerably higher than expected from the norms published by Porteus. The scores on this test are expressed as a 'Test Quotient', representing 'test age' as a percentage of chronological age. A T.Q. of up to 120, which would be considerably above average, was attained by over a half of the boys (53 per cent, N=407). There was a pronounced negative skew of the distribution of scores—that is there was a bunching of scores of 35 per cent of the boys within the T.Q. range 120 to 130.

Since it is clear from the Matrices and other evidence that our boys were not excessively intelligent, there must be some reason for the usual standards not being applicable. Possibly these boys were unusually practised, for some of them mentioned that they did the mazes published in their comics. Since these data were collected, some work by Professor Vernon (1965, p. 13) of London University Institute of Education has shown that 'the present day performance of English schoolboys is much superior to Porteus' norms' so the findings from the present sample are not really anomalous.

Fortunately the number of boys tested was sufficient for individuals to be assessed in relation to the distribution of scores within the Study sample itself. The correlation between Porteus T.Q. and Matrices I.Q. (r = ·40), indicated that the two tests were to some extent measuring similar qualities.

(c) *The Boys' Physical Growth.* The heights and weights of all but six of the boys were measured at age 8 to 9. This was done without jackets or shoes, and generally using the same height calipers, by the psychologist, working in the medical room at each school. A constant of 0·76 kg. was substracted in each case to allow for the average weight of clothes worn by boys of 8 to 9 years. The results were compared with figures for a large normal sample obtained by Dr J. A. Scott (1961), whose methods of measurement were closely followed. There are some inaccuracies in the method, since no difference between summer and winter clothes was allowed for, and a large boy of nearly 10 may perhaps wear twice the weight of clothes that a small boy of 8 will wear. Nevertheless, the comparison in the following Table shows a consistent and probably valid difference. The raw figures have been corrected (by linear regression) to allow for the boys' different ages at the time of measurement then converted into a frequency distribution by percentile rank. (See Table II (3).) The Table includes data from the repeat measurements taken at age 11, when, in this Study, some allowance for the variable weight of clothing was made.

TABLE II (3)

Distribution of Heights and Weights of Boys in Terms of Percentile Rank

J. A. Scott's Study:	N		3rd	10th	25th	50th	75th	90th	97th	100th
Present Study Sample	405	Height at age 8–9	2·5	12·3	31·6	61·2	81·7	94·6	98·8	100
	402	Height at age 11	2·7	11·4	28·4	60·2	83·8	95·0	99·0	100
	405	Weight at age 8–9	2·2	7·9	25·1	54·3	75·0	88·4	96·0	100
	399	Weight at age 11	2·8	7·8	21·8	52·6	74·4	89·5	96·2	100

Percentiles

It is evident from Table II (3) that although the weight distribution of our boys was very similar to that of the larger study (which covered over 2,000 boys of similar age range), their height was markedly inferior. As much as 61·2 per cent of our boys were as short as the shorter half of the normal schoolboy population. It follows that in terms of body build our sample had a predominance of boys whose height to weight ratio was low. This finding was to be expected in view of the social class structure of the Study sample. Studies of physical measurements such as those of J. M. Tanner (1961) and R. W. Parnell (1958) have shown that body-build is related to class, the lower socio-economic classes tending to have a smaller height/weight ratio, due to a relative excess of individuals of mesomorphic (sturdy, muscular) physique who are heavy for their height. Not only did the Study sample show a tendency to a lower height/weight ratio when compared as a group with a larger and more diverse population, but the tendency was also apparent within the sample for those of the lower social classes to have the smaller height/weight ratios.

In view of the association between mesomorphic physique and criminality, which emerged from the researches of W. H. Sheldon (1949) and the Gluecks (1956) in America, as well as from T. C. N. Gibbens (1963) study of an English borstal population, height/weight ratio is of special interest in relation to delinquency. Each boy was allocated to one or other of three types on the following system. First heights and weights were separately scored on eight point scales according to each boy's percentile rank[11] on the divisions shown in Table II (3). A boy was classed as *heavily built* (i.e. mesomorphic or endormorphic) if his height score was lower than his weight score; *balanced* if his height and weight scores were equal (that is in the same percentile range), and *lightly built* (ectomorphic) if his height score was greater than his weight score. Of the 405 boys rated, 160 fell into the heavily built class, 81 into the lightly built class. The heavily built boys were significantly more frequent among those of the lower socio-economic classes. Being heavily built was also related to being badly behaved, although the trend did not reach statistical significance. (See Appendix II (D).)

(d) *A Glimpse of Commencing Delinquency.* The first impression of the boys at their schools was much as expected in view of the general character of the neighbourhood. In brief, they were a somewhat underprivileged group, starting out with few social or educational assets, but generally free from those gross signs of physical neglect or malnutrition which occur in seriously poverty-stricken communities. Although retarded in height, the boys were fully up to average in weight, so in all probability this feature had more to do with the naturally sturdy, mesomorphic body-build of working-class males than with any dietary deficiency. Likewise, their range of scores on non-verbal tests of intelligence was that of a normal population of this age, whereas in a grossly deprived group one would have expected to find some retardation. On the other hand, in educational attainment the boys were distinctly below average, which was scarcely surprising in view of the poor schooling and lack of interest in education of many of their parents. Even among those of the boys who were of bright intelligence, very few were advanced in reading. However, though the majority of the boys were backward in reading and verbal skills, this disadvantage, like most others observed in the course of the research, was more relative than absolute. Only about 12 per cent were unable to read more than one or two words on the test, and some[12] illiterates were accounted for by pupils from the school for the educationally subnormal. Although about a quarter of the sample failed to respond meaningfully to a simple personality questionnaire designed for this age group (see p. 44 and Appendix III (B)) indifferent motivation and lack of practice in concentration on verbal tasks doubtless accounted for much of this blockage.

Within the sample, individual boys differed widely in the degree of social disadvantage experienced. These variations, which are described in more detail in later chapters, were found to be related to differences in performance and behaviour which were quite evident even at the age of 8 or 9. As time passes it should become clear how much importance should be attached to these early troubles as precursors of unrest and delinquency in later life.

Whatever the future findings may reveal, it would seem that the sample has been fortunately chosen for research into delinquency, in that the boys came from a fairly ordinary working-class urban community, free from special problems of racial conflict or extensive unemployment, where the kind of delinquent behaviour commonly encountered would probably be typical of similar areas throughout the country. The incidence of juvenile offences would be expected to be relatively high, but not particularly unusual. In fact, judging from the records of their older brothers, about one in seven of the boys in the Study will have one or more findings of guilt at a juvenile court by the time they reach the age of 17. Of course there will be many others with equal or worse behaviour problems who will not necessarily come to the notice of the courts, but whose difficulties will be known to the investigators.

At the time of the latest count (October 1968), when all had reached or passed the age of 14 years, fifty-six boys (13·6 per cent) had already been found guilty by a juvenile court on one or more occasions. Of these, eight were found guilty for the first time at age 10 or less, six at 11, six at age 12, and ten at age 13. Apart from these official offenders, the courts had taken action in respect of a further seven boys under 14 either for non-attendance at school or as in need of care, protection or control. (Some of these boys were also delinquent in behaviour according to the reports of parents or other informants, or according to their subsequent court records.) Finally, a further eighty boys, not included in the above categories, were reported to have committed delinquent acts, mostly thefts, outside their homes before they were 14 years according to statements by parents, teachers, police or neighbours. In short, even before the age of 14, thirty boys (7·3 per cent) were official delinquents and a further eighty-seven (12·2 per cent) had appeared at court or been reported for delinquent behaviour.

These preliminary estimates of incidence of official delinquency do not suggest a particularly high level, especially considering the general character of the sample. In J. W. B. Douglas' (1966) national sample, all of whom were born in 1946, 15 per cent of the boys had been cautioned or convicted for an offence by the time they reached 17 years of age, which is just about the same as the incidence of convictions among the older brothers of boys in this Study. In the Social Medicine Research Unit's survey of an East London borough, reported by Power (1967), 25 per cent of boys had been convicted by the time they were 17 years of age, and it was further found that having appeared at juvenile court for the first time the chances of a boy making a second appearance within one year were about 50 per cent.

NOTES

[1] The local authority schools were selected by the education authority on the basis of the number of boys required for the research and the willingness of the headmasters to participate in the scheme. The church school was approached by the investigators on account of its immediate proximity. No Roman Catholic school was included because the church authorities took so long to consider whether to grant permission that the sample was completed before any decision had been reached.

[2] These were subsequently amalgamated. From the researchers' point of view, it was an added complication having to deal with two administrations, but this was a condition requested by the education authorities, who did not want all of the schools used for the Study to be taken from one administration only.

[3] The number N in brackets indicates where, owing to lack of information about certain boys, the percentages are based upon something less than the total sample of 411.

[4] However, 55·6 per cent of the boys rated as coming from poor homes, compared with only 21·3 per cent of those from comfortable homes, belonged to social classes IV or V, although boys belonging to these two classes comprised 36·8 per cent of the total sample.

[5] To be exact, this meant the number of children, surviving at least a year, born to the parents before our boy's tenth birthday. Siblings of all categories living away were also counted, when their existence was known, provided only that they had once been members of the boy's nuclear family. Especially in the case of the unco-operative families, or of illegitimate births, it may be that siblings existed who were unknown to the investigators.

[6] Although there were 411 boys in the Study, these included 14 pairs of brothers, so there were only 397 different families in this count. Except where otherwise stated, however, the numbers in this report are normally based upon the boys, the same parent being counted twice in the case of brothers.

[7] Since no Roman Catholic primary school was included in the Study, it may be that the sample was somewhat deficient in Catholic boys compared with the neighbourhood in general. A rough calculation, based upon numbers of births recorded in the local Catholic Parish register, suggested that about 23 per cent of boys in the district were baptised Roman Catholics, which would mean that the numbers of Catholics in our sample were not far below the average. Of course, since none were attending their own church schools, they could not be regarded as representative Catholics.

[8] Expressed as a percentage of the total of boys aged eight or over attending the schools, the annual average of boys found guilty was 1·5 per cent in the Study schools of Area A, and 1·4 per cent in the Study schools of Area B. For all schools in areas A and B the corresponding figures were 1·4 per cent and 1·3 per cent respectively.

[9] One possible exception was the rating of 'conduct disorder severe', which was made by the P.S.Ws on only 5·2 per cent of boys in school A compared with much larger percentages in other schools. However, this could have been an artefact of rating habits. For instance, A was the first school inducted to the Study, and it could be that rating standards became stricter later on. A discussion of the criteria and validity of this rating appears on p. 42 and Appendix III (A).

[10] This was done on the assumption of a linear regression. Permission to use the test and norms was given by Dr Douglas and Mr Douglas Pigeon of the N.F.E.R.

[11] Due allowance for age having been made.

[12] Nine boys.

[13] Only a minority of the boys were still under the age of 10 when, by the Children and Young Persons Act, 1963, the age of criminal responsibility was raised from 8 to 10 years.

III
Assessing Conduct and Personality at Age Eight

1. *Teachers' Ratings of Conduct in School*

Misbehaviour by young children in the classroom is known to be a frequent precursor of delinquent behaviour in later years. Whether such conduct is the result of inadequate training at home, or of the child's individual disposition, the manifestations are much the same: the boy tends to be defiant and aggressive, to lie and steal, and to rebel against adult prohibitions. He also fails to develop the habits teachers try to foster, he is neither punctual nor regular in attendance; even though he may be of sound potential ability, he does not exert himself academically and is difficult to teach. He may be noticeably unkempt or dirty in appearance, and his relations with his classmates do not run smoothly.

A number of previous studies have demonstrated the effectiveness of teachers' observations of young schoolchildren as predictors of future delinquency. For example, A. J. Reiss (1951) in Chicago, in a survey of 1,110 white male juvenile delinquents, between the ages of 11 and 17 years, all of whom had been put on probation, found that one of the background features most significantly correlated with being convicted again while on probation was being classified as badly behaved by school authorities. W. C. Kvaraceus (1961), working in Boston, applied his own Delinquency Proneness Scale to a large sample of children attending junior high schools, and then followed up their delinquency records for three years. He found that teachers' reports of bad behaviour correlated more closely with subsequent delinquency than did the results of the psychological test. In a predictive research by Hathaway and Monachesi (1953), using the Minnesota Multiphasic Personality Inventory on a large sample of children in junior high schools, who were subsequently followed up at intervals up to 10 years, it was again found that whereas the test scores related only slightly to future delinquency, teachers' opinions concerning which children were behaving like potential delinquents proved comparatively effective predictors. Out of the total sample, 13·9 per cent of the boys were identified by teachers as potential delinquents, and of this high risk group 45 per cent in fact became delinquent.

B. B. Khlief (1964), studying school records in Kansas City, made an analysis of the spontaneous comments in the cumulative reports made by teachers during each child's career at school. Derogatory items concerned with poor work habits, poor attitude to school, objectionable personality traits, and misconduct were used to rate children on a scale of disturbance. High scores derived from the school records of previous years were found to be significantly correlated with court appearances at age 14 to 16.

It appears that school misbehaviour is of greater prognostic significance when it occurs at an early age. In the Gluecks' (1950) mammoth research, comparing 500 male delinquents with 500 non-delinquents matched for age, intelligence and area of residence, they found that 95·6 per cent of the delinquents seriously misbehaved themselves at school, whereas only 17·2 per cent of the non-delinquents were reported to have done so. Furthermore, of the boys who did misbehave badly, 59·6 per cent in the delinquent group, compared with only 19·8 per cent in the non-delinquent group, were reported to have done so for the first time at the age of 9 or earlier.

In England, D. H. Stott (1964) has developed a questionnaire for teachers, the Bristol Social Adjustment Guide, which asks about specific items of their pupils' classroom behaviour, and purports to identify potential delinquents. Stott showed that delinquents were distinguishable from others by the high frequency with which items indicative of a hostile or unfriendly attitude to adults, quarrelsomeness among peers, or aggressiveness were reported by teachers. He showed that among juveniles put on probation, those with high scores on such items were re-convicted with significantly greater frequency.

Of the various techniques available for obtaining ratings of child behaviour from teachers the most suitable for the present purpose was the questionnaire, devised by J. W. B. Douglas (1964) in the course of a national survey of the health and education of a cohort of British children, and given to teachers of 10-year-olds. The form was modified, with the author's permission, to meet the special circumstances of this Study. Two questions (5 and 8) were changed in wording because the Education Authority would not allow teachers to be asked about their pupils' homes or parents. The form had to be somewhat abbreviated, since in this Study teachers were asked to complete the questionnaires for all the boys in their class, and this meant filling in some twenty forms. It was also slightly changed so that it could be appropriately used at age 8 and 9, and repeated at age 10 to 11. The final version used is reproduced as Appendix I (A).

It has been demonstrated that teachers vary considerably in their standards of rating conduct (Hartshorne and May, 1928). J. W. B. Douglas (1964, p. 64) noted that children attending private schools were assessed relatively unfavourably by their teachers, although coming from the middle classes, whose children are generally reported to be more hard-working, one would have expected them to get better reports. He concluded that the teachers in private schools were probably applying stricter standards. In the present Study, one teacher categorized 30 per cent of her (A stream) boys as 'difficult to discipline', whereas some teachers assigned no boys at all to this category.

The teachers' rating form was filled in for all the boys. Co-operation was good, and twenty-four different class teachers contributed. The forms were scored on a points system for various items of undesirable behaviour mentioned, including, in order of seriousness, truanting, difficult to discipline, does not try to be a credit to his parents, noticeably dirty or untidy, lazy, difficult with his peers due to aggressiveness, seriously distractable, not specially good at anything, or outstandingly bad in at least one activity. The maximum possible of bad points amounted to thirty, and although no boy reached this total some of the worst behaved ones came very near to it.

When the scores for all the boys had been calculated, the data were considered class by class, according to the teacher who made the assessments. A boy was identified as badly behaved if his score fell among the uppermost quartile of the scores allocated by his teacher, and well behaved if his score was in the lowest quartile of his teacher's ratings.[1] This method of grouping into badly behaved, averagely behaved and well-behaved boys allowed for the difference in the strictness or leniency of particular teachers, but it meant that individuals with exactly the same score might be differently categorized. The use of only three categories might seem crude, but given the nature of the data it was doubtful if a finer grading would have been meaningful, and in fact the system identified effectively groups of boys who were distinctly different in many other respects.

Although the teachers' ratings were collected on a rather different system, it is of some interest to compare the responses of teachers in this Study with those reporting on boys in the National Survey. From the comparison which is set out in Appendix I (A), Table I A (1), it seemed that the present sample contained an excess of lazy and ill-disciplined boys compared with the national average. The evidence is not conclusive, however, since the effect of having the same class teacher rate a large number of boys all at once may have been to encourage raters to use the extreme categories more often than teachers in the national survey, who only rated one or two boys each.

The majority of the Study boys retained the same ranking when reassessed three years later, just before leaving their primary schools, on the basis of fresh reports from a different set of teachers. Of the 388 boys rated a second time at age 11, and classed as 'good', 'average' or 'bad', 55·5 per cent were in the same category as before. Only ten (2·6 per cent) had changed from one extreme to the other, five out of eighty-five changing from good to bad, and five out of eighty-eight changing from bad to good.

2. Conduct Disorder Rated by P.S.Ws

A different assessment of behaviour disorder in the boys was made by the psychiatric social workers. The case record forms which they completed had places for noting a wide range of specified items of relevance. Twelve of these were taken into account in rating boys on what was called 'Behaviour Disorder'. These were wandering away from home, stealing from home, truanting from school, lying, stealing outside the home, sexual misbehaviour, quarrelling, tempers, cruelty, destructiveness, jealousy and defiance. Five items were recorded simply as absent or present, but the first seven were each graded on rating scales indicating the severity of the problem. For example *lying* had a four-point scale defined as follows:

(i) Frequent habitual first reaction is to deny or distort facts. Compulsive lying where no immediate purpose served, or lying as a characteristic pattern for gaining own ends, even when the truth would be as effective. So characteristically he is mistrusted by those with whom he has more than casual contact.

(ii) More frequent than average. Lies habitually in any emergency to serve immediate purpose. Includes easily detected impulsive lies as well as complicated distortions.

(iii) Lies occasionally to avoid scolding, punishment or under pressure to make a good impression, but not characteristic in all situations. Includes frequent wish-fulfilment lies.

(iv) Never lies, due to unusual and rigid honesty.

The P.S.Ws were asked to look through each of their schedules on all these points, to read through any relevant comments they had made on the record forms, and then, on the basis of their total impression of each case after all the individual items had been set down, to allocate their boys to four grades of behaviour disorder: absent, minimal, moderate or severe.

Scrutiny of these ratings showed considerable inconsistency between the P.S.Ws in the type of boy identified as behaviour disordered. For this reason the method of rating had to be simplified, taking into account no more than six basic items (lying, stealing at home, stealing outside, destructiveness, quarrelsomeness and defiance), and basing the final rating on an item count rather than a global impression. Some account of how and why this was done is given in Appendix III (A). The final, modified rating of *conduct disorder* appeared to be more reliable than the original assessment, and this was the one used in all subsequent tabulations. The scale had three points, no conduct disorder (262 boys), moderate disorder (62 boys), and severe disorder (60 boys), leaving 27 not rated.

3. *A Combined Assessment of Boys' Conduct*

The teachers' ratings of conduct in the class situation (see p. 38) and the P.S.Ws' ratings of conduct disorder were correlated ($r = 0.29$), but by no means identical, which is hardly surprising considering that some boys are angels outside and devils at home, or vice versa. In fact, of the 262 boys rated free from conduct disorder by the P.S.Ws, 40, that is 15.3 per cent, were placed in the worst behaviour category by their teachers. In some of these cases the lack of complaint on the part of the parents may have been due to their own slack standards. Of 83 boys rated well-behaved by teachers, only 7, that is 8.4 per cent, had a severe degree of conduct disorder according to the P.S.Ws.

On the assumption that the combined opinions of independent judges would give a more discriminating assessment, a final rating of the boys' conduct was obtained by amalgamating the ratings of teachers and P.S.Ws.[2] The combined rating scale of conduct ranged from one point for boys rated 'good' by both teachers and P.S.Ws, to five points for boys rated 'bad' by both judges. (The exact system of points allocation, including the twenty-seven boys rated by teachers only, is indicated in Appendix III (A), Table 1.) It seemed reasonable to suppose that the thirty boys placed in the worst category by both judges would represent the most seriously troublesome cases.

Here are a few examples of contrasting ratings on the combined scale of conduct:

Case 321 (Rated 1, the best category of conduct)
In response to the specific questions, this boy's class teacher reported that he was a very hard worker, with no outstandingly good or bad subjects, who had no trouble in concentration, no difficulties with other

children, who was noticeably clean and tidy and not difficult to discipline. The teacher added, 'He is a born comic, eager and lively. He never seems to get despondent. He will keep trying at something he finds difficult.'

The P.S.W. noted that he always comes straight home from school, never wanders off or truants, never known to steal and on the rare occasions that he tells a fib he owns up if challenged. He is able to stand up for himself and doesn't mind a scrap, but he doesn't look for trouble. If he loses his temper it is soon over.

Case 41 (Rated 3, an intermediate category of conduct)
In answer to the specific questions the teacher gave the same responses as in the previous case 321, except that this boy was only 'average' in school work. The teacher added this comment: 'A quiet boy, does not mix well with all the other boys but keeps to his own small group.'

The P.S.W. recorded some more adverse comments. 'He doesn't fight, but he teases and bosses other children. He can't hold his own and comes home crying if attacked. On the whole he avoids occasions for strife.' His mother complained that he often sulks. 'He feels hard done by, you can't talk to him, he makes a pretence of listening but he's not really taking things in.'

Case 18 (Rated 5, the worst category of conduct)
The teacher reported he was a poor worker, bad in writing and reading, with no outstandingly good subject. He lacked concentration, was only average in cleanliness, and was difficult to discipline, but he had no difficulties with other children. The teacher added, 'He seems to have some sort of grudge against life, I haven't got to the bottom of it. Sometimes he is extremely difficult and at other times he is very willing to help. . . .'

His mother told the P.S.W. he was 'a problem, always up and down'. He was always late in coming home from school and would swear black was white to get himself out of trouble. He was quarrelsome with other boys and he had very severe tempers, when he would lock himself in his room and be liable to hit anyone. Once he attacked his father with a knife. He was defiant to his parents, refusing to do as he was told. He was very jealous of his younger brother, and he was often moody and miserable, complaining and feeling persecuted.

As will be seen in later chapters, poor conduct, on the combined ratings of P.S.Ws and teachers, was closely associated with a number of background factors traditionally regarded as conducive to delinquency. In anticipation of the discussion to follow, Table III (1) gives just one example, namely the highly significant association between poor conduct and poor family income. Only 13·3 per cent of boys from 'comfortable' income families received the worst rating (5) on conduct, whereas 46·7 per cent of the boys from 'inadequate' income families were so rated.

TABLE III (1)

Boys' Conduct (Combined Ratings) against level of Family Income

	Boys' Conduct (Combined Ratings of Teachers and P.S.Ws)										Total No. of boys rated on income	
Family Income	Good				Average		Bad					
	I		II		III		IV		V			
	N	%	N	%	N	%	N	%	N	%	N	%
Comfortable	29	42·0	53	33·5	29	32·6	7	14·3	4	13·3	122	30·9
Adequate	30	43·5	81	51·3	36	40·4	24	49·0	12	40·0	183	46·3
Inadequate	10	14·5	24	15·2	24	27·0	18	36·7	14	46·7	90	22·8
TOTAL	69	100	158	100	89	100	49	100	30	100	395	100

$\chi^2 = 31·02$ with 8 d.f., $p < ·001$

4. Assessments of Neurotic Tendency

(a) *Psychological Testing.* Some means of assessing neurotic tendency in boys was clearly needed in view of the widespread assumption that this is an important factor in delinquency. An obvious first choice was the Junior Maudsley Personality Inventory (Furneaux and Gibson, 1961), a questionnaire that has been used with English children to measure an individual's position along the two important personality dimensions of neuroticism and extraversion. According to Eysenck's (1964) theory, persons with a high degree of both neuroticism and extraversion are prone to hysterical, psychopathic and criminal behaviour. Such personality types may not account for the entire delinquent population, but they constitute an important element.

Unfortunately, the Maudsley Inventory proved impractical in this Study because of the low level of reading ability and verbal comprehension of many of the boys. A simplified instrument was therefore constructed, to measure similar variables, but in a manner adapted to semi-literate boys of this age. In this new test all the items applied specifically to boys, the wording was made of elementary simplicity, and the items were printed on separate cards and illustrated pictorially. To reduce defensiveness in the face of potentially embarrassing questions, the test was presented as if its purpose were to assess reading ability. The boys were given the test individually and were asked to look at and if possible to read the illustrated cards, each of which depicted some significant action in the life of a boy of about their own age. They were told to put the card into either of two boxes which had the labels 'Same as Me' and 'Not the Same'. Thus, if the card bore the legend 'Other boys bully him', with a picture depicting the situation, and the boy put it in the 'Same as Me' box, this would be taken as an admission that he thought himself bullied by other boys.

Some further particulars are given in Appendix III (B). The results of the test, scored on scales of 'neuroticism' and 'extraversion', lent support to the idea that the characteristic delinquent type is a personality who is high on both these traits (Trasler, 1962). Table III (2) shows the proportion of badly behaved boys (i.e. rating four or five on the combined assessments of teachers and P.S.Ws) in the four personality groupings identified by the personality test scores. As predicted, the group of neurotic extraverts contained a significantly higher proportion of badly behaved boys than the other groups. However, the differences were not very great, and among all personality groupings, including the neurotic extraverts, only a minority were badly behaved. Thus, though the relationship between these personality features and anti-social behaviour seems a valid one, it is probably not close enough to have much practical value for prediction in the individual case.

TABLE III (2)

Conduct against Personality Inventory Rating

Conduct (ratings of P.S.Ws and Teachers)	Stable Introvert No.	%	Neurotic Introvert No.	%	Stable Extravert No.	%	Neurotic Extravert No.	%
Average or good (I, II or III) Conduct	52	91·2	52	86·7	67	84·8	60	75·0
Bad (IV or V) Conduct	5	8·8	8	13·3	12	15·2	20	25·0
TOTAL	57	100	60	100	79	100	80	100

$\chi^2 = 7·25$ with 3 d.f. N.S.
Comparing the Neurotic Extravert category with all the rest, $\chi^2 = 5·38$ with 1 d.f., $p < ·05$

(b) *Interview Reports of Nervous Disturbance in Boys.* Nervous disturbance among the boys was also assessed independently by the P.S.Ws, mostly on the basis of symptoms reported to them by mothers, but occasionally supplemented by information from medical agencies or other outside sources. Particular care was taken in the part of the record form used for transcribing this information to make the inquiry as specific as possible. Seventeen symptoms were listed on the forms, and the instruction guide requested the P.S.Ws to mark each one according to whether the items was asked about, whether it was reported not present, or whether it was said to have occurred, in which case they were asked to give an account of the severity and duration of the symptom, stating the boy's age when it occurred. The items included such things as tics, sleep disturbances, speech disorder, enuresis and special fears, followed by a general question about 'Any other symptoms?' Definitions, and in some instances code ratings of severity were set out in the instruction guide.[3]

Here are three examples to show how the P.S.Ws allocated differing degrees of severity to the symptoms reported to them:

Case 22 (Rated 'minimal degree' of nervous disturbance)
This boy was described as over-active, always fidgety, always doing something. Even when watching T.V. which he likes, he has to be very interested indeed before he can sit still. At the time of interview he was said to be enuretic. His mother reported that this had begun some three months previously, and that he wet himself about once a week. She thought it was due to troubles at school. No other specific symptoms were mentioned.

Case 81 (Rated 'moderate degree' of nervous disturbance)
The boy was rated unfavourably in regard to appetite disturbance, moodiness, fears and psychosomatic disorder. He suffered from asthma and was described as a nervous, excitable, highly-strung child who became moody and irritable, particularly when his asthma was bad. He tended to grizzle at the least thing, and to get wheezy and rather panicky. He was afraid of the dark and would leave his bedroom door open with the light on in the passage outside. He was fussy about food and some days would eat only very little.

Case 18 (Rated 'severe degree' of nervous disturbance)
This boy was rated unfavourably on sleep disturbance, restlessness, obsessionality, and moodiness. His mother described up and down moods which she put down to jealousy and insecurity. He would look miserable, and go into his room and shut the door. He had had nightmares since 6 years of age, waking up terrified and shouting for his mother. He bit his nails. He was obsessionally fastidious about cleanliness, re-washing cutlery, scrubbing his hands and feet repeatedly at night. When upset, he would occupy himself tidying his cupboard. He would refuse to wear a tie if he could not get it straight. When the time to leave for school approached he would constantly watch the clock. He also had trouble with speech, getting his words mixed up, and he had had treatment for this for three years.

These categories of severity were necessarily highly complex and subjective judgements, and there was evidence that they were considerably affected by the level of intelligence and communicativeness of the mother, who was the main informant. (The matter is discussed in some detail in Appendix III (C).) Nevertheless, in spite of the shortcomings of the rating scale of nervousness there must have been some validity to the identification of boys with a severe degree of nervous disturbance, all of whom had a considerable array of symptoms reported. The incidence of severe nervous disturbance (41 boys out of 382 rated), 10·7 per cent, was not unduly large considering the nature of the sample. Rutter's (Rutter and Graham, 1966) survey (of an Isle of Wight population of 10 to 11 year old children) identified as sufficiently disturbed to warrant psychiatric treatment. 89 boys out of a total population of 2,193, that is 8·1 per cent of boys, assuming that the sexes were equally distributed in the original sample. In this Study, only a minority of the forty-one disturbed boys were receiving any special treatment. Up to November 1964, only fourteen of them had been referred to child guidance or special clinics (like those for enuresis or speech defects), although in later years a few more of them found their way to clinics. Moreover, of those who were professionally examined, not all received effective help, some had diagnostic interviews only, whilst others failed to attend subsequent appointments.

TABLE III (3)

Teachers' Ratings of Boys' Conduct against P.S.Ws' Ratings of Nervous Disturbance in Boys

		\multicolumn{4}{c}{Nervous Disturbance Ratings:}			
		Absent or minimal		Moderate or Severe	
		No.	%	No.	%
Teachers'	Good	71	24·5	13	14·1
Ratings of	Average	160	55·2	48	52·2
Conduct	Bad	59	20·3	31	33·7
	TOTAL	290	100	92	100

$\chi^2 = 8·8$ with 2 d.f., $p < ·025$

Table III (3) shows that there was a significant tendency for the same boys who were identified by P.S.Ws as nervous to be picked out as badly behaved by teachers. An actual example of this kind, Case 18, has already been quoted on pp. 43, 46. Another, Case 32, is quoted on p. 56. This overlap between nervousness and antisocial behaviour[4] suggests that some of the boys with anxiety symptoms at age 8 or 9 are destined to swell the ranks of the delinquents when they grow older. The idea that juvenile delinquents are often drawn from among the ranks of neurotic children meets with resistance from educators and legal authorities, who view them as bold, bad characters rather than sufferers. Moreover, research studies, such as that of Ivy Bennett (1960), have generally supported the view that typical neurotics and delinquents are sharply contrasted in personality, social outlook and family background; the former being anxious and conflict-ridden, the later being care-free rebellious and lacking in social standards. It may be, however, that some of the boys who are predominantly anxious and inhibited at age 8 will become predominantly rebellious and uninhibited as they approach adolescence.

5. *Psychomotor Performance*

(a) *The Porteus Mazes.* A careless, clumsy performance on tests requiring dexterity and fine control of movements is believed to be characteristic of certain delinquents. In investigations at the national centre for training and research on delinquency at Vaucresson (Bize, 1964; 1965), near Paris, groups of ordinary schoolchildren and groups of juvenile delinquents have been compared on a variety of tests of motor skills, such as finger agility, accuracy of movement in threading a ring along a curled rod without letting it touch (a popular fairground game) and speed of placing small metal rods in rows of holes. The investigators concluded that juvenile delinquents performed significantly differently from normal juveniles on many of these tests, not on account of lack of basic motor control in elementary tasks of co-ordination, but because of ineptitude in the more complex tests involving thought as well as movement. The delinquents were particularly inferior in tasks demanding a balance between speed and accuracy, tending to concentrate on speed to the detriment of accuracy, as if incapable of deliberation and reflection before action. A number of such studies (Anthony, 1960) have shown that socially disturbed individuals, and notably delinquents, give anomalous responses when tested with apparatus designed to measure accuracy of psychomotor performance. Perhaps this is one reason for the offensive driving habits of men with a criminal record (Willett, 1964). Of course questions of motivation, caution in avoiding errors, patience, and persistence enter into these tasks, as well as sheer skill in the control of movement, so that the reasons why delinquents tend to perform badly may be quite complex.

One of the earliest demonstrations of defective psychomotor

performance on the part of delinquents arose from the use of the Porteus Mazes which, as described in Chapter I, were included among the tests given to the Study boys at age 8. According to Porteus (1942), 'There is a marked tendency of delinquents as a group to carry out a simple task, such as drawing through a maze design, in an inexact, heedless, slipshod or nervous manner, and to neglect instructions, especially when that task is incidental to the solution of a more immediate or overt problem'. By scoring them according to the manner in which they are filled in, apart from their correctness, the Porteus Mazes can be made to yield a Qualitative or 'Q' score believed to be indicative of delinquent trends. The Q score is obtained by counting a variety of stylistic errors (such as cutting corners and touching or crossing the borders of the maze path) which the subject may perpetrate during the test.[5] The specially useful feature is that the subject does not know, when taking the test, that this aspect of behaviour is under scrutiny. The chief purpose of including the mazes in this battery was not to confirm that established delinquents tend to give high Porteus Q scores (Docter and Winder, 1954), but to see if the scores would have predictive value when the test was applied to a predelinquent age group (Sanderson, 1945).

(b) *The Gibson Spiral Maze.* In order to explore further one aspect of the Porteus Mazes, namely the slipshod performance characteristic of disturbed individuals, the psychologist developed a new technique, the *Spiral Maze Test* (Gibson, 1965), which is quick and easy to score, and takes only about two minutes to administer. It consists of a spiral path, bordered by heavy black lines, which is printed on a large card. Obstacles, represented by the letter O in heavy type, are scattered along the pathway. The subject has to trace round the path with a pencil or ball-point pen, from the centre outwards, in an anti-clockwise direction, and as quickly as he can, but without cutting across the obstacles or touching the edges of the path. The subject's performance is timed with a stop-watch, and he is urged to go as fast as he can. An error score is produced by summing penalty points, e.g. one for every time the subject's pencil touches the printed lines of the spiral or the obstacles, two for every time the pencil actually penetrates. The error score is adjusted according to the time taken to complete the maze, so that in effect the final score is a rating which compares the subject's accuracy of performance with the average performance of a person of the same age who takes the same length of time.

On this test, well-adjusted persons are both quick and accurate. It was anticipated that high Error scores, indicative of careless performance, would be given by the more maladjusted or badly behaved boys, and in fact this proved to be the case (Gibson, 1964).

(c) *The Tapping Test*. This test, based on the work of G. A. Foulds (1961), is another measure of psychomotor performance. This was introduced into the battery of individually administered tests[6] some time after the commencement of the Study, but 82 per cent of the boys tried it. Each boy was given a pencil and told to tap with it as fast as possible on to a blank paper for ten seconds. The test appears to be one of speed of movement, but actually it is the area covered by the dots which forms the basis of the test score. Some subjects are restrained in their movements and produce a small neat patch densely covered with dots. According to Foulds' theory, the extra-punitive personality type tends to expansive movements which cover a large area with dots. The hypothesis which justified the use of the test in the present Study was that boys with delinquent potentialities would tend to scatter their dots more widely. Although the rationale of this test is less obvious and more speculative than that of the maze tests, it takes only a minute to administer, and it was thought it might prove useful as an adjunct to the other psychomotor measures. In point of fact the scores did show a slight but significant positive correlation with bad conduct as rated by teachers ($r = \cdot 17$).

(d) *The Body Sway Test*. One other test, included under the general heading of psychomotor performance, consisted in having the boy stand upright, blindfolding him with opaque goggles, and then measuring how much he swayed in response to the suggestion that he would now feel as if he were falling forwards (Himmelweit and Petrie, 1946). Some boys found the test unpleasant or anxiety provoking. For this and other reasons it was given to 373 boys only, and the 9 per cent who did not take the test may have been a somewhat untypical group. Most of the boys (216) hardly swayed at all, some (81) swayed steadily forwards in direct response to the suggestion, whereas a minority (76) swayed backwards and forwards erratically, sometimes losing balance in one direction or another. This 'static ataxia' type of response was made by 31·5 per cent of the boys with poor conduct ratings from their teachers, compared with only 15·2 per cent among the well-behaved group, which was a statistically significant difference.

(e) *Combined Psychomotor Scores*. Each boy was given a combined score[7] for all four psychomotor tests on the assumption that a series of measures would give a better assessment of performance than any single test. Boys who did not take a particular test were allocated the modal rating they achieved on other tests. On this system only three cases had to remain unscored because too few tests had been given.

TABLE III (4)

Psychomotor Performance (Combined score of Four tests) against Boys' Conduct (Combined Ratings of P.S.Ws and Teachers)

Psychomotor Score:	Good				Conduct Ratings: Average				Bad	
	I		II		III		IV		V	
	No.	%	No.	%	No.	%	No.	%	No.	%
Good	41	59·4	69	43·4	30	30·9	11	20·8	3	10·0
Average	22	31·9	66	41·5	49	50·5	27	50·9	13	43·3
Bad	6	8·7	24	15·1	18	18·6	15	28·3	14	46·7
TOTAL	69	100	159	100	97	100	53	100	30	100

$\chi^2 = 44·98$ with 8 d.f., $p < ·001$

Table III (4) shows the relationship between bad behaviour (on ratings by teachers and P.S.Ws combined) and the final psychomotor scores. The figures show a steady increase in the incidence of poor psychomotor performance from 8·7 per cent in the best conduct category to 46·7 per cent among the worst boys. This is a straightforward, significant linear correlation, which, as subsequent analysis showed, held true at all three levels of family income, and thus could not be explained away as being due to a coincidence of clumsiness and misconduct among lower-class boys. In fact, psychomotor performance was more closely related to conduct than to any other major variable concerned with either the boys or their backgrounds, with the possible exception of intelligence.[8] These results confirm the importance of psychomotor performance in relation to social behaviour, showing in particular that a poor performance is unusual among socially conforming types.

6. *Popularity among Class-mates*

In this Study a measure of popularity among peers was obtained by the well-known technique of the sociogram, which depends upon asking subjects to make choices from among fellow members of their group or class those whom they like best. At least in normal schools the delinquent-prone members are apt to be among the less popular (Croft and Grygier, 1956), whereas good conduct and popularity tend to go together (Sugarman, 1968, p. 50). This may not hold true in all circumstances. For example David Hargreaves (1967) showed that in the lowest educational stream of the secondary school where he worked adherence to conformist and academic values earned unpopularity.

The present research was inspired by the work of D. Harper (1965) who showed that the response of schoolboys of about 13 years of age to such questions are highly predictive of subsequent delinquency among those rejected by their class-mates. In Harper's research the question was posed in a negative form also, the boys being asked to write down the names of other boys in the class whom they would *not* like to sit next to them. In the present Study, this was not done, because it was thought that the boys might not co-operate so cheerfully if they were asked to write down such critical or humiliating opinions about their class-mates. Instead, they were asked to name their four best friends from among other boys in the class in order of their preference. The boys were given copies of a duplicated class list with all their names on which to make their choices. The girls in the class were issued with corresponding lists of girls' names so they would be similarly occupied during the test.

Even though phrased in positive terms, the results of the test gave measures of unpopularity as well as popularity, since the socially rejected boys were chosen by few or none of their classmates. Sociometric scores were obtained for 358 boys only, since some did not belong to a class as they were working in small groups having special tuition, and a few had been absent from school so much due to illness or other reasons that they could not be considered as regular members of the group.

The test results can be used to reproduce the structure of the whole class in terms of individuals' social relationships. This is best demonstrated in diagrams showing for each individual which boys choose him, and which he is attracted to. In this way it can be seen at a glance that some boys belong to popular cliques, the members of which choose each other, and are also chosen by outsiders, while other boys are social isolates to whom no one seems attracted. However, for present purposes, a simple popularity score has been used, based upon the number of times the boy was chosen by others.[9]

Table III (5) sets out the relationship between ratings by classmates and ratings by teachers, showing a highly significant tendency for boys rated poorly as to conduct to be unpopular among their peers. This result was due to the teachers' contribution to the conduct assessment, for the relationship between the boys' unpopularity ratings and the P.S.W.s' assessments of conduct disorder was negligible (r = ·06). Apparently behaviour complained about by mothers had little relevance to a boy's popularity, whereas behaviour disapproved by teachers tended to cause him to lose status among his class-mates. The popularity ratings could not have been influenced by direct suggestion from the teachers, however, since the test was conducted by the psychologist independently. Unpopularity was slightly more prevalent among boys from lower-income families, but the positive correlation with poor conduct held true within all three income groups, so it could not be due to both teachers and pupils viewing the lowest classes with disfavour. It may be true in some penal establishments for juveniles, or in some very rough delinquent neighbourhoods, that rebels in the schoolroom win high status among their peers, but in the present setting, and at the age of 8, it was the better behaved boys who were generally the more popular.

cf. interaction

TABLE III (5)

Boys' Conduct against Boys' Popularity among Peers

	Boys' Conduct (Combined Ratings of P.S.Ws and Teachers)								
Peer Rating:	Good				Average		Bad		
	I		II		III		IV		V
	No.	%	No.	%	No.	%	No.	%	No.	%
Unpopular	15	21·7	78	52·0	55	59·1	28	62·2	19	67·9
Popular	54	78·3	72	48·0	38	40·9	17	37·8	9	32·1
TOTAL	69	100	150	100	93	100	45	100	28	100

χ^2 (Kolmogorov-Smirnov Test) = 16·49 with 2 d.f., p < ·001

7. Summing Up the Picture at Age 8

As can be seen from previous tables, as well as from the matrix of correlations displayed in Appendix VI (A), in all the measures of individual characteristics so far mentioned (including intelligence, scholastic attainment, neurotic tendency, psychomotor performance, and peer ratings) poor scores invariably correlated significantly with adverse ratings of conduct by the teachers (or by the teachers and P.S.Ws combined). The correlations were highest between poor conduct and poor psychomotor performance, but since this and most of the other adverse individual characteristics were themselves positively inter-correlated it was clear that no single feature could be regarded as the predominant or exclusive factor in misconduct at this age. From this all too obvious and expected conclusion it follows that in studying the antecedents of juvenile misbehaviour one must be concerned, from now on, with combinations of factors and relationships between factors rather than with any single cause and effect.

The results of repeat assessments at age 11 showed that on most measures, including teachers' ratings of misconduct, the rankings of the majority of the boys were not grossly different from what they had been three years previously. This suggests that the assessments at age 8 may well prove to have considerable long-term predictive value in respect to future delinquency. Meantime, it seems appropriate to see how far it is possible to identify from the data collected at age 8 which boys appear, by virtue of their present behavioural and personality characteristics, to stand in particular risk of becoming delinquent.

8. *Identifying Boys at Special Risk of Delinquency*

On the assumption that nothing predicts future delinquency so well as present misconduct, an attempt was made to combine all sources of information about the boys' behaviour at age 8 to 9 into a single, composite assessment which would serve to identify a group consisting of the most rebellious, worst-behaved, and generally 'difficult' characters in the Study sample. The over-riding feature of the boys in this category was their liability to various forms of disapproved conduct calculated to hurt or annoy others. We called them the 'acting out' boys, borrowing a psycho-analytic term and using it (as the analysts themselves often seem to do) in a loose and purely descriptive sense.

The five elements which were amalgamated to produce the acting-out category consisted of bad conduct ratings by teachers, presence of conduct disorder according to P.S.Ws' ratings, the lowest grade of popularity on the choices of class-mates, scores on the self-reporting personality test indicative of traits of combined neuroticism and extraversion and finally attendance at the school for the educationally subnormal. This last criterion was included because troublesome behaviour was often the main reason for the placement of these boys in an E.S.N. school. Actually, only seven boys were included in the acting out group on these grounds who would not otherwise have appeared there, and all seven had been rated adversely as to conduct by either P.S.Ws or teachers.

One advantage of combining ratings from different sources is that a false or inaccurate rating on any one variable is likely to be outweighed by all the rest. Hence the combined assessment may be expected to have greater reliability than its individual components. Another advantage is that allowance can be made where the rating on any particular measure is missing, provided other relevant measures are available. A predetermined system was fed into the computer to enable cases to be counted in which not all of the defining criteria were available. Finally, seventy-seven boys were identified as troublesome 'acting-out' characters who may be expected to prove particularly prone to delinquency as they grow older. Since the conduct assessments by teachers and P.S.Ws formed two important elements in the definition of the acting-out group, there was a considerable overlap between this and the group of eighty-three boys allocated to the worst categories on the conduct ratings of teachers and P.S.Ws combined. In fact, fifty-six (that is 72·7 per cent) of the seventy-seven acting-out boys were included among the eighty-three with bad conduct ratings. However, for reasons just stated, the 'acting-out' assessment, on account of its relative comprehensiveness, may be expected to be somewhat more efficient as a measure of delinquency proneness. Time will tell.

Meantime, taking as a criterion of early delinquency the thirty boys found guilty by a juvenile court of an offence (i.e. one sufficiently serious to have been recorded by the Criminal Record Office) on one or more occasions before reaching the age of 14 years, 12·9 per cent of the seventy-seven acting-out boys have become early delinquents compared with 5·9 per cent only of the rest of the boys. On the same basis, 18·1 per cent of the eighty-three boys with the worst conduct ratings have become early delinquents compared with 4·6 per cent among the remainder of the sample.

A further indication of the predictive value of the acting-out category, at least in the immediate future, was provided by the results of the social workers' continued inquiries during the years 1965/6, when the boys were mostly about 12 years old. Table III (6) shows that of the boys of this age about whom there were complaints of behaviour problems as many as one-third belonged to the acting-out group; whereas of those who had no behaviour problems reported only 8·8 per cent belonged to the acting-out group. Incidentally, in the minority of cases in which parents were unco-operative, and no information was available to the social workers concerning a boy's present behaviour, as many as 19·6 per cent belonged to the acting-out group. This was yet another example of no news being bad news, since family resistance to inquiry was often an unfavourable sign.

TABLE III (6)

Behaviour Difficulties in Boys (at about age 12) reported to social workers against the Acting-out Classification

	Number of Boys	Number classed as acting-out	Percentage classed as acting out
No behaviour problems reported	217	19	8·8
Behaviour difficulties reported (including court appearances)	148	49	33·1
Parents uncooperative and information lacking	46	9	19·6
TOTAL	411	77	18·7

In order to illustrate the kind of disturbance which made up the acting-out group, here are two typical examples. The first boy appeared in the worst category (V), and the second being one in the average category (III), on the conduct ratings of teachers and P.S.Ws combined.

Case 32
When first seen at the age of 8, this boy was living in rather poor and crowded conditions in an old slum house. His mother appeared anxious and harassed. She described him as an aggravating boy, extremely restless and fidgety, prone to temper tantrums and screaming bouts when he wanted attention or could not get his own way. He was also hypochondriacal, and subject to bad dreams, and was jealous of his brothers and apt to quarrel and fight with them. With his mother he was alternately clinging and defiant. He made friends, but usually with the noisier type of boy, and complained he was bullied. He hated school and often stayed off or ran home to his mother. His school teacher commented that he dribbled and lisped and was at times very babyish, becoming violent when he did not get his own way, and truanting frequently. Up to the age of 13 there were no complaints of actual delinquency in this boy's case, but both his father and elder brother had been convicted.

Case 232
This boy came from a poor family with a large number of children. His parents were both rather dull, and with bad health records. The teacher commented that he often turned up late and dirty-looking, and that he was dull, lacking in concentration and extremely childish. The sociometric test showed he was not popular with other boys, and he produced

poor scores on psychomotor testing. Various social workers considered this a problem family and had tried to help but were put off by the father, who was very aggressively independent, very strict with his children, and not amenable to advice. Mother commented on the boy's slowness, laziness and untidiness, but otherwise she had no serious criticism of his conduct and no significant nervous troubles to report. Some of his brothers were duller and more overtly troublesome or maladjusted. He himself reached the age of 13 with no court appearances and no complaints of delinquency recorded against him.

TABLE III (7)

Relationships of Boys Classed as 'Acting-out' to other Variables

Variable:		No.	Percent rated 'Acting-out'	Significance[1] of difference
Criminality of Father	No record	310	16·5	
	1 Conviction	50	24·0	$p < ·02$
	2+Convictions	29	37·9	
Family Size	Only child	41	17·1	
	2 to 5 children	303	15·8	$p < ·01$[2]
	6 or more children	67	32·8	
Physical Neglect of boy	Not neglected	349	14·9	$p < ·001$
	Neglected	49	49·0	
Social Handicap	Nil	182	11·5	
	Moderate	174	19·0	$p < ·001$
	Severe	55	41·8	
Mother's Personality	Stable	333	15·6	$p < ·001$
	Unstable	49	44·9	
Father's Personality	Stable	321	17·4	N.S.
	Unstable	47	27·7	
Parents' Marriage	Satisfactory	284	15·8	$p < ·01$
	Disharmonious	89	30·3	
Parental Rules	Not lax	309	14·5	$p < ·001$
	Lax	66	36·4	
Non Verbal Intelligence (Matrices)	Bright (>110)	122	13·9	
	Average	203	16·7	$p < ·01$
	Dull (<91)	86	30·2	
Body Build	Not 'heavily built'	246	13·4	$p < ·001$
	'Heavily built'	159	27·0	
'Combined' Psychomotor Disturbance	Low (<5)	351	15·4	$p < ·001$
	High (⩾5)	77	33·8	

[1] Levels of significance are based on χ^2 values obtained from the raw figures.
[2] Here the 3rd category is compared with the other two.

One of the great problems of child welfare is how to get at those most in need. It has already been remarked how large a proportion of the boys considered to have 'severe' nervous disturbance received little effective help. The seventy-seven 'acting-out' boys were nearly all actual or potential social problems, but less than half came from families in contact with clinics, childrens' departments, or other social agencies. Even among the minority under official notice the help given was sometimes minimal—for example grants for clothing, or free school meals—and often focused upon some other member of the family than the 'acting-out' boy himself. This tends to confirm the impression that for every child effectively dealt with by the welfare services, another one or two, with problems equally severe, slip through the net.

Assuming that the 'acting-out' boys include a significant number of future delinquents (perhaps more especially the persistent and serious delinquents) it is of interest to note what special characteristics they have apart from their troublesome behaviour. Some of these are set out in Table III (7). It appears that boys of dull intelligence compared with those of bright intelligence; heavily built (? mesomorphic) compared with lightly built (? ectomorphic) boys; those poor on psychomotor tests compared with those of satisfactory performance; are all at least twice as frequent among the acting-out category. Other features significantly associated with 'acting-out' include having a father with more than one criminal conviction, coming from a large family, having a mother of unstable personality, having parents who are lax in disciplinary rules, or coming from a family of poor socio-economic standards (social handicap). These very important concomitants of present, and probably also of future, acting-out behaviour are concerned with individual family backgrounds, and form the subject matter of the subsequent chapters.

NOTES

[1] Theoretically the proportions of boys in the good, average and bad categories should have been $\frac{1}{4}$, $\frac{1}{2}$ and $\frac{1}{4}$. Since a difference of only one point of scoring sometimes meant the inclusion or exclusion of a sizeable percentage of the class, it was not always possible to divide the classes exactly in quarters. The actual numbers were 85, 226 and 100 respectively.

[2] The cases not rated by the P.S.Ws on the conduct disorder scale were allocated, in the first instance, according to their earlier impressionistic assessments of behaviour, or else, when no other information was available, on the teachers' reports only, so that finally every boy received a rating on the new conduct scale.

[3] For example, 'Tics' was defined as 'Any mannerism other than nail-biting, thumb-sucking, masturbation or stammering'. (These other items were recorded elsewhere.) It was graded in three categories as follows (the definitions being taken from Macfarlane et al. (1954)):

   i. Compulsive, pronounced, tic-like behaviour occurring daily whether obviously ritualistic or not, and whether involving only small muscle groups. Either severe or frequent, or less severe but going off many times a day. (By severe is meant involvement that compels attention of anyone.)

ii. Persistent mannerisms. Less often or severe than (i). Obvious enough to be noticed by anyone. Clearing throat, sniffing, hunching up shoulders, squinting, twitching of any facial muscles, tapping with feet, etc.
iii. Absence of observed mannerisms of tic-like behaviour, except when child is overfatigued or under emotional pressure, or few minor transitory mannerisms, for example rubbing eyes.

[4] The relationship is only tentative, since teachers' reports were available to the P.S.Ws and could have affected their ratings. Furthermore, certain items of behaviour, such as refusal to go to school on account of anxiety, might count as both an indication of nervous disturbance and a piece of misconduct. There was some evidence that P.S.W. A, whose nervousness ratings differed from those of her colleagues, had a greater tendency to consider boys with behaviour problems as having nervous disturbance.

[5] All records were scored rigidly in accordance with Porteus' instructions. However, the norms for the Q score given by Porteus (*op. cit.*, p. 93) refer to adults and teenagers, and do not apply to the present sample, since it is known that younger boys give much higher Q scores. The best comparative data for present purposes were obtained by Sanderson (1945), who tested separate groups of school children aged 9, 12 and 15 years respectively, and found that the mean Q score dropped significantly between the ages of 9 and 12, but did not decline much thereafter. The average Q score of her 9-year-old group was 40·8, close to that obtained by the present sample in which the median score was 35·4. The mean, which is presumably what Sanderson meant by 'average', would be a little higher.

[6] At age 11, 180 boys were retested individually on the tapping test, and of the sixty-seven boys who originally produced a small scatter (0 to 6 cm.) forty-one did so again, and only six produced a wide scatter (over 12 cm.). However, the fifty-six boys who scattered widely on first testing were more or less equally distributed among all three scoring categories on repeat testing. It would seem that only the low scores at age 8 predict well a boy's future status. A further 142 boys had a repeat test at 11, but given as a group test to the whole class. This change in conditions destroyed the test retest relationship because the presence of others was found to have lessened restraint and influenced the boys to more widely scattered dots!

[7] The score levels which determined the weightings are as follows:

		Weighted Score:		
		0	1	2
I	Porteus Q Score	0–25	26–60	61+
II	Spiral Error (corrected)	0–95	95–105	106+
III	Tapping Test	1–2	3–7	8–9
IV	Body Sway Test	Ataxia nil	Ataxia 1·5–3	3·5+

[8] Among bright boys, with an I.Q. of over 110 on the Matrices, only 5·8 per cent produced poor psychomotor scores, compared with 20·4 per cent among average boys and 33·7 per cent among dull boys of I.Q. 90 or less ($p < ·001$ on a χ^2 test of significance).

[9] Since the raw score varied with the size of the class—the more boys the more choices to distribute—the scores were grouped into quartile ranges for each class separately, and each boy was rated on a four point scale of popularity according to which quartile his score belonged.

IV

Assessing Adversities of Home Background

1. *Broken Homes, Separations and Child Neglect*

In this chapter some of the basic features of the boys' home backgrounds are described, with particular reference to the way these matters were assessed. In each instance this is followed by an account of the relationship of the background features to the boys current behaviour, as expressed in the combined ratings as conduct by P.S.Ws and teachers.

The Study sample did not include any inmates of local authority childrens' homes, so the number of boys from broken families was relatively small. It was not easy to specify the incidence precisely owing to the difficulty of defining a broken home. At the age of 9 years, forty-four boys (10·7 per cent) were living in anomalously constituted or incomplete families.[1] These were made up as follows. Father had died in ten cases, mother in four cases. The natural father was permanently away due to divorce, separation or desertion in twenty-one cases, mother in six cases, and both parents in three cases. Of these forty-four cases of permanent family breaks, twenty-one had occurred before the boy was aged 3. These family breaks did not necessarily mean that a boy was permanently deprived of parental care, since some were well settled with step-parents or foster parents. At the time of intake, only six boys had no acting mother, although twenty-four had no acting father.

Here are two examples to show the widely differing levels of disturbance included under the general heading of 'broken homes':

Case 662 (Father deserted, various separations from mother)
This boy's father deserted the home shortly before he was born. His parents had not married, but had lived together for some years in a very stormy relationship. At the age of 6 months he was taken into the charge of the children's department because his mother had to enter hospital for prolonged treatment of a chronic illness. He did not return to her for eight years. In this period he was himself admitted to hospital several times, and had a number of changes of foster homes. During all of the time his mother visited him only once.
Complaints about the boy's conduct began when he was 4, when he

was reported to have screaming attacks, severe temper tantrums, and to be erratic and obstinate in behaviour and almost compulsively disobedient. When he returned to his mother at the age of 8 there were immediate complaints from her and from his school about lying, pilfering, temper outbursts, incessant talking in class and neglect of school work.

Case 30 (Father deceased)
This boy's own father died when he was only 8 weeks old, but his mother married again quite quickly and he had been brought up by a step-father ever since he was one year of age. The step-father was reported to have become very keen on the boy. The mother's second marriage had proved reasonably happy and stable and the birth of further children had not led to any obvious tensions. His behaviour at home and at school aroused no special comment, and on most of the items concerning home circumstances and parental management this family was given favourable ratings.

Apart from permanently broken homes, great importance has been attributed to temporary separations of infants from their parents as a cause of bad behaviour in later years. The psychiatric social workers, therefore, were asked to inquire of every mother interviewed whether her boy had ever been separated from one or both parents. The record forms had a special space for recording this, and the instruction guide directed that all separations, except for odd days, should be noted, and that the duration and circumstances should be specified, as well as the age of the child at the time.

In practice, the P.S.Ws found this task peculiarly difficult. Some of the mothers were vague or casual in their recollections, and there was reason to believe that certain separations, for instance those due to a father's imprisonment, tended to be suppressed, and that other incidents tended to be forgotten, especially so perhaps by the duller mothers or the harassed mothers of large families. Owing to the complexity of the information sought, and the large number of other topics being covered, the P.S.Ws' notes on separations were often incomplete. Accordingly, this section of the background inquiry was continued after 1964 by subsequent social workers, who repeated the questions, and established a considerably larger number of separations than had originally been recorded.[2] Even so, perfect coverage is clearly unattainable by retrospective inquiry from mothers.

In all, seventy-one boys were reported to have had one or more separations from their mother (or acting mother), of more than one month duration and while they were still under 6 years of age. Twelve of these boys have already been mentioned as coming from anomalous family situations. In the remaining fifty-nine cases, the circumstances of the boy's longest separation from mother were classified as follows:

Boy in hospital 26
Boy at home, mother in hospital 14
Boy at home, mother temporarily deserted 1
Boy temporarily in care of local authority because:
  (i) Parents ill or mother confined 6
  (ii) Housing problems 5
  (iii) Parental violence 1
Boy temporarily with relatives because of:
  (i) Holidays 3
  (ii) Mother's confinement 1
  (iii) Mother having emigrated 2

Rather more boys were reported to have had separations from their fathers because, in addition to those due to hospitalizations and housing problems, there were also separations due to fathers being in the services, in prison, or taking jobs away from home.

Looking at the variety of circumstances responsible for separations, it seemed hardly likely that this general heading could have much criminological significance. The forty cases of early separation due to hospitalization of either mother or boy might be thought to comprise a fairly distinct group, but even within this category there were important variations. For instance, where a mother spent repeated periods of months at a time in a mental hospital this was a very different situation from absences due to comparatively short-lived physical illness. Of the remaining nineteen cases of separation, some were clearly the result of family disorganization, or of parental inability to weather a crisis without outside assistance.

Neglect of the physical appearance, hygiene or feeding of a child might be thought to provide a particularly strong indication of adverse home background. At a late stage of the social background inquiry, rather as an afterthought when the record forms were almost completed, the P.S.Ws marked forty-nine cases 'boy physically neglected', meaning that evidence of past or present neglect had been found. This was a global impression, rather than the result of specific inquiry, and indeed P.S.W. B rated proportionately twice as many boys 'neglected' as did P.S.W. A. Nevertheless, the P.S.Ws' ratings of neglect correlated fairly highly ($r_{tet} = 0.71$, $N = 398$, $p < .001$) with the answer 'noticeably below average' given by teachers in response to the question, 'When he comes to school in the morning is he a clean and tidy boy (compared with others in his class)?' A little under a half of those rated 'neglected' by P.S.Ws were also rated 'dirty' by teachers, and vice versa. In fact, whatever the precise grounds for the ratings, 'physical neglect' was an item that correlated significantly with a number of other items of parental mismanagement perceived by the P.S.Ws, as well as with a number of unfavourable features of the boys themselves, such as poor conduct according to teachers' ratings, and poor psychomotor performance.[3]

TABLE IV (1)

Boys' Conduct against various Home Adversities

Number of boys in each category of conduct (on P.S.Ws' and teachers' combined ratings)

Number of boys who experienced:	Total Boys		Satisfactory (I or II)		Moderate (III)		Bad (IV or V)	
	No.	%	No.	%	No.	%	No.	%
Anomalous family constitution	44	100	22	50·0	9	20·5	13	29·5
Early temporary separation from mother[1]	59	100	26	44·1	15	25·4	18	30·5
Information lacking (on separation and/or neglect)	26	100	4	15·4	11	42·3	11	42·3
Physical Neglect Present[1]	24	100	8	33·3	7	29·2	9	37·5
Information complete and no family anomaly, separation or neglect	258	100	171	66·3	55	21·3	32	12·4
TOTALS	411	100	231	56·2	97	23·6	83	20·2

[1] Excluding those already counted under previous headings.
12 boys from anomalous families experienced maternal separation.
A total of 49 boys experienced physical neglect.

Table IV (1) displays the association between poor conduct in the boys and the three items of home background adversity so far mentioned. Each category of adversity, anomalous family constitution, maternal separation, and physical neglect, compared with the remainder of the sample, was associated with a more than doubly raised incidence of badly behaved boys.[4] The table also shows that the small number of boys about whom background information was not available, owing to their parents being unable or unwilling to co-operate, were a particularly badly behaved group. (In their case, of course, the conduct ratings were mostly derived from teachers or outside informants.) This suggests, as do many subsequent tabulations, that difficulty in obtaining information is often associated with family disturbance, and is therefore an interesting and important item. It also means, unfortunately, that some of the

64   PRESENT CONDUCT AND FUTURE DELINQUENCY

families of greatest criminological interest are among the most difficult to get to know and to assess.

The example below is of a case classified as 'no information' in Table IV (1), although in the course of time considerable information of an adverse kind was received from various outside sources. The subsequent example provides a contrast, showing that 'no information' does not necessarily imply unfavourable circumstances; it can mean that a family is particularly respectable and particularly anxious to preserve personal privacy.

Case 851
It was never possible to interview this boy's parents. His mother was extremely hostile towards all authorities, and although encountered on her doorstep several times she continued highly suspicious, believing that the investigators intended to single out her son for unfavourable attention, and remaining unconvinced by all assurances to the contrary. Information received subsequently, mostly from probation officers dealing with the boy's older siblings, revealed a state of affairs in the home which, had it been known at the time, would have attracted unfavourable ratings on a large number of topics.

Father was said to be a weak man, dominated by his wife. He had been admitted as a patient to a mental hospital more than once, and was diagnosed as an inadequate psychopath. Mother was described in reports as aggressive, unco-operative and untrustworthy. She quarrelled constantly with her husband, spent a large part of her time drinking in local bars, and had deserted the home on various occasions. Both parents were considered to be unconcerned and neglectful in regard to their children's education and welfare. The boy in our Study was a persistent truant, liar and thief who first appeared before the juvenile court at the age of 12.

Case 042
This boy's family background was at first something of a mystery, and many of the ratings concerning upbringing and parental behaviour were recorded 'not known'. Initially father said he did not want anyone discussing his family and mother said she 'didn't agree with' surveys of this kind. It was known, however, that father had a sound and regular job, that the family were not in financial want, and that the parents were interested in their children's education and in contact with the schools. An older sibling was at a grammar school, while the boy in our Study was of average performance at school with no known behaviour problems. His father was thought to be somewhat authoritarian.

When the P.S.W. finally succeeded in securing these parents' co-operation it was possible to confirm the impression that the boy came from a substantially normal background, so that had it been possible to assess this family on the various items of parental attitude and conduct covered in other cases the ratings would have been generally favourable, erring, if anything, on the side of over-anxiety and over-control, rather than on the side of laxness or negligence.

Looking back at the figures in Table IV (1) it appears that the more elusive adversities, such as physical neglect or parents unco-operative, are probably more powerful influences than the more easily defined categories of broken homes and parental separations. Indeed, it may well be that events such as occasional hospitalizations, or even loss of a parent by death, become important in relation to the incidence of behaviour disorder only in families who are already vulnerable on account of other troubles. The conclusion that temporary separation from mother is not, in itself, an outstandingly important adversity, agrees with the findings of a number of recent investigations. Mary Ainsworth (1965), in her careful review of research on the maternal deprivation hypothesis, concluded that the circumstances associated with separation were at least as important as the fact of separation itself. In a survey of a group of 112 families on the National Health Service list of a London medical practice, Anthony Ryle (1967, pp. 97, 102) found a somewhat larger incidence of anomalous families and temporary separations from parents than in the present Study, but in Ryle's sample these adversities bore no significant statistical relationship to the children's behaviour disturbances. In a Swedish study reported by Jonsson (1967), comparing a sample of institutionalized juvenile delinquents with a control group of unselected schoolboys, a very substantial difference in incidence of separation from mother in the first five years of life emerged, 84 per cent in the case of the delinquents, only 38 per cent in the case of the controls. However, as the author pointed out, the delinquents had been selected for commitment partly on the basis of broken homes and missing parents, and there was a much larger incidence of young unmarried mothers in the delinquent group. On the other hand, among the minority of the control group who had experienced separation, social adjustment was no worse than among those who had never been separated. This finding illustrates the fallacy of generalizing from institutionalized delinquents.

2. *Working Mothers*

According to ideas widely accepted among social workers, one might expect a young boy to be affected adversely if his mother has a job outside the home. At the time of their first contact with the families the P.S.Ws inquired of the mothers (or acting mothers) whether they went out to work either part time (i.e. six hours or less per day) or full time (i.e. over six hours). The distinction between full-time and part-time work was particularly important, since the neighbourhood was one in which married women commonly undertook office cleaning jobs for limited hours.

TABLE IV (2)

Teachers' Rating of Boys' Conduct against Working Mothers

	\multicolumn{6}{c}{Teachers' Rating of Conduct:}	
	Good		Average		Bad		Total
	No.	%	No.	%	No.	%	Boys
Mother has no job	26	31·0	87	41·2	54	60·7	167
Mother works part-time	37	44·0	70	33·2	22	24·7	129
Mother works full-time	21	25·0	54	25·6	13	14·6	88
TOTAL	84	100	211	100	89	100	384

$\chi^2 = 17·66$ with 4 d.f., $p < ·01$

Table IV (2) shows that the boys whose mothers stayed at home had the highest incidence, and those whose mothers went out full time had the smallest incidence, of poor conduct. In other words having a working mother was a favourable rather than an unfavourable factor. This was confirmed by the correlational analysis (see Appendix VI (A)), which showed that mother *not* working correlated positively with most of the other indubitably adverse items such as 'physical neglect' and 'low intelligence'.

This result was largely due to the fact that the mothers of boys from large families of six or more children comparatively rarely went out to work, coupled with the fact that boys from large families were more often badly behaved. Nevertheless, even when the sample was divided into three groups according to family size (i.e. only child, two to five children, six or more children) and comparisons were made within each group, though the contrasts were much reduced, it remained true that the incidence of badly behaved boys was slightly greater where mother had no job. At each level of family size mothers who worked part time were more often to be found in association with the better behaved boys.

A plausible interpretation of these findings would seem to be that in the Study neighbourhood the more effectual mothers had the initiative to work, while the less effectual ones stayed at home. Having a mother at home all the time did nothing to counteract the adverse effects of belonging to a large-sized poor family.

3. Financial Hardship and Social Handicap

It has already been explained (see Table III (1), p. 44) that the three grades of family income, assessed by the P.S.Ws as comfortable, adequate or inadequate, were surprisingly closely correlated with the boys' conduct ratings. The inadequate income had 35·6 per cent of boys with poor conduct ratings (IV or V), compared with only 9·0 per cent of badly behaved boys in the comfortable income group.

It is sometimes argued that the reputed bad behaviour of the children of poor families is exaggerated by a tendency of middle-class raters to judge such children unduly harshly. In the present instance, since the P.S.Ws had more detailed knowledge of family income and background than the teachers, any such bias might be expected to show itself more strongly in their contribution to the combined conduct ratings. In fact, the teachers' ratings correlated more highly with family income (r = ·29) than did the P.S.Ws' ratings (r = ·09).

An attempt was made to obtain a more sensitive measure of social handicap than the P.S.Ws' rough estimate of family income level. For this purpose seven separate items of social adversity were taken into account, and if a boy had more than half of these (or more than half of the number of items about which information was available) he was considered to have a 'severe' degree of social handicap. If none of the seven items was recorded as present he had no social handicap, otherwise he had a 'moderate' degree of social handicap. Five of the items involved have already been described, namely; (i) family income inadequate; (ii) Grade V manual on the Registrar General's scale of socio-economic status; (iii) very unsatisfactory housing; (iv) large-sized family, i.e. six or more children; and (v) child physically neglected. The remaining two items were rated by the P.S.Ws and consisted of (vi) interior of house very neglected; and (vii) family supported by social agencies. Accommodation was rated 'very neglected' if a family kept their rooms conspicuously badly, that is in a dirty or very untidy condition. As far as possible this was a judgement of poor standards of upkeep inside the home, regardless of the satisfactory or unsatisfactory quality of the housing itself. 'Supported' families were defined as those known to have obtained financial help frequently from the National Assistance Board (as it was then) or from other social agencies, those listed as problem families by the local social welfare agencies, and those dependent on emotional or financial support from probation officers, hospital social workers, etc., but excluding those dependent purely for reasons of sickness. This category included the very badly off and very bad managers.

Here are two examples to illustrate how social level, as assessed by the social handicap classification, appears to pervade every aspect of family life:

Case 243 (No social handicap)
A small family living in a pre-war council flat, in somewhat cramped accommodation, but with basic facilities provided. Furnishings and household equipment were adequate, and although rather shabby by local standards, they were well looked after. Both parents were working, mother part time, and their income was adequate, although leaving little to spare for social activities or family outings. Father, a quiet man of stable temperament, had a record of very steady employment. The parents' domestic life was contented. They were a home-centred couple who enjoyed their children, and were spontaneous and unanxious in handling them. They both valued consistency and took pains to present a united front. The children were free of any noteworthy neurotic or behavioural difficulties.

Case 802 (Severe social handicap)
A large, poor family well known to social agencies. They had been evicted for non-payment of rent on several occasions, and at the commencement of the Study they were occupying an old terraced house that had been requisitioned by the council. The street was notoriously dilapidated, but this house was even worse than most, with broken windows, battered front door, and a yard filled with old iron and other rubbish. Inside the house plaster was peeling off the walls, and on account of a leaking roof the whole family was encamped on the ground floor in rooms of striking squalor, crammed with boxes and junk. Nevertheless, the mother tried to keep the floors clean and saw to it that they had a fire blazing irrespective of temperature, but on the whole she was considered a bad manager. The family were known to obtain goods on hire-purchase in order to sell them again; and father had served a prison sentence for this. For a long time father declined to claim national assistance because, he said, the officials taunted him with his prison record. As a result they fell into even worse rent arrears and debts. Originally a skilled tradesman, father's work performance had deteriorated in recent years, and he complained of both nervous and physical disabilities.

While there was no outward evidence of marital conflict, mother assumed the dominant role in the household. It was her aggressiveness and persuasiveness that won for the family a good deal of financial help from various organizations. Father was on the whole passive and uninterested in his attitude to the children, although given to occasional violent outbursts of temper. He had refused psychiatric aid.

All of the children of secondary school age had been before the juvenile court. The boy belonging to this Study was excessively timid and phobic, scholastically backward and a chronic truant.

The category 'severe' social handicap was a more extreme rating than inadequate family income, and was given to only fifty-five boys.

It was very closely associated with bad behaviour, as can be seen from Table IV (3), which tabulates social handicap against conduct ratings. Of the severely handicapped group 41·8 per cent were rated badly behaved (IV or V) and, as may be seen in Table III (7) p. 57, 41·8 per cent fell into the 'acting-out' category; whereas of those boys free from social handicap only 11 per cent were rated badly behaved and only 11·5 per cent fell into the 'acting-out' category. The inadequate income category, and to an even greater extent the severe social handicap rating, obviously reflected a generalized social deficiency in certain families which had wide ramifications in terms of the competence, attitudes and behaviour of the parents concerned, and of the educational and social adjustment of their children. Indeed, this general social factor proved to be the most powerful discriminant of 'good' boys and 'bad' boys of all the measures recorded in this first phase of the Study. Of the fifty-five boys with severe social handicap, 16·4 per cent proved to be early delinquents (i.e. convicted under 13 years of age), compared with only 3·1 per cent among the rest of the sample.

TABLE IV (3)

Social Handicap against Boys' Conduct
(Combined ratings of P.S.Ws and Teachers)

Social Handicap Category:	Satisfactory I No. / %	II No. / %	Moderate III No. / %	IV No. / %	Bad V No. / %	Total Boys No. / %
Nil	40 / 58·0	85 / 52·5	37 / 38·1	14 / 26·4	6 / 20·0	182 / 44·3
Moderate	26 / 37·7	66 / 40·7	42 / 43·3	26 / 49·1	14 / 46·7	174 / 42·3
Severe	3 / 4·3	11 / 6·8	18 / 18·6	13 / 24·5	10 / 33·3	55 / 13·4
Total	69 / 100	162 / 100	97 / 100	53 / 100	30 / 100	411 / 100

$\chi^2 = 47 \cdot 46$ with 8 d.f. $p < \cdot 001$

This result echoes the findings of innumerable previous studies, all of which point to a heavy concentration of bad behaviour (and also of parental pathology and of individual maladjustments) among boys of the lowest social level. To quote just one example, Kellmer Pringle (1966), in a survey of 11,000 7-year-olds, found that social behaviour at school, especially among boys (as assessed by the

Bristol Social Adjustment Guide completed by teachers) was strongly associated with social level. Boys whose fathers' occupations were in the lowest group V on the Registrar General's classification had a much greater chance of being rated 'unsettled and maladjusted'. The fact that the association proved even closer in the present Study was probably due to the use of the social handicap rating, which was a more sensitive index of the social level of a family than father's occupational group.

4. *Parental Disharmony*

In view of the disturbing effects upon children of conflicts between their parents the P.S.Ws were asked to pay particular attention to this topic in their interviews, to ask parents specifically about their marital difficulties, and to record any indications of conflict. Originally the P.S.Ws' record forms included a four-point rating scale of parents' marital adjustment, but this proved difficult. The rating standards of the three interviewers were so discrepant that for the purpose of statistical analysis a simple division into satisfactory marriage and disharmonious marriage was all that could be obtained. Of 373 boys rated, 89, that is 23·9 per cent, were said to have experienced parental disharmony.[5] As with most of the P.S.Ws' assessments of parents, ratings varied remarkably according to socio-economic circumstances. The proportion of boys with 'parental disharmony' was four times as great among the 'inadequate' income group as among the 'comfortable' income group. As expected, bad conduct in boys was significantly and positively correlated with parental disharmony; but the relationship was not the same at all social levels. The comparison is displayed graphically.

Figure IV (1) shows parents' marriage against boys' conduct on three separate graphs, one for each level of social handicap.[6] The two graphs representing boys from families free from social handicap, or with only moderate social handicap (the dotted and interrupted lines) both show convincing upward trends. The percentage of boys from disharmonious marriages steadily increases as one goes from the good to bad conduct categories. The boys from the poorest homes, however, represented by the continuous line graph, show no such trend. Regardless of what conduct category they belonged to (and relatively few were given good conduct ratings) a half of the socially handicapped boys came from disharmonious parental homes.

This result, and others to be mentioned later,[7] suggest that the factors responsible for juvenile misconduct may not always be the same at different social levels. In this instance one might argue that

ASSESSING ADVERSITIES OF HOME BACKGROUND 71

whereas in most homes signs of marital disharmony go with a considerably increased risk of juvenile misbehaviour, in the minority of severely handicapped families, the presence of marital disharmony, in the context of multiple economic and social adversities, adds little to the already high risk of juvenile misbehaviour. Another possible explanation of (or contribution to) this result could be a tendency on the part of the P.S.Ws to assess the poorer families, who squabble openly, rather more harshly than the better off and socially more successful families, who try to keep their troubles concealed as long as possible. If such a tendency existed it would follow that visible disharmony would have more serious implications in the better class families.

FIG. IV (1)

Relationship between Boys' Conduct (combined ratings) and Parents' Marriage at three Levels of Social Handicap

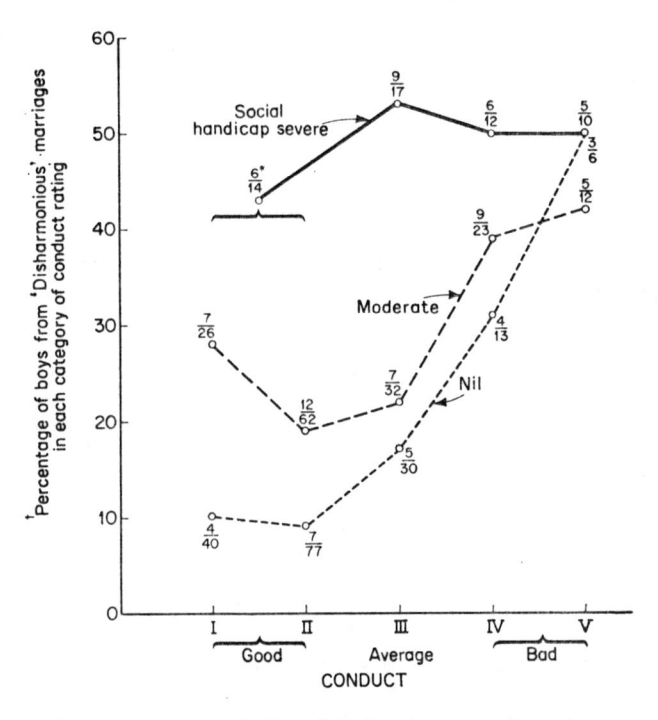

Percentage of boys from 'Disharmonious' marriages in each category of conduct rating

CONDUCT

* Conduct categories I and II combined owing to small numbers.
† The actual numbers of boys from which these percentages were obtained are shown against each point on the graph.

The following two examples of badly behaved boys from conflictual parental homes illustrate the difference between social levels. The first boy was not unusual for one in the severely socially handicapped category, but the second was exceptionally badly behaved for one classed as having no social handicap:

Case 283 (Poor conduct, severe social handicap and parents' marriage 'disharmonious')
A large family living in rented furnished rooms in a dilapidated house, from which they were subsequently evicted for rent arrears. Owing to the nature of his trade father was frequently unemployed during the winter. Mother took occasional work as a cleaner, but the money available for housekeeping was clearly inadequate.

Both parents were themselves born illegitimate and had experienced unhappy and disrupted home backgrounds. Father was a pathologically jealous husband who strenuously restricted all his wife's activities, while at the same time accusing her of a bewildering number of infidelities and disclaiming parentage of his children, towards whom he was harsh, punitive and physically violent. There were frequent rows between the parents, accompanied by physical as well as verbal abuse. The control of their children was a particular source of conflict, each parent taking up an extreme attitude, father one of severity and strict control, mother one of laxness and neglect.

The boy in our Study was reported to be an habitual liar, both spontaneously and when trying to avoid trouble. He was also a persistent truant and absconder, wandering off and staying away half the night as well as missing school. He frequently pilfered from home.

Case 453 (Poor conduct, no social handicap, parents' marriage 'disharmonious')
This was a small family of good material standards living in a well-equipped house. Both parents were working full-time at white-collar jobs. Psychologically, however, the home atmosphere was adverse and conflict ridden. Father was an extremely dogmatic, self-opinionated man of domineering ways. Mother was frustrated and resentful of her husband's attitude. There was severe sexual disharmony between them. Mother openly criticized her husband, describing him as suffering from an underlying sense of inferiority. She herself was notably anxious and unsure of herself. She was cold, critical and rejecting in her attitude to her children, whom she described in most negative terms. She strongly disapproved of her husband's approach, which she considered too lenient, as well as over-anxious, and hence liable to make the children too dependent.

The boy in our Study was described as quarrelsome, defiant, destructive, jealous and uncontrollably bad tempered. He was said to be cruel to animals, and he had poor reports as to conduct from his school. His mother was particularly annoyed by his attention-seeking and clinging behaviour.

5. Parental Mismanagement and Its Relation to Poor Conduct in Boys

(a) *Six Items of Parental Behaviour.* The assessments of parental child-rearing behaviour made by the P.S.Ws included the following six ratings:

   (i) Boy physically neglected.
   (ii) Parents uninterested in boy's education.
   (iii) Inconsistency between parents in handling boy.
   (iv) Lack of parental vigilance.
   (v) Laxity in rules.
   (vi) Lack of praise from parents.

The assessment known as *Boy physically neglected* has already been discussed. (See p. 62.) It was used as one of the criteria to define socially handicapped families, since the rating correlated substantially with most of the major features of social adversity.

The comment *Parents uninterested in the boy's education* was made according to the following descriptive definition: 'Does not know how the child is progressing, appears unaware of interests, progress or problems. Negative attitude to school. Does not bother to attend functions or to see teachers.' There was a space on the record form for noting whether a parent visited the boy's school 'regularly', 'occasionally' or 'never', but otherwise the rating was made impressionistically. It was based mainly upon mother's attitude, unless for some reason father came prominently into the picture, and was on a three-point scale from 'very interested', through 'average interest', to 'uninterested'.

Inconsistency between parents in their handling of the boy was defined as 'sufficient to be confusing to the child, or to permit him to play off one parent against the other, or to enable him to avoid conforming with either'. If the parents claimed complete agreement between themselves, or if there seemed to be no more than a normal amount of disagreement between the parents' standards, or if the parents concealed their disagreements from the child, the rating was 'not inconsistent'.

Vigilance was intended as a judgement of the watchfulness of parents, their closeness of supervision. Under-vigilance was defined as 'careless or heedless of the child's activities'. The instruction guide suggested that the P.S.Ws should ask parents, 'What does he usually do when he is out? Do you know where he is when he goes out? Do you know who he is with?' Over-vigilant was described as 'watching the child too much and asking him for detailed explanations of all his activities'. The average or normal rating on this three-point scale corresponded to ordinarily watchful parents.

Lax Parental Rules was a global impression recorded by the P.S.Ws in November 1964. It was a three-point scale representing the degree of strictness or laxity of parental control over the boy, ranging from 'rigid' through 'average' to 'lax', with the majority of the sample placed in the 'average' category. Relevant data occurred in two places on the P.S.Ws' record form. One was an item in the discipline section called 'special rules' where parents were graded into three categories according to whether they rigidly enforced rules about punctuality, bedtime, television viewing, manners, choice of playmates and tidying up; or were fairly consistent in rules but not rigid; or rarely, if ever, enforced rules and let the boy do much as he pleased. The other relevant item was an inquiry into methods of punishment, with spaces for recording whether or not specified techniques (e.g. slaps, scolds or nags, ridicule, severe corporal punishment) were used by mother or by father. Comments on the choice and severity of punishments were used by the P.S.Ws as an indication of strictness or laxity of control. Where there was inconsistency of control, an alternation between strictness and laxity, an 'average' rating was recorded. The correlation of $r = \cdot 32$ between laxity of parental rules and parental under-vigilance shows that the two assessments, though related, were far from identical. Rules reflected the enforcement of parental control, vigilance reflected a wider aspect of parental concern and conscientiousness.

Parents never praise, a comment made in about 10 per cent of the cases, was considered by the P.S.Ws to be an important indication of a certain parental attitude. There was a specific question on the record form asking about what parents do when the boy behaves well, e.g. praise, reward, special privileges or no recognition. Those who got no recognition from either parent were put down as 'never praised'.

A positive rating on any of these six items was clearly an unfavourable comment on the parents' handling of their boy. All six ratings were positively inter-correlated (see Table IV (4)), which means that the presence of any one of these unfavourable items was associated with an increased probability of other unfavourable items also being reported.

Table IV (4) shows further that all of the six ratings were positively correlated with poor conduct in boys as assessed by the teachers. This suggests that each item of parental mismanagement has a contribution to make towards the sum-total of misconduct in boys. However, as in the example of parental disharmony, which has just been discussed, the picture was complicated by the fact that all items of adverse parental behaviour were significantly more frequent among boys from poor families, the 'inadequate income' group.

(See Appendix IV (B).) Therefore, in order to elucidate the true relationship between specific items of parental mismanagement and misconduct in boys, the socio-economic status of the family had to be taken into account.

TABLE IV (4)

Inter-correlations between six assessments of Parental Child-rearing Behaviour and Teachers' Ratings of Poor Conduct at School

	1	2	3	4	5	6	7
	Boy physically neglected	Parents uninterested in boy's education	Inconsistency between parents	Parents under-vigilant	Parents lax in rules	Parents never praise	Teacher rates boy's conduct poor
1. Boy physically neglected	—	·33	·26	·30	·43	·16	·30
2. Parents uninterested in boy's education		—	·20	·27	·18	·27	·25
3. Inconsistency between parents			—	·22	·13	·21	·15
4. Parents under-vigilant				—	·32	·22	·20
5. Parents lax in rules					—	·04*	·07*
6. Parents never praise						—	·12
7. Teacher rates boy's conduct poor							—

* Not statistically significant

(b) *Relationships between Upbringing and Conduct at Different Social Levels.* In some instances the relationship held good at all income levels. Taking the conduct categories in order I to V (according to the combined opinions of teachers and P.S.Ws) the proportions of boys with 'parents under-vigilant' and with 'inconsistency between parents' increased step by step from the best behaved to the worst behaved group, and the same trend appeared in all three income sub-divisions. On the other hand, the comment 'boy physically neglected' bore no relationship whatever to boy's conduct in the 'comfortable income' segment of the Study sample for the reason that affluent boys were almost never neglected. In both the inadequate and middle-income brackets, however, there was a clear tendency for boys in the inferior conduct categories to be more often rated physically neglected. (See Table IV (5).) The only difference was that in all conduct categories physical neglect was less often recorded in the middle-income group than in the inadequate-income group.

TABLE IV (5)

Boys' Conduct against Rating 'Physical Neglect' by Income Level

Boys'Conduct (Combined Ratings of P.S.Ws and Teachers)

	Good I No. Rated	% Neg-lected	II No. Rated	% Neg-lected	Average III No. Rated	% Neg-lected	IV No. Rated	% Neg-lected	Bad V No. Rated	% Neg-lected
Inadequate Income Group	10	0·0	24	25·0	24	50·0	18	44·4	14	50·0
Adequate Income Group	30	0·0	79	5·1	35	8·6	24	16·7	12	25·0

When income level was allowed for, the variable 'parents never praise' became quite insignificant in relation to conduct. Likewise, the relationship between boys' conduct and 'parents uninterested in education' largely disappeared, except in the inadequate income group. In other words, parental lack of interest in education was largely a reflection of social class, and in itself of little importance as a determinant of misconduct. This is illustrated by the graphs in Appendix IV (C) (3), which show no consistent upward trend in the proportion of 'uninterested' parents as one progresses from left to right from the good to bad conduct categories. The only suggestion of any such trend occurred in the inadequate income group among whom 'uninterested' parents were always common but relatively less frequent among the better behaved boys.

A positive interest in education (parents rated 'very interested') was quite unusual among the poorer families, only twelve boys in the inadequate income group being so rated; but all but one of these boys were in the well-behaved categories, i.e. rated I or II on conduct. This suggests that an unusual interest in education on the part of poor parents is a good sign, and likely to be associated with unusually good behaviour among their boys.

Laxness of parental rules was positively associated with poor conduct at all income levels, although it was rarely reported (only seven cases) among the comfortable income group. The other end of the scale, 'parental rules strict' (as opposed to 'lax' or 'average'), was associated with good behaviour in the inadequate income group, and bad behaviour in the comfortable income group. 'Strict rules' would appear to be helpful only at the lower income levels. This paradox might be due to the rating 'strict', when applied to better class families, meaning fussy and nagging, whereas applied to poor homes it might just mean more particular than their sub-standard neighbours. An 'average' or 'moderate' strictness of rules was associated with good behaviour at all income levels.

The items 'parental vigilance', and 'parental interest in education', which have just been discussed, provided further interesting examples of the significance of parental behaviour varying according to the socio-economic level of the family. Over the whole sample, there was a slight but positive correlation ($r = \cdot 14$) between parental under-vigilance and poor educational achievement of the boys (as measured by the quotient obtained in the Mechanical Reading Test.) There was also a positive correlation, which might reasonably have been anticipated, between parental lack of interest in education and poor reading by boys ($r = \cdot 29$). On subdividing the sample according to the three income levels, these correlations were found to be due almost entirely to the low income group, among whom there was a striking association between better reading ability in boys and above average parental vigilance, or above average interest in education on the part of parents. In the higher income groups these items of parental behaviour bore no significant relationship to boys' reading ability. (The findings are displayed in greater detail in the graphs in Appendix IV (C)). A possible interpretation of these findings is that boys handicapped by social adversity are liable to become poor readers unless stimulated by exceptional parents, whereas in better class homes boys usually learn to read adequately regardless of their parents' attitude to education or degree of 'vigilance'. These results are somewhat different from what was found by Kellmer Pringle (1966, p. 151) in her study of a sample of 11,000 Seven-Year-Olds. She reported a general correlation between parents' interest in their children's education and boys' reading attainments; but within particular social classes it was the Registrar General's occupational Groups I, III and IV, and not the lowest Class V, which produced the significant associations. In the sample studied by J. W. B. Douglas (1964, p. 156), however, as in the present Study, it was among children at the lowest social level that parental interest in education appeared to make the most difference to scholastic performance at age 8.

These findings concerning the varying relations between parental behaviour on the one hand and boys' conduct and performance on the other show that the significance of family background features depends upon the social context. An item that has a favourable connotation in a poor home may be a bad sign in a better off home, or an item that has definite implications in one social setting may have no importance in another. The Gluecks (1962, pp. 105, 116) had earlier reached rather similar conclusions in their great studies of juvenile delinquents. They found that delinquency-producing factors operated selectively according to social circumstances, and that it was the combined impact of social and individual factors which counted more than single factors. Thus, low verbal intelligence was more closely related to delinquency if the boy concerned came from a poverty-stricken home, and emotional lability was more closely associated with delinquency if the boy came from a broken home.

The matter becomes still more complicated if one takes account of the possibility that standards of rating may vary with social class. For instance, better-off parents are expected to be interested in their children's education, and may be at pains to give the impression that they are so even if it is not really true. This could result in a larger proportion of better-off parents being inaccurately rated on this item, which in turn could account for the apparent lack of relation between boys' conduct and parental interest among those from the better-off homes. The question of the validity of interview ratings is considered in greater detail in a later chapter.

6. *Parental Attitude and Quality of Discipline*

Because so many investigators have found parents' attitudes of crucial importance in the genesis of juvenile delinquency, it was decided to ask the P.S.Ws to make a particularly careful judgement about this. The system of categorizing attitudes was based upon the definitions used successfully by the McCords (1959, pp. 88–99) in connection with the Cambridge-Somerville Study. The descriptive definitions in the P.S.Ws' instruction guide read as follows:

Exclusive categories of maternal attitudes (based upon McCord)
1. *Loving normal.* In general kindly and affectionate. Not over restrictive, does not exhibit any signs of marked anxiety or neurosis. Enjoys companionship of her children and has a zest for life.
2. *Loving anxious.* Similar in personality to the over-protective mothers. Differs from them to the lesser extent to which they restrict boy's activity. More generalized anxiety—exhibited not only in relation to their children, but in other areas of their lives. They exhibit an inordinate degree of anxiety.
or
Loving neurotic. Mothers with permeating anxiety reaching the level of an apparent neurosis or latent psychosis. Mothers who are

affectionate towards their boys, but preoccupied with their emotional problems and their symptoms caused by these conflicts.
3. *Over-protective* (as a form of domination = subtle rejection). Strong anxiety about the boy. Strenuously attempts to protect him. Rigorously restricts son's activity. Child treated as if he were still in an infantile stage.
4. *Cruel* (= active rejecting). Uses verbal and/or physical abuse, makes it clear to the boy that he is heartily disliked. Dominates him and shows him no affection.
5. *Passive*. Weak, ineffectual, phlegmatic in manner, playing only a minor role in the family, leaving direction and discipline to other people in the home. An 'I cannot be bothered' attitude governing relationship with their sons.
6. *Neglecting*. Not just emotional passivity, but total indifference to the boy. Neglects his physical and psychological needs. Seldom exhibits any sign of affection.
7. *Absent*. Permanently absent. Separation or divorce. If natural mother has left the home and is replaced by a step-mother or mother substitute, classify substitute mother in appropriate category.

The categories of loving anxious and loving neurotic were finally amalgamated into one group because the P.S.Ws found them difficult to distinguish, and because their rating standards differed markedly when they tried to make the distinction.

Fathers' attitudes were categorized as follows:

1. *Warm*. Enjoy their children, kind in their treatment and show affectionate concern.
   As a group cordial, friendly, relaxed. Open in their treatment and dealings with children. This includes some who are over-protective and anxious, others who are restrictive, and others who are highly demonstrative, or taciturn.
2. *Passive*. Play subsidiary role in family life, generally withdrawn. Some leave discipline and control entirely to wife, but are kind and thoughtful.
3. *Cruel*. Overtly and vehemently reject and terrorize their children. Rule the family with firm grip, are verbally and/or physically violent with the children and their wives—aggressive men who dominate the lives of those around them.
4. *Neglectful*. Seem indifferent to the welfare of children. Ignore or overtly reject them. Show complete absence of attention or concern for their families.
5. *Father absent*.

It turned out that the proportions of the present sample with anything other than 'normal' or 'warm' ratings on parental attitudes were rather small, generally less than one fifth the incidence reported by the McCords. This may have been a quite realistic assessment,

80 PRESENT CONDUCT AND FUTURE DELINQUENCY

since the McCords were dealing with a sample deliberately selected on grounds of high delinquency potential; but as a consequence of their small numbers in this Study the boys with cruel, passive and neglecting fathers or mothers had to be taken together as a single group for the purpose of statistical comparison. On the whole they represented a group of boys in most unhappy circumstances, as may be judged from some of the following examples:

Case 41 (Mother rated 'Loving anxious')
Mother was an anxious, depressed woman with quite severe neurotic symptoms; intelligent, thoughtful with considerable insight, but overloaded with guilt. She admitted to an anxious reaction to most situations in life, but claimed that this did not affect her handling of the boy. But clearly she had been over-protective, at least in the past. Until the boy was 9 years old he was never allowed out to play in the courtyard or in the adjacent park, and he had never been to the cinema on his own. The mother identified very closely with this boy, and feared that he may have inherited her own temperament. She was constantly afraid that something would happen to him and she seemed to have conveyed her anxiety to the boy. For example, the dangers of electricity were so much emphasized that the boy was too frightened to switch on the electric fire. At 9 years of age he refused to go away on the school holidays because this meant leaving mother.

Case 533 (Mother rated 'Neglecting')
This boy was reared by a step-mother who seemed to be completely lacking in warmth. She said, quite openly and without sign of guilt, that she was not interested in him and had never been able to take to him as there was something about him she could not like. She and her husband had no contact with the school, and she was astonished to learn the boy was doing so well. She talked about him as if he were a casual lodger. He was given freedom to come and go as he pleased, and at age 10 he was making his own evening meals, his step-mother having told him he must learn to look after himself as she could not always be there to do things for him. She told the P.S.W. that neither she nor his father could find much good in him.

Case 523 (Mother rated 'Cruel')
This mother was extremely rejecting and probably both cruel and harsh in her handling of the boy. She was quite clear that she had not wanted him when he was born. She had wished for a girl, and was so disappointed she could not bear to look at the baby and asked for him to be taken away. She could not bear to breast-feed him, finding the process nauseating. When he grew to be a handsome infant, she got used to him being a boy and idealized him and over-protected him out of guilt for not having wanted him in the first place. In later years, however, as he got to an age to be troublesome in behaviour, she again wanted to be rid of him, often telling him so, saying he was mad and a devil, and threatening to send him to a boarding school. Her discipline

was erratic and haphazard, sometimes harsh and cruel, but at times when it pleased her she could be indulgent and spoiling. She regarded his difficult behaviour as retribution for her not wanting him when he was born.

Case 803 (Mother rated 'Cruel')
Mother was a domineering, aggressive woman with poor emotional control. 'I open my mouth and everything comes out', she said. She was very dissatisfied with her marriage and devoted much of her energy to putting her boy to rights, constantly nagging and shouting at him. She was highly disparaging in her comments about him to the P.S.W., referring to him as a 'measly milk-sop' who could not stand up for himself. She considered him the black sheep of the family and clearly favoured her daughter. She seemed to recognize the boy's need for affection, but she resented it greatly, and would push him away saying 'I haven't got time'. When he got into trouble she would rush to his defence, and then attack him soundly for it later. She asserted that she believes one needs to be hard, independent and selfish in order to get on in life.

Case 532 (Mother rated 'Over-protective')
Mother was a very intelligent woman, but a perfectionist, with unrealistically high expectations of her children. She was strict about most things, particularly about manners and tidiness. She was extremely vigilant in controlling and supervising, questioning the boy closely about his activities, and constantly admonishing him. She believed it necessary to urge and push the boy, and clearly she did so unremittingly. She feared the influence of local children, and discouraged her boy from mixing. Until he was of school age he had no companionship from other children, but played alone in the garden, and at 9 years of age he was rarely allowed out of his parents' sight except in school, and he never went anywhere alone. If he wanted to play in the local park his mother would accompany him. Until he was 10 years old she regularly helped him to wash and dress.

Case 104 (Father rated 'Passive')
Father was described by his wife as a selfish, unpredictable man who took little interest in the family and left her to cope on her own. Although overtly resenting this, she appeared to fall in with it very readily. For example, she would tell the children to keep away from father and not to annoy him, and she would conceal from him the children's misdeeds because he was apt to hit them very hard when he got into a temper. Father liked to go out a lot, and was very sociable, but mother preferred to be home. She obviously enjoyed being the person to whom all the family turned, the one who made the decisions and dealt with crises.

Case 281 (Father rated 'Neglectful')
Father was a poor provider, an irregular worker, rather feckless and erratic. He had deserted the family on several occasions. He showed no interest in the children and allowed the home to get into a very poor

state materially. He left all discipline to his wife, only taking part when she begged him desperately to intervene because the children were getting completely beyond her control.

Within what might be described as the 'normal' ratings of parental attitude, a considerable diversity existed as the following examples show:

Case 271 (Paternal attitude 'Warm')
Father was a man of considerable intelligence and ability, determined that his son should make use of the educational opportunities which he had been denied himself in a previous generation. He was vigilant, conscientious and over-concerned and over-identified with his son. He helped his son with homework, kept in touch with the school, and encouraged the boy in outside activities. He tended to be strict, to worry about his son's casual approach to life, and to punish rather severely, for instance by keeping the boy at home and away from his friends every evening for a week. Fundamentally he was anxious and over-identified with the boy.

Case 763 (Paternal attitude 'Warm')
Father was very indulgent and tolerant, quite unprepared to bring up his children on any other principle than giving them what they want and trusting that they will grow up well. He left the boy to pursue his own friends and interests, but, he said, 'If the boy needs something I have to give it to him, even if I go without. I remember what it was like to go without and so I let my kids have anything they like.'

Case 122 (Maternal attitude 'Loving normal')
The P.S.Ws described this mother as very affectionate and kindly, but lacking in confidence. She reported that she had always been quiet and timid as a child, very dependent on her mother, and that she still hated to be aggressive or tough or to take decisions. It appeared that she leant on her husband a good deal, leaving it to him to punish the children, while she herself tended to be lax and inconsistent in her discipline. Nevertheless she watched over her children a lot, and was easily upset and worried if they got into any trouble.

Case 033 (Maternal attitude 'Loving normal')
This was a very vigorous and capable mother. Although she worked full time she made a point of attending school functions. She was kindly but firm in handling the children, believing in respecting their individuality, and interesting herself in their different pursuits. She encouraged them to be self-reliant, and perhaps had some tendency to push them into independence rather too quickly, but on the whole she was tactful, sensitive, humorous and loving in her approach.

Discipline also was categorized separately for each parent on a system somewhat similar to that used by the McCords. Every rateable case was allocated to one of five categories of maternal discipline and paternal discipline. These were called respectively normal, erratic, lax, strict and very strict. Erratic discipline meant erratically varying standards of strictness or laxity. Lax was defined as 'No disciplinary rules. Children go their own way.' This classification differed in two ways from the parental rules scale mentioned earlier; it included the additional class of 'erratic' type discipline, and it was a double rating, one for each parent. An assessment of the emotional quality of maternal and paternal discipline was made by noting, for each of the parents, whether they 'spoilt', 'harshly disciplined' or were 'uninterested' in their attempts to control the boy. 'Spoilt' meant over-loading with attention or with material things, 'harsh' meant a certain cruelty or brutality of method, and 'uninterested' implied a lack of concern about training the boy.

TABLE IV (6)

Maternal Attitude and Discipline related to three degrees of Social Handicap

	Boys with Social Handicap:					
	Nil (n=182)		Moderate (n=174)		Severe (n=55)	
	No.	%	No.	%	No.	%
Maternal Attitudes:						
Normal	94	51·7	97	55·8	30	54·5
Loving anxious	42	23·1	30	17·2	10	18·2
Over-protective	21	11·5	13	7·5	2	3·6
Cruel, Passive or Neglecting	13	7·1	19	10·9	10	18·2
Not rated or not applicable	12	6·6	15	8·6	3	5·5
	182	100	174	100	55	100
Maternal Discipline:						
Normal	92	50·6	71	40·8	14	25·5
Erratic or lax	36	19·8	59	33·9	34	61·8
Strict or very strict	38	20·8	28	16·1	4	7·2
Not rated or not applicable	16	8·8	16	9·2	3	5·5
	182	100	174	100	55	100
Quality of Maternal Discipline:						
No special comment	128	70·3	120	68·9	38	69·1
Spoiling	24	13·2	12	7·0	3	5·5
Harsh	12	6·6	22	12·6	9	16·4
Uninterested	3	1·7	5	2·9	1	1·8
Not rated or not applicable	15	8·2	15	8·6	4	7·2
	182	100	174	100	55	100

This last was the least commonly recorded quality of parental discipline, and, perhaps naturally, it was reported of fathers much more often than of mothers. As with all of the P.S.Ws' assessments of parents, attitude to boy and qualities of discipline were closely tied to the social level of the family.

TABLE IV (7)

Paternal Attitude and Discipline related to three degrees of Social Handicap

	Boys with Social Handicap:					
	Nil ($n=182$)		Moderate ($n=174$)		Severe ($n=55$)	
	No.	%	No.	%	No.	%
Paternal Attitude:						
Warm	138	75·8	124	71·2	24	43·6
Cruel, Passive or Neglecting	22	12·1	21	12·1	25	45·5
Not rated or not applicable	22	12·1	29	16·7	6	10·9
	182	100	174	100	55	100
Paternal Discipline:						
Normal	87	47·8	74	42·5	16	29·1
Erratic or lax	28	15·4	45	25·9	24	43·6
Strict or very strict	48	26·4	30	17·2	10	18·2
Not rated or not applicable	19	10·4	25	14·4	5	9·1
	182	100	174	100	55	100
Quality of Paternal Discipline:						
No special comment	122	67·1	113	64·9	28	50·9
Spoiling	15	8·2	13	7·5	2	3·6
Harsh	14	7·7	13	7·5	14	25·5
Uninterested	15	8·2	10	5·7	7	12·7
Not rated or not applicable	16	8·8	25	14·4	4	7·3
	182	100	174	100	55	100

Tables IV (6) and (7) show clearly that unfavourable ratings, such as mother or father 'cruel, passive or neglecting', 'harsh' or 'erratic or lax' were much more commonly attributed to boys in the socially handicapped group, the group which corresponded to the lowest social level. The contrasts between the social groups were even more marked in relation to fathers than to mothers, which is perhaps understandable in view of the predominance of the father in determining the social status of a family. However, such extreme contrasts must be treated sceptically. Among the ratings on fathers in the socially handicapped group one might have expected, in view of the difficulty of interviewing these elusive men, a high proportion of unrateable cases. The fact that this was not so suggests that the P.S.Ws were less inclined to reserve judgement in the case of socially handicapped families. The rating paternal discipline 'erratic' was particularly suspect, in that it was held to apply to a third of the inadequate income group compared with about an eighth of the other income groups.[8] Whatever the true reasons for the very close link between socio-economic circumstances and parental attitude and discipline, it follows that social level must always be allowed for in considering the relation of these factors to misconduct in boys.

7. Parental Attitude and Discipline in Relation to Boys' Conduct

In spite of the gross variation in incidence of anomalous parental attitudes and discipline at different social levels, the relations between these variables and boys' conduct were surprisingly close, and in many respects they held true throughout all sections of the sample. Thus, maternal discipline 'normal' correlated negatively ($r = -\cdot 36$) and maternal discipline 'erratic' correlated positively ($r = \cdot 42$) with poor conduct on the combined rating scale of P.S.Ws and teachers, and these relationships were similar at all three levels of income or social handicap. Maternal attitude unfavourable (i.e. cruel, passive, neglecting or absent) was also significantly related to bad conduct (see Table IV (8)) and this also held true at all social levels.

TABLE IV (8)

Boys' Conduct against Maternal Attitude

Maternal Attitude Rated:	Good I No.	%	II No.	%	Average III No.	%	Bad IV No.	%	V No.	%
Cruel, passive neglecting or absent	6	8·7	9	5·8	15	18·3	9	19·6	9	30·0
None of of these	63	91·3	147	94·2	67	81·7	37	80·4	21	70·0
TOTAL	69	100	156	100	82	100	46	100	30	100

$\chi^2 = 16\cdot 66$ with 2 d.f., $p < \cdot 001$, using the Kolmogorov-Smirnov test to compare the frequency distributions.

Paternal attitude and discipline were much less closely related to boys' behaviour. There was a general tendency at all income levels for 'normal' paternal discipline to go with good conduct ratings, but it was too slight to be statistically significant. Neither 'strict' paternal discipline nor 'erratic' paternal discipline showed any detectable association with good or bad conduct at any income level. There were only ninety-two cases in which father's attitude was rated as anything other than 'warm', and it was impossible to demonstrate any connection with conduct, except for a slight but statistically insignificant association between 'warm' fathers and well-behaved boys. This result pointed to the conclusion that parental influence upon conduct in boys derived almost exclusively from the mother. However, it might be that if the P.S.Ws had been able to see as much of the fathers as they saw of the mothers their assessments of fathers would have yielded different results.

Two aspects of maternal behaviour appeared to have different connotations according to social levels. In the better income groups, the rating 'loving normal' mother correlated with good conduct in boys; but in the inadequate income group there was no consistent relationship with conduct. This might be interpreted to mean that a good maternal attitude is powerless to combat bad behaviour when social circumstances are very poor. Alternatively, it could be that the assessments of the poorer mothers, owing to communication difficulties, were less discriminating. In the better income groups, where mother was rated 'loving anxious or over-protective' there was an increased likelihood of poor conduct in boys. Paradoxically, in the inadequate income group the trend was reversed, the anxious or over-protective mothers having better behaved sons. Once again, the interpretation is uncertain. The anomaly might arise from the difficulty of assessing the poorest families, or it might be that, where mothers have to combat serious social adversities, a certain level of anxiety is realistic and beneficial.

Much the same results were obtained when parental attitude and discipline were compared with the 'acting-out' category instead of with the crude conduct ratings, except that the significant associations with unfavourable maternal features were even more marked, and lax paternal discipline emerged as a significant factor in the subgroup of comfortable income. (Details are given in Appendix IV (D).) Since the P.S.Ws' ratings of boys' conduct formed only a small part of the acting-out categorization, which incorporated the results of two psychological tests as well as teachers' ratings, these findings showed that the relationships were not to be explained away as due to the P.S.Ws' tendency to give unfavourable ratings to both boys and parents in certain families.

8. Parental Attitudes to Child-Rearing as Revealed by Questionnaire Responses

The parents were given questionnaires (one for fathers, one for mothers) which asked them to circle the answers 'agree' or 'disagree' against a sequence of statements of opinion about child-rearing. It was hoped, by this means, to obtain some measure of each parent's position in respect to the basic dimension of authoritarianism-permissiveness, and, in the case of mother, on the dimension of over-concern under-concern as well. The development of these inventories as described, and specimens of the forms used are shown, in Appendix IV (E). As administered in this Study the inventories consisted of thirty-three items each, but on the fathers' form five buffer items, not concerned with authoritarianism, were included in order that the general tenor of the questionnaire should not appear too obvious.

Of the 411 boys, completed inventories were obtained from the mothers of 291, and from the fathers of 232. This was a poor response indeed, especially considering that over a period of more than two years the social workers continued to remind the parents about the inventory and to encourage them to return the forms.[9] In twenty-one cases, either there was no mother left in the home, or else she was illiterate or foreign speaking, and for similar reasons no father was available in thirty-four cases, but the bulk of the missing cases were due to unwillingness or resistance on the part of parents, many of whom promised to complete the forms and never did so, or said they had already posted them, although they had not been received. It would appear that self-completing questionnaires are not a very effective means of surveying a population of this character. A better response was obtained later to questionnaires administered verbally by the social workers themselves in the course of their interviews.

In the better class 'no social handicap' families 75·3 per cent of the boys had a mother's form completed, and 65·9 per cent had a father's form; but in the lower class of 'severely socially handicapped' families the percentages were 63·6 per cent and 36·4 per cent, respectively. As in other contexts throughout this Study, it was the fathers in the poorer families who were the most elusive. There was a very significant association between lower social class and education of mother, and failure to complete the attitude inventory by both parents. This is shown in Appendix IV (E), Table IV E (1). There was much less association between father's socio-educational status and the likelihood of a form being completed. This suggests that it was the mothers, who generally had closer contact with the Study than the fathers, who mostly determined the degree of parental co-operation.

A group of twenty-five boys who for any reason had been to a juvenile court before reaching the age of 13 (see page 105) had attitude inventories completed by both parents in only eight cases, that is 32 per cent, as compared with 56 per cent in the remainder of the sample; a statistically significant difference (p < ·05). This was yet another example of unfavourable features associated with non-response or non-co-operation. Such findings are not peculiar to the present Study. For instance, in Rutter's (Rutter and Graham, 1966) survey of 10 to 11 year-old schoolchildren, he found that, among the minority whose parents failed to complete questionnaires, nearly double the usual proportion were identified as anti-social from teachers' reports.

In view of these findings about the non-responding section of the sample, it was not surprising to discover that, while misconduct in boys was in some degree linked with inventory ratings indicative of parental authoritarianism and maternal under-concern, it was equally, if not more strongly, linked with absence of an inventory rating. The results are shown in Table IV (9).

TABLE IV (9)

Inventory Ratings of Parental Attitude against Teachers' Ratings of Boys' Conduct

Parental Attitude:	Boys rated poor on conduct No.	%	Other Boys No.	%	Total No.	%
Mother's authoritarianism:						
Low	7	11·9	52	88·1	59	100
Average	43	24·2	135	75·8	178	100
High	16	29·6	38	70·4	54	100
No Response	34	28·3	86	71·7	120	100
Mother's under-concern:						
Low	12	25·0	36	75·0	48	100
Average	39	19·5	161	80·5	200	100
High	15	34·9	28	65·1	43	100
No response	34	28·3	86	71·7	120	100
Father's authoritarianism:						
Low	5	12·5	35	87·5	40	100
Average	33	24·4	102	75·6	135	100
High	14	24·6	43	75·4	57	100
No response	48	26·8	131	75·2	179	100

N.B. Values of χ^2 of the difference between the two categories of boys by Teachers' Ratings, 6·92, 6·14 and 3·59, for each table respectively. $\chi^2 = 7·82$ with 3 d.f. for p < ·05, so none of the tables quite reaches statistical significance.

Considering the effort put into the development and administration of the parental attitude questionnaire, the rather slight connection between parental attitude and boys' conduct was something of a disappointment. Moreover, we found only a very slight connection between P.S.W. ratings and questionnaire findings. For example, the P.S.W. rating 'maternal discipline normal' was to some slight extent associated with low scores on maternal authoritarianism. Further, by picking out the most unfavourable categories of maternal attitude and discipline on the P.S.Ws' ratings, a slight association was found between these and the extreme categories of maternal over-concern and under-concern on the questionnaire ratings. These relationships, and also a suggestive association between P.S.W. ratings and authoritarianism in fathers, are displayed in Appendix IV (E), Tables IV E (2), (3) and (4).

In Ryle's (1967) survey of parents in a general practice, he used a similar scale of authoritarianism based upon A. N. Oppenheim's questionnaire, but found no significant relationship between parents' scores and children's conduct or social adjustment. He also found no consistent relationship between the questionnaire assessments of parents' attitudes and his social worker's assessments based on interviews. Faced with this conspicuous lack of correspondence between inventory ratings and interview assessments, Ryle confessed faith in the greater validity of the latter. It may be that parents responses at a personal interview are more revealing or of greater relevance in practice than the opinions they are willing to register on a form.

In this Study, certainly the P.S.Ws' ratings of parental attitudes appeared more helpful than the self-reporting inventory ratings, in so far as they correlated the more highly with the important variables of conduct and performance in boys. However, in this Study the two sets of ratings were not meant to be assessing exactly the same attributes. Moreover, the P.S.Ws' ratings had the advantage of covering a larger proportion of the Study population, including many parents whose extreme attitudes had led to refusal to complete the questionnaires. One can only conclude that the self-completing attitude inventory technique has very serious limitations when one is dealing with a rather sensitive topic among a somewhat resistive population containing many uneducated individuals.

9. *Physical and Mental Health of Parents*

(a) *P.S.Ws' Assessments.* The P.S.Ws recorded an impressionistic judgement of each parent's state of health, based upon the informant's own description, occasionally supplemented by independent medical reports. Physical health was rated 'poor' if the parent was suffering from some definite disorder, or was generally ailing, even though no definite diagnostic label was available. No actual check-list of diseases was used, but such conditions as epileptic fits, recurrent peptic ulcers, asthmatic attacks or chronic bronchitis earned a rating of 'poor' health. The whole period of contact from the time of intake up to November 1964 was considered in relation to this rating, but illnesses before that,[10] if a parent had recovered fully and apparently permanently, were not counted. Twenty-seven per cent of boys (382 rated) were considered to have physically unhealthy mothers, and 22 per cent of boys (360 rated) were thought to have unhealthy fathers.

The mental health of each parent was considered under two headings, neurotic tendency and unstable personality. Presence of any of the classic neurotic symptoms (e.g. chronic anxiety, tension states, depression, phobias, hypochondriasis, somatic complaints of emotional origin, and psycho-somatic diseases clearly associated with emotional tension) warranted a positive rating, and two categories were identified, moderate or severe. A few parents with psychotic symptoms were placed in the severe neurotic group. Independently of this assessment, a parent was categorized as being of unstable personality if he displayed such peculiarities as abnormally erratic behaviour, abnormal temper outbursts, or could be described as psychopathic, very immature, or of hysterical personality. Broadly speaking, this category was intended to identify the behaviour disordered individual who may not necessarily have any anxiety symptoms.

The following two examples, of a neurotic and an unstable mother respectively, illustrate these contrasting forms of personality disturbance; both, as it happens, were associated with very badly behaved boys—conduct ratings 5.

Case 422 (Mother with 'Severe neurotic tendency')
The mother described herself as very nervous, and was under treatment from her doctor for this, but she had never had to go into hospital. She had bouts of intense and irrational anxiety, for which she was given sedatives, but she tried to manage without taking them because she was afraid of becoming addicted. She was obsessional about cleanliness, especially in relation to food, and found it necessary to take most elaborate precautions. She had a severe facial tic and also such a phobia of travel that she could never go away for a holiday. She was hypochondrical about internal ailments, and once when she had a mild food poisoning she refused to eat for a long time, lost a great deal of weight, lost interest in the home, could not cope with housework, and became quite depressed. In the ordinary way she was quite the reverse, that is

over-active and hurried, taking on too much to do in order to stave off her anxieties.

The boy was rated poor as to conduct (category 5). He was openly defiant to his mother and covertly so towards his father. He seemed to enjoy fighting, and would get into fearful tempers with his brothers. He resented any interference. He was apt to embroider stories to make himself look big. The class teacher described him as thoroughly lazy, lacking in concentration and difficult to discipline. In his younger days he had also shown nervous traits, that is moodiness, restlessness, fidgeting and intolerance of noise.

Case 032 (Mother 'Unstable')
This boy, who was rated very poor on the conduct scale (category 5), was described as wild, aggressive and violent tempered, always fighting and sometimes really hurting his opponents. Very restless, destructive and defiant, spiteful and jealous to his siblings, with a huge chip on his shoulder, although quite insensitive to the feelings of others. He was also said to be a persistent liar and a thief.

His mother was an intelligent woman who could be lively and charming at times, but was subject to bad moods and violent tempers. She came from a deprived, rejecting background herself, and seemed incapable of giving consistent mother love. She described herself as erratic and unstable and said 'I'm just not fit to live with at times'. She was living in comparative stability at the time this Study began, but up to a few years before she had cohabited erratically with a succession of 'husbands', moving from place to place and deserting her children, who had all experienced periods of neglect and rejection and had all been in and out of the care of the Children's Department.

There were some significant inter-correlations between the assessments of parental mental and physical health. Physical ill-health of mother was significantly correlated with neurotic tendency of mother, and neurotic tendency of mother with unstable maternal personality. The same relationships held true of the paternal variables, with the level of correlations even higher. There were also significant correlations between maternal and paternal health, between maternal and paternal neurotic tendency and between unstable personality in mother and father. In other words, if a boy had a mother unhealthy in respect of one measure he was more likely to have a mother unhealthy in other respects and also more likely to have a father unhealthy in one or more respects. The assessment of mother's personality as unstable was particularly likely to be associated with a similar evaluation of father. These inter-correlations are displayed in Table IV (10).

As before, parental characteristics were found to be closely tied to the social level of the family. This was particularly evident in the ratings of unstable personality and poor health. For example,

Table IV (11) shows that severe social handicap was seven times as frequent among boys with unstable mothers than among those with mothers of stable personality. Neurotic tendency, on the other hand, was less closely associated with poor circumstances than either ill-health or instability.

TABLE IV (10)
Inter-correlations between six assessments of Parents' Mental and Physical Health

	1	2	3	4	5	6
1. Mother's physical health poor	—	·25	·20	·15	·09	·13
2. Mother with neurotic tendency		—	·18	·14	·12	·18
3. Mother of unstable personality			—	·15	·05	·28
4. Father's physical health poor				—	·23	·15
5. Father with neurotic tendency					—	·35
6. Father of unstable personality						—

There were so few boys from the better off families who had unstable mothers that one cannot but wonder whether recognition of the superior social competence of certain families may not have

TABLE IV (11)
Association between Parental Health and Social Handicap

Parental Rating		No. of boys rated	Percent rated as having 'severe social handicap'	Significance[1] of difference
Mother's physical health	Normal	280	8·2	p < ·001
	Poor	103	27·2	
Mother's neurotic tendency	Nil or Moderate	310	11·6	p < ·1
	Severe	73	20·5	
Mother's personality	Stable	333	7·5	p < ·001
	Unstable	49	51·0	
Father's physical health	Normal	282	7·1	p < ·001
	Poor	79	35·4	
Father's neurotic tendency	Nil or Moderate	339	13·0	p < ·1
	Severe	30	23·3	
Father's personality	Stable	321	9·3	p < ·001
	Unstable	47	44·7	

[1] Significance based on χ^2 comparison of the raw figures.

made the P.S.Ws insensitive to adverse features of personality in these cases. Whatever may be the correct interpretation of the close link between social circumstances and parental personality, it is clear that deductions about the effect of parental personality upon boys can only be made properly after taking account of comparisons within groups of similar social level. Otherwise, variations due to a whole constellation of factors subsumed under the general heading of social handicap might be wrongly attributed to the single factor of parental personality.

(b) *A Questionnaire Assessment of Neuroticism in Mothers.* An independent measure of neurotic tendency among mothers was obtained by giving them a questionnaire, a modified and shortened version of the Cornell Medical Index. The C.M.I. is made up of a list of symptoms, both mental and physical, and the respondents are asked to ring 'yes' or 'no' against each one according to whether they themselves suffer from the item in question. It has been found that neurotics tend to claim a large number of symptoms, and that a high rate of positive endorsements discriminates effectively between neurotic patients and normal groups.

The development of a shortened version for use in this Study has been described in detail elsewhere (Gibson, Hanson and West, 1967). We were fortunate in being supplied with C.M.I. responses collected by Professor K. Rawnsley and Dr A. N. Oppenheim from other samples of neurotics and normals. In an analysis of this data, it was found that endorsement of physical symptoms was as effective in identifying neurotics as endorsement of items concerned with fears and tension symptoms. The shortened version of the questionnaire excluded overt questions about mental health, excluded ambiguous and repetitive questions, and consisted of a total of seventy-five items, applicable to women. (See Appendix IV (F).)

As with the parental attitude questionnaire, a large proportion of the sample failed to complete the form,[9] and non-responders were found to include unduly high proportions of poorer families, troublesome boys, unstable mothers and so forth. Nevertheless, the questionnaire ratings corresponded surprisingly closely with the relevant P.S.W. ratings, namely, 'mother's neurotic tendency' and 'mother has had psychiatric treatment'. In other words, it was the same mothers who complained about their nervous symptoms to the P.S.Ws or to their doctors who also endorsed many symptoms on the questionnaire. (Further details are shown in Appendix IV (F).)

10. Parental Health and Temperament and Sons' Behaviour

Considering the probable effects of parental temperament, one might expect neurotic mothers to have nervous sons, as in the example (*Case* 41) quoted on p. 43. Some such associations were found, but to no more than a slight extent. There was a statistical relationship of borderline significance between the P.S.Ws' ratings of nervous tendency in mother and son respectively. There was also a slight association between nervous boys, as rated by the P.S.Ws, and neurotic mothers, as assessed independently by the health questionnaire. (See Tabulations in Appendix IV (F).)

A more definite association was found between nervous mothers and badly behaved sons. The combined ratings by P.S.Ws and teachers of poor conduct in sons were very significantly associated with the independent health questionnaire scores of neuroticism in mothers. There was also a small but significant correlation (r=·13) between the P.S.W. assessments of nervousness in mothers and the independent ratings by teachers of poor behaviour at school. (See Appendix IV (F).) Furthermore, the tendency for boys with mothers scoring high on neuroticism to be rated badly behaved more often than other boys held true at all three levels of social handicap. The association could not be explained away as the result of both neuroticism and poor conduct being class linked.

Physical health of mothers, and physical health of fathers, had no consistent relationship with either nervous disturbance or poor conduct in boys.[11]

As might have been expected, having an unstable mother was a particularly unfavourable item, being closely linked with bad conduct. The association was only partly the result of the concentration of unstable mothers at the lowest social level. There were just five boys with unstable mothers in the comfortable income group and fifteen in the adequate income group, too few for the association with poor conduct to reach statistical significance, although the same trend was discernible. Within the inadequate income group however, the association was particularly striking. Of the twenty-nine worst behaved poor boys (rated 4 or 5 on the combined assessments of P.S.Ws and teachers), 48·3 per cent had unstable mothers, whereas only 11·8 per cent of the thirty-four best behaved poor boys (rated 1 or 2) had unstable mothers. The following example shows a typical constellation of poor home, unstable mother and badly behaved boy:

> *Case* 721 (Severe social handicap; unstable mother; nervous and badly behaved boy)
> This boy had attended a child guidance clinic for severe temper tantrums

and other complaints. He was also unsatisfactory in conduct, being at times stubborn and defiant. He was apt to provoke other children, although when actually attacked he would become timid.

The family inhabited a grimy uncared-for home in damp neglected property. Father was an unskilled labourer. Health visitors' reports suggested that the boy had been physically neglected from babyhood.

The mother, who was rated 'unstable', was described as immature, unreliable and prone to unrealistic fantasy and self-dramatization. She discussed her numerous problems with evident satisfaction, but did little to solve them. She wilfully defied medical advice. She spent on luxuries while necessities were wanting. She had twice deserted her family. She was most erratic in discipline, constantly threatening punishment, rarely carrying out her word. With both husband and son she appeared at the same time both to encourage and to resent their dependence upon her.

In marked contrast to the clearly adverse associations with unstable mothers, having an unstable father bore no significant relationship to a boy's conduct rating, either in the sample as a whole or within the three groups of income level or social handicap. This was an odd finding in view of the importance paternal personality is said to have in the successful socialization of sons (Andry, 1960), and especially considering that, in the context of this Study, the 'unstable' category included all those with psychopathic traits and serious behaviour problems whose influence is believed to be particularly noxious (Robins, 1966). Maybe at this age (i.e. 8 to 9 years) boys' behaviour depends much more on the personality of mother than of father; but it is hard to reconcile this with the observation, quoted earlier, of significant links between fathers' discipline and boys' behaviour. Since the rating 'unstable father' was for the most part inferred at second hand from adverse comments made by mothers it may have been less valid and hence less discriminating than similar assessments of the mothers themselves.

11. *Summing up the Effects of Home Background*

The most outstanding finding from the results reported in this chapter was that a family's general social level, as revealed in income, or in the complex of variables we have called 'social handicap', was a closer concomitant of misconduct in boys than most of the individual characteristics of parental attitude or behaviour. On the other hand, nervous disorder in boys, as assessed by the P.S.Ws, was not significantly related to income level ($r = \cdot 02$). This curious contrast between the social backgrounds of nervous and behaviour-disordered boys is in conformity with expectation from previous research (Bennett, 1960), but it may nevertheless have been somewhat exaggerated by the greater difficulty of assessing nervous symptoms from the limited reports of mothers in the lowest income group.

Some of the family factors most closely correlated with misconduct in boys, such as physical neglect of children (Table IV (1), p. 63) or unstable maternal personality, were largely confined to the lower social levels, and for that reason had less importance in relation to the behaviour of boys from the more affluent homes. On the other hand, certain aspects of parental behaviour, such as erratic maternal discipline, deviant attitudes to children (i.e. cruel, passive, neglecting), parental carelessness or 'under-vigilance', or inconsistency between parents in handling their children, although more frequent in the lower income group, occurred sufficiently often throughout the sample for it to be possible to demonstrate significant associations with boys' misconduct at all social levels. Certain other features, however, appeared to have different connotations at different social levels. Marital disharmony between parents was definitely linked with poor conduct in most of the sample, but not among the boys from the socially handicapped group, even though among that group a half of the marriages were rated disharmonious. In contrast, having parents who were very interested in a boy's education bore no relation to his conduct, except among the inadequate income group, where this was a relatively unusual feature.

Where relationships differed according to social level, it was usually the lowest and most deprived group that proved the exception. It was certainly more difficult to make some of the assessments in the case of the poorer families with whom the P.S.Ws did not have very close rapport, and this may have led to some anomalous and mistaken impressions. One suspects, for instance, that some of the marriages in the poorer families were rated adversely on account of the general aura of squalor and unsatisfactoriness surrounding these unfortunates, and that in reality they may have been less disharmonious than they seemed. On the other hand, there were probably some genuine differences in family dynamics at different levels. Parental behaviour that might not ordinarily have much bearing upon school performance or conduct, such as special interest in education, might have had a more favourable effect where social circumstances were so bad that a boy would otherwise be expected to be retarded and badly behaved. Maternal anxiety and over-protectiveness, which was generally an unfavourable feature, did seem to have a good effect when it occurred in a context of real social adversity.

The investigation of parental attitudes by questionnaire produced very little of relevance to boys' conduct. The mother's health questionnaire, however, did appear to give a valid measure of maternal neuroticism, and to correspond closely to the P.S.Ws' interview impressions; but the predicted connection between nervous boys and nervous mothers, although present, was only very slight. Contrary to expectations (Rutter, 1966), parental health did not seem to have much influence upon either conduct or nervous disorder in the boys. Finally, it was observed that, in general, mothers' attitudes and behaviour were more closely related to the boys' conduct and performance than were father's characteristics. This probably reflected the greater influence of mothers at this age; but the effect may have been exaggerated by the P.S.Ws' lesser degree of contact with fathers, leading to less efficient assessments of paternal features.

It may seem that a great deal of effort has been spent documenting the obvious, namely that socially deprived, unloving, erratic, inconsistent, and careless parents tend to produce badly behaved boys. But the main point of the exercise has been to try to produce some elementary quantitative measures of all these features so as to see how they stand in relation to each other, and how they rank in importance as factors in juvenile misconduct now, and as predictors of juvenile delinquency later.

NOTES

[1] A further six boys were known to be the offspring of cohabitation rather than legitimate marriage, but since they were living with both natural parents in normal family circumstances they were not counted as anomalous.

[2] This was an exception to the rule, otherwise strictly followed, to count in the analysis of early behaviour and background only those items assessed and recorded before November 1964. One other exception was made in the matter of questionnaires addressed to parents, some of which were completed at a later date. (See pp. 87, 93.)

[3] For further details see Appendix IV (A).

[4] The question arises here, and in many of the findings reported later on, whether the association between some unfavourable item and poor conduct may not be due entirely to the concentration of both badly behaved boys and family adversities among the poorest section of the sample at the lowest social level. Using a scale of 'social handicap' to identify three social levels (see p. 67 ff.), and analysing the boys who had been separated from mother in each of the three social groups, it was found that some association between separation and poor conduct existed at all levels. But the other items of adversity listed in Table IV (1) occurred too rarely outside the lowest social level for an analysis of this kind to be applied.

[5] The rating was made on the situation as it existed at the time of intake into the Study when the boys were 8 to 9 years old. In the case of marriages that had terminated in the not too distant past the assessment was made retrospectively, but fourteen cases, mostly boys who had been fatherless since infancy, were rated

'not applicable' and a further twenty-four 'not known' on account of absence of information.

[6] Defined on p. 67.

[7] See especially Appendix IV (C).

[8] A special examination of these assessments revealed an unusual number of alterations at this point on the record form, suggesting that the P.S.Ws must often have had second thoughts on this rating. There was also a curiously close correspondence between fathers with a criminal record and fathers rated erratic in discipline. Furthermore, a list prepared by the P.S.Ws naming fathers they suspected were criminal showed even closer correspondence with erratic discipline than did the final list of convicted fathers obtained from the Criminal Record Office. The P.S.Ws would not agree that this evidence indicated bias in their ratings, but it seems probable that certain disagreeable or disreputable fathers generated a negative halo which greatly increased the likelihood of their being described as 'erratic'.

[9] On account of the very slow response, these questionnaire scores were not included in the first analysis, which was based on data available in November 1964. The analysis reported here includes all questionnaires returned by the end of year 1966.

[10] Assessments of past ill-health were attempted, but proved unreliable. (See p. 132.)

[11] Considering the sample as a whole, there was in fact a just significant relation between poor conduct of boys, on the combined ratings of P.S.Ws and teachers, and both mothers' health poor and fathers' health poor. (For conduct against mothers' health, $\chi^2 = 11 \cdot 14$ with 4 d.f., $p < \cdot 025$; for conduct against fathers' health $\chi^2 = 9 \cdot 51$ with 4 d.f., $p < \cdot 05$.) However, the association was amply accounted for by the ubiquitous variable of 'social handicap', the severely handicapped group having a considerable excess of both bad boys and unhealthy parents. Considering each social level separately, no significant relationship was found. In fact, in the severely handicapped group the tendency ran in the opposite direction, that is the better behaved boys had unhealthy mothers rather more frequently than the badly behaved boys, but the numbers were too small to make any certain deductions.

V

Some Special Criminogenic Factors

1. Criminality in the Family

(a) *The Incidence of Criminal Convictions.* It is commonly assumed that criminal behaviour on the part of parents or elder siblings is an important factor in predisposing boys towards misconduct; but firm evidence on this issue remains surprisingly scarce. As with so many of the factors under consideration, the interpretation of any correlations that may be found present considerable difficulty. The likelihood of a boy having a delinquent sibling increases with the number of children in the family, and of course for both parents and siblings the likelihood of a criminal conviction is much greater among the poorer families. Hence, it needs to be demonstrated that any association between bad behaviour in boys and criminality among their families is not merely the consequence of both features being commoner in lower class families.

Information concerning convictions for indictable offences of parents or siblings was obtained by searches carried out at the Criminal Records Office at Scotland Yard and by searches through the archives of various local authority Children's Departments. These sources were supplemented by statements from the parents themselves, by information from nearby probation offices, and occasionally from teachers. The tabulations in this section concern all criminal convictions known to the Criminal Records Office which occurred before November 1964.[1] In the case of juveniles, all findings of guilt were counted, but court appearances for 'care, protection or control', or for non-attendance at school, were excluded from the figures in this section.

Out of a total of 401 boys, eighty-two, that is 20·5 per cent, had a father with one or more criminal convictions.[2] Since there are no published statistics of the proportion of the male population with a criminal record it is impossible to compare this figure with a national average. However, it has been estimated by Rose and Avison (Radzinowicz, 1952, p. 129), from an analysis of the age distribution of first offenders in the Criminal Statistics of England and Wales 1962, that 29·5 per cent of males and 7·1 per cent of females will be convicted of an indictable offence during their life span, 25·7 per cent of males being convicted before reaching their fortieth birthday. The fathers in this sample had for the most part passed their peak age for criminality some twenty or more years previously, when crime rates were much smaller. An estimate by Trenaman (1952) and Emmett, similar in principle, but based on the crime rates for 1938, yielded an expectation of 11 per cent of males convicted sometime during their life. These authors pointed out that in poorer working-class districts the expectation was doubled. A further difficulty in making comparisons is that unmarried men are convicted more often than married men, but unmarried men were excluded by the method of selection of the present sample.

Table V (1) shows the numbers of boys with a convicted father, mother, elder brother and elder sister respectively. Altogether, over one-third of the boys had had one or more family members convicted.

TABLE V (1)

Numbers of Boys with one or more Relatives Convicted
(up to November 1964)

Relative:	No. of boys with specified relative(s) known to have been convicted	Percentage of total 411 boys
Father or acting father	82	
Absent father (in 10 cases with no acting father)[1]	4	20·9
Mother or acting mother	30	7·3
Any of the above	99	24·1
Elder brother	54	13·1
Elder sister	12	2·9
Any of the above categories	140	34·1

[1] These were not included in subsequent tabulations since none of them were at home for any substantial period of their boy's life, and none of them had direct influence upon their boy's upbringing.

The records of convictions were of very varying degrees of seriousness. Of the eighty-two boys with a convicted father only thirty had a father with a record of two or more convictions since reaching the age of 17, and only twelve had a father with more than three such convictions. Of these twelve persistent recidivists, only four committed serious crimes involving substantial amounts of property or considerable personal violence. There were eight boys whose fathers' only recorded convictions were as juveniles, but possibly this number would have been larger had the records of juvenile convictions of the last generation been more complete.

It was noticeable that the age of a boy's father had a significant connection with the frequency with which a criminal record was found. Those boys with younger fathers, born after 1929, had the highest proportion with convictions, which perhaps reflected the increasing liability of more recent generations to court appearances. Those with older fathers, born before 1915, had a slightly higher proportion with more than one adult conviction, which was consistent with their longer period at risk (see Appendix V (A)).

The percentage of older brothers convicted was rather high. Of a total of 117 brothers who had grown beyond the juvenile age range (that is all those born before 1948) who were identified and their names searched for at the Criminal Records Office and in Children's Departments, forty-seven, that is 40·2 per cent, were found to have had one or more convictions by November 1964. The expectation of future convictions for all the boys in the sample is not necessarily quite so high. These grown-up brothers of young boys naturally tended to come from the larger sized families, and such families contribute a disproportionate share of delinquents.

(b) *The Significance of Criminal Convictions.* The concentration of delinquent relatives in particular families was very marked. The fact of having a convicted mother increased the likelihood of a boy having a convicted father more than three times. Among boys who had older brothers, the fact of having a brother convicted increased the likelihood of having a convicted parent one and a half times.

Families in which one or other parent had had some isolated conviction, perhaps many years previously, were not noticeably different from most others in the sample, but where several members of a family had been convicted repeatedly multiple social problems were very likely to be found, as in the following instance:

Case 31 (Problem family associated with criminality)
Although he came from a very disordered home background, this boy had a satisfactory rating as to conduct (category 2), but he was attending a school for the educationally subnormal, and he got into trouble subsequently. By the time he reached 13 years of age he had already appeared at juvenile court and been found guilty on more than one occasion.

His father had been convicted many times, and five of his older siblings had also been convicted. Father was an unskilled manual labourer, addicted to heavy drinking and gambling, and prone to violent rages. He knocked his wife about frequently. She was a dull, worn woman who was subdued and terrified by her psychopathic husband. The children were exposed to thoroughly inconsistent discipline, oscillating between their soft, loving but over-indulgent mother and their harsh, punitive and cruel father. In addition, the children's clothes, hygiene and food were obviously neglected, and the living accommodation was in an appalling state. This notorious family was being dealt with by a formidable array of social agencies.

The implications of the findings concerning fathers' criminality were fairly clear. The rating scale of father's convictions (nil, one, or more than one) correlated positively and significantly with the basic features of social handicap, such as low family income ($r = \cdot 12$), large sized family ($r = \cdot 17$) and poor housing ($r = \cdot 15$). Indeed, among the group of boys identified as having a severe degree of social handicap, the incidence of convicted fathers was 38·2 per cent, compared with only 11·1 per cent among those with no social handicap. Although over the sample as a whole poor conduct on teachers' ratings correlated significantly with father's criminality ($r = \cdot 15$); within each of the three levels of social handicap there was no significant tendency for the worst behaved boys to have more convicted fathers. In short, it would seem that the fact of having a convicted father represented one of a cluster of adversities commoner at the lower social levels, but as an item in isolation it was of little importance as a determinant of misconduct in boys of this age.[3] Some further account of the characteristics of boys with criminal fathers occurs in Chapter VII, p. 126, in connection with the discussion on the validity of the assessments of family background.

2. *Dullness, Retardation and Misconduct*

(a) *Duller Boys are more Trouble-Prone.* Lack of intelligence is no longer believed to be an important feature of badly behaved juveniles. As more refined tests have developed, which are less dependent upon scholastic experience, differences in mean intelligence quotients between delinquent and non-delinquent groups have tended to diminish very substantially, if not to disappear altogether. On the other hand, scholastic retardation, not necessarily associated with lack of potential intelligence, remains a striking characteristic of juvenile delinquents (Eilenberg, 1961).

The boys in this Study were of normal population standard on tests of non-verbal intelligence, although below average in reading and scholastic attainment generally, as was only to be expected in a sample containing large numbers of families belonging to the lower socio-economic levels. (See p. 18.) Over the sample as a whole, below average intelligence, and scholastic retardation, were both significantly associated with bad behaviour. Table V (2) shows that 73 per cent of the boys in the worst conduct category were below average on the verbal comprehension test, compared with only 42 per cent of the boys in the best conduct category.

TABLE V (2)

Verbal Comprehension against Boys' Conduct
(Combined Ratings of P.S.Ws and Teachers)

	\multicolumn{10}{c}{Conduct Rating:}
Verbal	\multicolumn{2}{c}{Good}			\multicolumn{2}{c}{Average}			\multicolumn{2}{c}{Bad}	
Comprehension	I		II		III		IV		V	
	No.	%	No.	%	No.	%	No.	%	No.	%
High Quotient (>100)	39	58·2	47	30·9	24	25·3	7	13·2	8	26·7
Not High (⩽100)	28	41·8	105	69·1	71	74·7	46	86·8	22	73·3

χ^2 (by the Kolmogorov-Smirnov test) = 14·96 with 2 d.f., $p < ·001$

There was a significant, positive association between misconduct and poor intelligence (as measured by the Raven's Matrices), and between misconduct and poor reading attainment. These trends held true at all three levels of social handicap, so they could not be just a social class phenomenon. (See Appendix V (B).) The converse expectation, that the more intelligent boys, and the superior readers, would tend to be well behaved, while true of the sample as a whole, was not found to be so among the socially favoured boys of the 'no social handicap' sub-group. Apparently intelligence and scholastic ability did nothing to protect the better-class boy from developing behaviour problems.

For the most part, the boys of the acting-out group (defined by unpopularity and 'neurotic-extraversion' as well as misconduct) shared the characteristics of the worst behaved boys as defined solely by the P.S.W.-teacher conduct scale. The findings concerning intelligence and conduct proved to be an exception. In the acting-out group the various grades of intelligence score were represented roughly in the same proportions as in the total sample, there was no over-representation of dullards. The only exception was among the twenty-three acting-out boys who were classed as severely handicapped, among whom those of below average intelligence, and those of poor reading ability, were both greatly over-represented. This suggests that where low intelligence and severe social handicap go together in the same unfortunate individual, the combination has a deleterious effect upon personality as well as being conducive to misconduct.

Is it certain that the duller boys are worse behaved than their social peers? The effect could be more apparent than real. At age 8, when the tests were carried out, a boy's co-operativeness and amenability to directions from an adult had a considerable influence upon his scores. Maybe the worst behaved boys appeared dull because they were not giving of their best. This is unlikely to be the whole explanation, however, for on re-testing at age 11, when scores may be expected to be less drastically affected by distractability or emotional resistance, misconduct and dullness were still associated. Another source of error might be the teachers' dislike of stupidity causing them to rate the duller boys poorly on conduct. In fact, the teachers' ratings of poor classroom conduct correlated more highly ($r = \cdot 30$) with low intelligence (the matrices test) than did the P.S.Ws' ratings of conduct disorder ($r = \cdot 12$). Maybe the classroom situation brought out the worst in the duller boys, or perhaps the teachers did not always distinguish between inattention or laziness and real intellectual handicap. Be that as it may, since the P.S.Ws' conduct ratings also correlated significantly with intelligence, teacher bias could not account for the entire effect.

Further evidence of the relation between intelligence and troubleproneness was obtained by comparing the statistics of appearances of boys at juvenile court with scores on the Matrices Test. Of the twenty-five boys under 13 years of age who were found guilty of an offence or brought before courts for non-attendance at school or as needing care and protection the majority, namely sixteen, came from the minority of eighty-six boys classed as dull (I.Q. ninety or less) on the test. In contrast not a single one came from among the 122 boys classed as bright (I.Q. 110 or more). The difference was statistically very significant.

(b) *Differential Effects According to Social and Intellectual Level.* In the previous chapter attention was drawn to the point that certain items of parental behaviour, notably 'parental vigilance' and 'parental interest in education' appeared to have different effects upon the child's conduct and educational performance according to the social level of the family. In the inadequate income families, above average parental vigilance, and above average parental interest in education (although both relatively unusual at that social level) were associated with better reading quotients in boys. In the adequate or comfortable income groups, however, there was no significant association. (See Appendix IV (C).) In view of the close link between intelligence and conduct revealed by the findings just described, it seems likely that both this factor and the social level of the family need to be taken into account when evaluating the effects of different methods of discipline and upbringing. A similar conclusion was reached by Conger and Miller (1966, p. 70) in a research on juvenile delinquents in Denver. They found that individual factors of personality had different implications for delinquency-proneness according to both the social and intelligence level of the child.

The problem is high-lighted in Table V (3). The left-hand column sets out the unfavourable characteristics which were commonly found in association with the twenty-five boys who appeared before juvenile courts at an early age. (These consisted of 20 boys found guilty of offences plus 5 who had been dealt with for non-attendance or as care, protection or control cases.) Over a half of these boys had parents in obvious martial conflict, a third had parents rated under-vigilant, and almost a half had parents lax in rules. All of these proportions were greatly in excess of the incidence levels in the sample as a whole. But if, instead of comparing these boys with the generality of cases, one compares them with others of the same social and intelligence level a very different picture emerges. The twenty-five boys who had appeared at a juvenile court were matched with twenty-five boys who were free from court appearances or reports of delinquency by parents, teachers, etc., and were of just the same level of social handicap (using all points of the 0 to 7 scale), and were also similar in intelligence scores.[4] The results appear on the right in Table V (3). They show that, after matching for social level and intelligence, the differences between delinquents and controls either disappear altogether or are greatly reduced. The non-delinquents have just as high an incidence of criminal fathers, lax parents and under-vigilant parents as do the delinquents. In short, the results point to the importance of low social class and low intellectual level as prime characteristics of young delinquents. In the absence of these prime factors specific items of faulty upbringing appear to have comparatively small weight as determinants of early delinquency. Naturally a great deal more evidence will be needed before this suggestion can be taken seriously.

3. *Conduct Incongruous with Background*

Conduct in boys correlated so closely with the family's degree of social handicap that it was quite unusual to find a well-behaved boy among the mentally handicapped, or a really badly behaved boy among the socially favoured. By looking closely at these exceptions, it was hoped to deduce something about the individual qualities which protect certain boys from the effects of a bad environment, and cause others to develop behaviour problems in spite of coming from good homes.

TABLE V (3)

Various Parental Attributes in Groups of Early Delinquents and Matching Non-Delinquents

Parental Characteristics		25 Boys who had appeared at Juvenile Court under age 13	25 Non-delinquent boys of matching social level and intelligence
Parents' Marriage	Satisfactory	11	18
	Disharmonious	13	7
	Not Assessable	1	—
	TOTAL	25	25
Parental Vigilance	Above average	2	1
	Average	12	17
	Below average	8	7
	Not Assessed	3	—
	TOTAL	25	25
Parental Rules	Rigid	4	3
	Average	5	11
	Lax	11	10
	Not Assessed	5	1
	TOTAL	25	25
Father's Criminal Record	No Conviction	17	14
	Convicted once	4	6
	Convicted more than once	4	5
	TOTAL	25	25
Father's Attitude to boy	Warm	12	17
	Passive	3	2
	Cruel	6	4
	Neglecting	1	—
	Not Assessed	3	2
	TOTAL	25	25

Very well behaved boys from bad backgrounds were so exceptional as to be almost non-existent. Of the fifty-five boys in the severely socially handicapped group, only three were in the best grade of conduct on the ratings of P.S.Ws and teachers combined, although a further eleven were rated free from conduct disorder by the P.S.Ws and of average behaviour by their teachers.[5] Of this total group of fourteen, eight developed definite behaviour problems or actual delinquency by the time they were 11 years old, and seven had delinquent siblings. Only four of the boys remained reasonably well behaved and had no delinquent siblings. In all these four cases the reason for the social handicap was poverty consequent upon death of a father rather than poor social standards or family disorganization. This suggests that what might be called accidental poverty has a much less deleterious effect upon boys' behaviour than the fecklessness and neglect of parents who are ineffectual providers.

The bad boys from good social backgrounds were considered next. There were six boys in the worst conduct category who came from favoured (no social handicap) homes. In their case it was at once obvious that in spite of their homes being adequate materially they were highly insecure psychologically. Five of the six mothers were rated as having a severe degree of nervous disturbance, coupled with an over-anxious or over-protective attitude to the boy. The sixth mother, although said to have only 'moderate' nervous disturbance, was classed 'unstable' in personality and 'cruel' to her boy. (Refer back to pp. 79, 90 for definitions of these terms.) Only one of the mothers and two of the fathers were rated 'normal' in their methods of parental discipline. These indications of serious family disturbances were further reflected in the P.S.Ws' graphic descriptions. Here is an example:

Case 271
In this home everything was tidily arranged and in perfect condition. It had taken the parents twenty years to build up their comfortable home, but now they had practically everything, including fitted carpets and proudly displayed furniture.

Both parents had had unhappy childhoods. The mother was much younger than any of her siblings, and had been over-protected by her mother. Her father had been in chronically poor health, and she thought her childhood had been both drab and lonely. The father came from a poor slum household, and had been brought up by a harsh and unpredictable father who was a drunkard, and by a mother who had shown him little affection, in an atmosphere of perpetual rows. Although he won a scholarship, he was made to leave school as soon as possible. He was a 'warm' father (see p. 79), keen to provide a better background for his son, but he was over-anxious and restrictive and it was clear the boy was being pushed too hard.

The mother complained of severe self-consciousness, which had been a handicap all her life, and had made her childhood a misery. She said, 'I have always been a bag of nerves, I blush and flush easily'. She still suffered from claustrophobia, insomnia, nightmares, severe tension headaches and a liability to panic. She felt bored, frustrated and lonely, and had practically no contacts outside the family and no outside interests; but she did not go out to work because her husband objected. One time the P.S.W. visited the boy was playing in the street. Although it was a warm day he was wrapped in thick woollens and he had to report back constantly to his mother, who kept him well in sight all the time. This was not on account of the traffic, for it was a very quiet street. She explained, 'I don't like him running wild in the street. I like to see where he is.' In fact he had not been allowed out at all before the age of 8. She said with some resentment that although he was usually clinging, once he got outside with his mates he would forget about her for hours.

In this case, in addition to his troublesome behaviour at home and at school, the boy was considered to have severe nervous symptoms, including insomnia, night terrors, food fads, as well as babyish clinging and dependency.

This case history illustrates a number of points about the group of bad boys from so-called good backgrounds. First, unhealthy features in the boy's psychological environment are all too obvious. Second, the difficulties experienced by the parents in handling their boy appear to reflect troubles they themselves have had in their own childhood. Third, the effect on the boy is to produce a combination of troublesome behaviour and nervous traits. Of the six boys in this group, only two were rated by the P.S.Ws as being free from significant nervous symptoms. Even these two had some symptoms, indeed one of them was continuing to wet his bed several times a week at the age of 11, in spite of treatment at a special clinic, while the other suffered from food fads, nail-biting, occasional nightmares and bullying at school. One may safely conclude at this age conspicuous misconduct among boys from materially secure homes is highly likely to be associated with obvious psychological disturbances in the parents as well as with concomitant nervous disorders in the troublesome boys.

4. *Brain Damage and Subsequent Misconduct*

(a) *The Background of the Theory.* According to a now fashionable theory, the difficult behaviour of some juvenile delinquents is caused by damage to the brain which may have occurred during the mother's pregnancy or at the time of birth. Minimal brain damage can be so slight that no permanent physical signs or substantial intellectual

SOME SPECIAL CRIMINOGENIC FACTORS 109

subnormality are evident on examination, and yet it can still be severe enough to provoke disturbance of behaviour many years later.

An early exponent of this view, B. Pasamanick (1956), conducted a survey in Baltimore of all children born after 1939 and referred to the Education Department on account of behaviour disturbances. These were compared with other children in the same school classes who had not been referred. (This meant that the control group was well matched for social class and area of residence.) Medical records of birth histories were obtained for the children in both groups. Almost every kind of abnormality or complication of child bearing was more frequently found among the behaviour disordered than among the control group. Excluding the negro minority, cases with two or more complications were twice as frequent among the behaviour disordered children.

Pasamanick and his colleagues were primarily concerned with abnormalities of pregnancy, particularly toxaemias and haemorrhage. Other workers have been interested in premature births and complications of delivery resulting in asphyxia of the baby with risk of brain cell damage from oxygen lack. All of these factors have been held to contribute to the likelihood of the development, years later, of one or other personality disturbance, including behaviour disorder, neuroticism or the so-called hyperkinetic syndrome (consisting of restlessness, impulsiveness and distractability).

A statistical association between disturbed behaviour in children, poor performance at school, or below average intelligence (not necessarily subnormality) on the one hand, and a history of complications of birth or mother's pregnancy on the other, has been demonstrated in a number of recent researches. Opinions differ about the meaning of this relationship, whether it is a question of direct cause and effect, or whether the association is due in whole or in part to adverse factors in the social and physical environment which increase the risk of both birth complications and behaviour disturbance.

This point was brought out by J. W. B. Douglas (1960) in connection with children weighing less that $5\frac{1}{2}$ lb. at birth and so presumably 'premature'. It is believed that premature babies have an increased fragility and susceptibility to vascular injuries during birth, and hence an increased risk of subsequent mental handicaps. Using material from a large national sample, Douglas matched his group of 'premature' children attending primary schools against controls of the same age whose fathers were of the same occupational class. He found that the premature group were of significantly lower intelligence and educational attainments, and on a teachers' questionnaire received more adverse comments on their discipline, concentration and attitude to work. Children in the 'premature' group were less than half as likely as the controls to gain grammar school places in the eleven plus tests. However, these differences were largely explained by the association of poor living conditions and low standard of maternal care with a high incidence of premature births. In the absence of these other factors, prematurity made no significant contribution to poor performance.

Other workers have come to the opposite conclusion. C. M. Drillien (1964), using a more stringent criterion of prematurity (4½ lb. or less),[6] compared a sample of premature children with their own siblings of normal birth-weight. On Stott's Bristol Social Adjustment Guide (a questionnaire about children's classroom behaviour, which can be filled in by teachers) the premature children gave significantly higher scores indicative of maladjustment than did their normally born brothers and sisters. Using a series of twenty-one pairs of twins, among whom one member of each was of markedly inferior weight at birth, Drillien applied the Maladjustment Guide when they were attending school and obtained consistently higher scores from those born underweight compared with their normal twins. Since adverse environmental factors may be presumed to be approximately equal in the case of siblings, and especially twins, the marked behavioural differences would appear to be in this instance a direct consequence of abnormality of birth,

(b) *The Present Investigation.* In order to obtain as complete information as possible about the obstetric history of the boys in this Study the following steps were taken. The mothers were asked, at interview, where the boy was born, and such particulars as they could furnish about his weight at birth and about any complications of pregnancy or delivery. In order to check this, medical records were scrutinized in all cases of births in hospital where the place of birth was known. In addition, the records of the local hospitals were searched in order to trace particulars of other boys in the sample whose place of birth was not previously known to the investigators.

Records of home deliveries were more difficult to obtain, since the midwives working in the area came from six different agencies, and some of these had not preserved their records. For example, the local District Nursing Association were most co-operative, but their registers from February 1951 to July 1952 were missing. The notes made by midwives employed by the Local Authority had been sent to the Public Health Division for preservation during the mother's child-bearing life span, but we were told that in practice they were destroyed after five years except in cases where the mother had more babies during this time.

By October 1964, when the inquiry was brought to a close, all but one of the records had been traced for the 273 boys known to have been born in hospital. For 131 boys known to have been born at home, some information from midwives or other professional records was available in about half the cases, while for the remainder there was only mother's unsubstantiated account of the confinement.

Abnormality of weight at birth, defined as 5 lb. 8 oz. or less, or over 10 lb., was recorded in twenty-one boys (N=393), of whom three were overweight. The underweight boys, amounting to 4·6 per cent, fall into the range generally defined as premature births, of which, according to a national survey, the expected incidence for male births is 6 per cent (Butler and Bonham, 1963, p. 133).

A majority of mothers gave approximately correct information about their boy's weight at birth. In 310 cases in which a mother's version could be compared with an independent record, the two were identical to the ounce in 61 per cent of cases, differed by less than 4 oz. in a further 12 per cent, and by a pound or more in 9 per cent. Mothers under-estimated as often as they over-estimated, so there was no systematic error in the direction of exaggerating the size of the baby.

Abnormalities of confinement were recorded on the following system. Any history of haemorrhage, mal-presentations or severe asphyxia of the baby was categorized as a 'severe' abnormality of confinement.[7] 'Moderate' abnormality included uncomplicated breech deliveries and slight degrees of foetal distress or asphyxia.[8]

Little difficulty was found in transcribing hospital records on this system, but other records were not always so full, and when information was from mother only the classification was necessarily very rough. The more serious complications of confinement would naturally be more likely to be sent to hospital (in some cases after labour had begun). As the perinatal mortality survey has shown (Butler and Bonham, 1963), births booked and delivered at home tend to have less complications and to carry about half the average risk of infant mortality. In this sample, in 272 hospital records, 40 per cent had either a moderate or severe 'abnormality' of confinement, compared with only 10 per cent of home deliveries, recorded by midwives. This very small percentage was in part due to inadequate information, especially where mother was the sole informant.

Abnormalities of pregnancy were recorded as a separate variable, graded as 'moderate' or 'severe'.[9] On this variable, it seems that adequate information was available only for 272 cases with hospital records, of whom 53 had a 'moderate' or 'severe' abnormality of pregnancy. Only 8 cases of abnormality of pregnancy were mentioned among 127 reports of home deliveries, but there must have been other cases not recorded. Some of the midwives' notes clearly referred to the labour only and not to the ante-natal period.

(c) *The Present Findings.* Each of the obstetric variables (birth weight, pregnancy and confinement) was examined for significant correlations with the measures of personality and performance obtained from teachers' ratings of conduct, from P.S.W. reports of nervous symptoms, from the cognitive tests of intelligence and attainment, and from the psychomotor performance tests. Inspection of the large matrix of correlations showed no significant relationships in any of these respects,[10] and no other relationships of any note. However, before concluding that the present sample shows no significant connection between birth history and subsequent behaviour, it was necessary to consider whether relationships may have been obscured by one or more of the following factors:

1. The inclusion in the computations of too many minor abnormalities of no importance in development.
2. The absence of a measure of combined obstetric adversity, which would take into account confinement, pregnancy and birth weight together.
3. The uneven coverage of information according to whether the birth took place in hospital.
4. The operation of intervening variables.

Scrutiny of the cross tabulations to see if the more extreme categories of 'severe' pregnancy abnormality or 'severe' abnormality of confinement produced some relationships with the boys' conduct or performance failed to yield any significant result. In the case of the pregnancy ratings, there were only fifteen instances of 'severe' abnormality, too few for statistical comparison. In the case of 'severe' abnormality of confinement there was no significant excess of badly behaved boys in the group.

An example of the possibility of an intervening variable being responsible for a suggestive trend occurred in connection with the sixty-one boys with a history of some abnormality of maternal pregnancy. Fifteen of these were rated bad on conduct by their teachers, only six were rated good. However, of the fifteen bad boys whose mothers had had an abnormal pregnancy, a majority (nine out of fifteen) had mothers rated poor in general health, whereas of the six good boys only one had an unhealthy mother. Thus, any tendency for the history of abnormality of pregnancy to be associated with bad behaviour might be due to mothers in poor general health having both bad boys and bad pregnancies.

In a further computer analysis, the abnormalities of confinement, pregnancy and birth weight were taken together, or in various combinations, and cross tabulated against behavioural variables. The purpose of this was to see whether any one item from the whole range of obstetric adversities, or any particular combination of items, might be related to subsequent behaviour. None of these analyses yielded a statistically significant result.

In all these analyses, the population with hospital records was considered separately, since in these cases the information was more detailed and reliable, and might be expected to yield clearer results. The hospital sub-sample was then further divided into first-born boys and boys with older siblings. The reason for doing this was the fact that the incidence of abnormality of confinement was (as expected) greater for the first-born. Some of these results are displayed in Appendix V (C). They yielded a number of statistical associations between birth history and behaviour in certain segments of the sample, but none that suggested any true causal link.

To sum up the results of this investigation; no significant overall relationship between obstetric abnormality and subsequent bad behaviour was demonstrated. It could be argued that this was because the sample was too limited in size to yield sufficient numbers of significant abnormalities. Nevertheless, the sample was sufficiently large, and contained enough boys with disturbed behaviour, to make clear that obstetric history could not be a factor of outstanding importance in relation to the generality of misconduct. This conclusion agrees with the results of a research by Sula Wolff (1967). She compared the obstetric histories of a hundred schoolchildren referred for psychiatric disturbances with those of a hundred normal controls and found no significant differences between the two groups in maternal age, birth weight or complications of delivery. In our own research, the demonstration of anomalous relationships in certain segments of the study population showed that apparently straightforward associations between birth history and later behaviour cannot be taken as convincing evidence of a causal connection. Certain intervening variables are of considerable, if not overriding, importance and must be taken into account. Among the more obvious complicating factors are mother's general health, the number of children she has had, her social circumstances, and her likelihood of being delivered in hospital. All of these are related on the one hand to the chances of producing a badly behaved child as a result of environmental influence, and on the other hand to the risks of experiencing (or at least of having officially recorded) some kind of obstetric complication. Any reported statistical relationship between birth history and behaviour cannot be properly interpreted without taking such factors into account. In the present Study we found only very slight relationships between obstetric histories and boys' behaviour. These relationships, which were limited to particular segments of the sample, could all be adequately accounted for by the factors just mentioned, without having to postulate any causal connection between obstetric history and conduct. These results cast serious doubt on the theory that minimal birth injury is an important factor in the generality of juvenile misconduct.

NOTES

[1] These data were not completed as soon as expected owing to the time taken to secure permissions for the searches, and owing to the necessity to repeat the searches in order to achieve more accurate results. In many instances the P.S.Ws had not recorded the exact Christian names and birth dates of all family members, or the maiden names of mothers, and these items had to be found subsequently by looking up birth and marriage certificates at Somerset House. Searches then had to be repeated using the additional or amended particulars. Even so, perfect accuracy is unattainable. A certain small percentage of cases are always missed when clerks are asked to check a long name list. Where evasive individuals have given incorrect particulars to authorities, the chance of finding their records is lessened, and where an individual has lived abroad for a long time his convictions would not necessarily be known in England. In the case of adults, whether the records of their juvenile convictions were on file at Scotland Yard depended upon the seriousness of the offence and the area where it was committed.

[2] Ten boys were counted 'inapplicables', because they had had no acting father since the age of 3. In point of fact, the absentee fathers of four of these boys had been convicted. In the case of the anomalously constituted families, where both a biological father and an acting father existed, it was the latter, the man who had actually been involved in the child-rearing process, upon whom the count was based.

[3] The principal components analysis (see p. 117 ff.) served to confirm this conclusion. Item 3, father's convictions, had a substantial loading of ·35 on the first component, general social handicap, but practically no loading on the second component, which represented family instability as perceived by the P.S.Ws. Paternal criminality was apparently much more closely related to social level than to individual family dynamics.

[4] In ten cases a perfect match was obtained, each member of a pair being in the same scoring category on Matrices I.Q., Reading Quotient and Verbal comprehension, while in the thirteen remaining pairs there was only one point of difference on one of the three tests.

[5] There were no boys rated as having conduct disorder by the P.S.Ws who were not also rated poorly behaved by teachers.

[6] This excludes most babies who are under weight but with a normal period of gestation.

[7] That is: bleeding after onset of labour and before second stage; forceps delivery, internal versions and Caesarian operations; abnormal presentations other than uncomplicated breech; asphyxia described as severe in records or

where normal breathing delayed by fifteen minutes or more; all cases described as 'foetal distress' or cerebral symptoms during perinatal period, and cases of prolonged labour (thirty hours plus) or inertia.

[8] Slight to moderate blue asphyxia described as such in records, where baby responded well to resuscitation, with good colour and breathing in not more than fifteen minutes. Slight foetal distress not occurring till well on in second stage.

[9] Into the 'severe' category went all cases of severe toxaemia and pre-eclampsia, or instances of albuminuria, or bleeding after the twenty-eighth week of pregnancy. Into the 'moderate' category went early bleeding, mild toxaemia without albuminuria, as well as co-existing organic diseases likely to have affected pregnancy (e.g. anaemia, pneumonia, renal and cardiac disease).

[10] The obstetric data used in the correlational analysis was subsequently checked and corrected for certain clerical errors and inconsistencies of rating, and the corrected versions have been used in the tabulations in this chapter. Had these been made before it is most unlikely that the general picture which emerged from the correlational analysis would have been any different.

VI

An Over-view of the Factors in Interaction

This chapter reports a first attempt to get beyond the contemplation of individual factors in isolation and to search for some meaningful pattern in the natural clustering and mutual influence of one variable upon another. As a first step, thirty-seven of the most important ratings, the ones on which the bulk of this report has been based, were selected for examination, and the inter-correlations between them all were calculated by computer and displayed in a 37 × 37 matrix, which has been reproduced as Appendix VI (A).[1]

Simple inspection of this matrix suffices to bring to light some interesting features. First, practically all the correlations were positive, and the few with negative values tended to be small and insignificant.[2] This preponderance of positive associations was achieved by arranging all the rating scales to run in the same direction, so that the top end of each scale, that is the highest scores, always represented the most adverse or unfavourable assessment. Thus in item 6, which was family income, the poorest income group had the highest score on that scale; whereas in item 27, which was intelligence, as measured by the progressive matrices test, the dullest grade of boy had the highest score. The matrix demonstrates clearly the tendency for unfavourable features, both of background and personality, to be positively correlated, that is to occur together in the same unfortunate individuals.

In one or two instances, notably item 8, 'mother has no job', or item 23, 'boy adventurous', it was not so obvious in advance which would be the unfavourable end of the scale. These were decided after the event, when it was found in practice that being a dare-devil, or having a mother who did no outside work, were generally associated with adverse ratings in other respects.

For convenience of display the variables in the matrix were grouped into three blocks. The first, items 1 to 9, concerned directly observable or factual points about the social background of the family, such as their income, housing, number of children, and the nature of father's occupation. The second block of items, 10 to 26, consisted of assessments by the P.S.Ws, which were for the most part of an inferential or judgemental nature. The third block, items 27 to 37, consisted of the results of tests or measures applied to the boys at their primary schools.

Within each block the inter-correlations were often quite high, which was only to be expected considering what they represented. Thus most of the items in the first block reflected adverse socio-economic factors, while those in the second block were concerned with adverse features in the individual home background, and those in the last block represented unfavourable ratings in classroom tests and reports. However, where the correlations were very substantial, say more than ·5, this was usually because the items in question were different measurements of the same phenomenon, such as having a low income and being supported by social agencies, or because the items were logically inter-connected, as for instance a boy's height and his weight. Within the first block the highest value was ·53, which was the correlation between family supported by social agencies and family of low income. Within the second block of items, the highest value, ·65, represented the correlation between early separation of boy from mother, and early separation of boy from father. This was a consequence of the fact that boys sent away from home for any reason were automatically separated from both mother and father. The next highest value within this block, ·48, was the correlation between item 11, disharmonious marriage, and item 13, inconsistency between parents in their handling of their boy. Within the third block, the highest correlations were ·72, between low weight and short stature, and ·67, between low performance on the reading test and low score on the verbal comprehension test.

In order to investigate the matter further the matrix of correlations was subjected to a principal component analysis. This is a mathematical technique for identifying the chief groupings of items responsible for the trends that can be seen in the matrix. In everyday language a principal component represents an important cluster of items, relatively closely inter-correlated among themselves, and accounting for some substantial part of the total pattern of correlations. In effect we have already noted, by inspection alone, what may very well be one such cluster in the group of items, prominent in the first block of the matrix, and all of them reflecting in varying degrees the fundamental factor of socio-economic adversity.

More precisely, the principal component is a hypothetical variable, or vector, deduced mathematically, which links the individual correlations of the matrix. The principal component represents a unique mathematical solution to any particular matrix, being that single vector which accounts for the maximum amount of the variance. Further components are calculated in descending order of importance. Each subsequent component is so calculated as to be by definition statistically independent of previous ones; that is the correlations between components are zero, and they are technically referred to as having 'orthogonal' axes. Each of the items has a separate correlation or 'loading' on each of the components extracted from the matrix. The nature of items with largest loadings gives an indication of the probable meaning or interpretation of the component (Hotelling, 1933; Lawley and Maxwell, 1963).

A diagram may help to make the situation clearer.[3] In Fig. VI (1), three of the items or measures, namely 'low family income', 'large family size' and 'mother's nerves bad' are represented by horizontal lines. The length of each line indicates the variance, or range of values which the item is seen to have among the different individuals in the Study population. The total variance of the population, if the three items were independent, would be shown by joining the lines end to end. In practice, the items are inter-correlated. Thus most of the large families fall into the low income group. These correlations are indicated by the amount the lines overlap, to a great extent in the case of income and family size, to a very small extent in the case of family size and mother's nervous state.

FIG. VI (1)

Schematic Illustration of Three Variables in Relation to each other and to the First Principal Component[1]

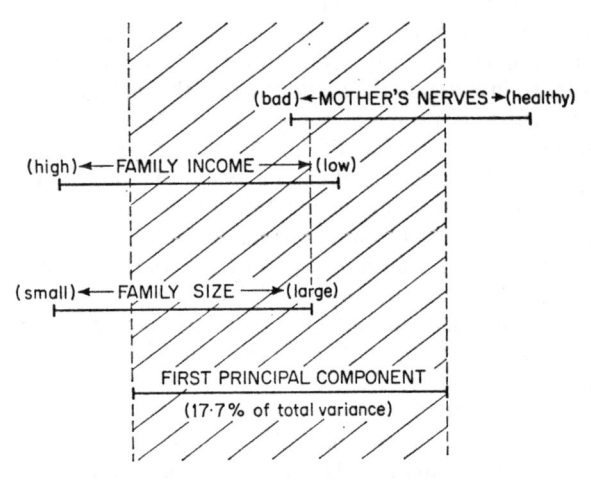

[1] *N.B.* This is purely illustrative and not a scaled representation of actual variances.

AN OVER-VIEW OF THE FACTORS IN INTERACTION 119

The shaded area between dotted lines represents an underlying general factor, the first principal component. Each item has a different amount of overlap or loading on this first component. The two social variables, income and family size, have much larger loadings on the first component than does the item 'mother's nerves'.

Fig. VI (2) illustrates the findings on a graph. The horizontal axis represents the first principal component (accounting for 17·7 per cent of the total variance). The items, represented by numbered circles, are ranged from left to right across the page according to the size of their loading on the first component.[4] Thus items 1, 6 and 10, that is 'supported family', 'low income' and 'boy physically neglected', which have the highest loadings on the first component (·70, ·64 and ·62 respectively), appear at the far right of the page, and are enclosed in one of the shaded circles for ease of reference. Items 5 'house interior badly kept', 4 'housing poor', 7 'large family' and 2 'low social class' (i.e. by father's occupation), also have high loadings on the first component (·55, ·43, ·51 and ·30 respectively). All of these, as well as the items 'low income' and 'physical neglect' already mentioned, were components of the combined rating entitled 'social handicap'. That particular combination was arrived at before the results of this analysis were available, but it would seem, nevertheless, that the general factor of socio-economic adversity identified by the principal component analysis is much the same as what has been referred to as 'social handicap' and roughly assessed by the three point scale used in previous tabulations. This result amply vindicates the view already expressed that in most comparisons between individuals in this Study, the social level of the family was a powerful discriminating factor. Only after allowing for this can other less dramatic relationships be investigated adequately.

The vertical axis in Fig. VI (2) represents the second principal component, which accounted for 7·3 per cent of the variance.[5] Items have either positive or negative loadings on this component, since they may be either positively or negatively correlated. Items positively related to the second component appear towards the top of the page, those negatively related appear towards the bottom, while those with no substantial relationship either way appear about the horizontal axis, which is the zero level. The axes representing the two components have been drawn proportional in length to the respective amounts of variance included, namely 17·7 per cent and 7·3 per cent. This was done to illustrate the relative importance of each component. A variable such as item 25 'boy nervous', which has loadings of approximately ·1 and ·2 on the two components, is positioned comparatively close to the zero point because the larger loading was on the less important component.

FIG. VI (2)

Loadings of the items of the Correlational Analysis on two Principal Components

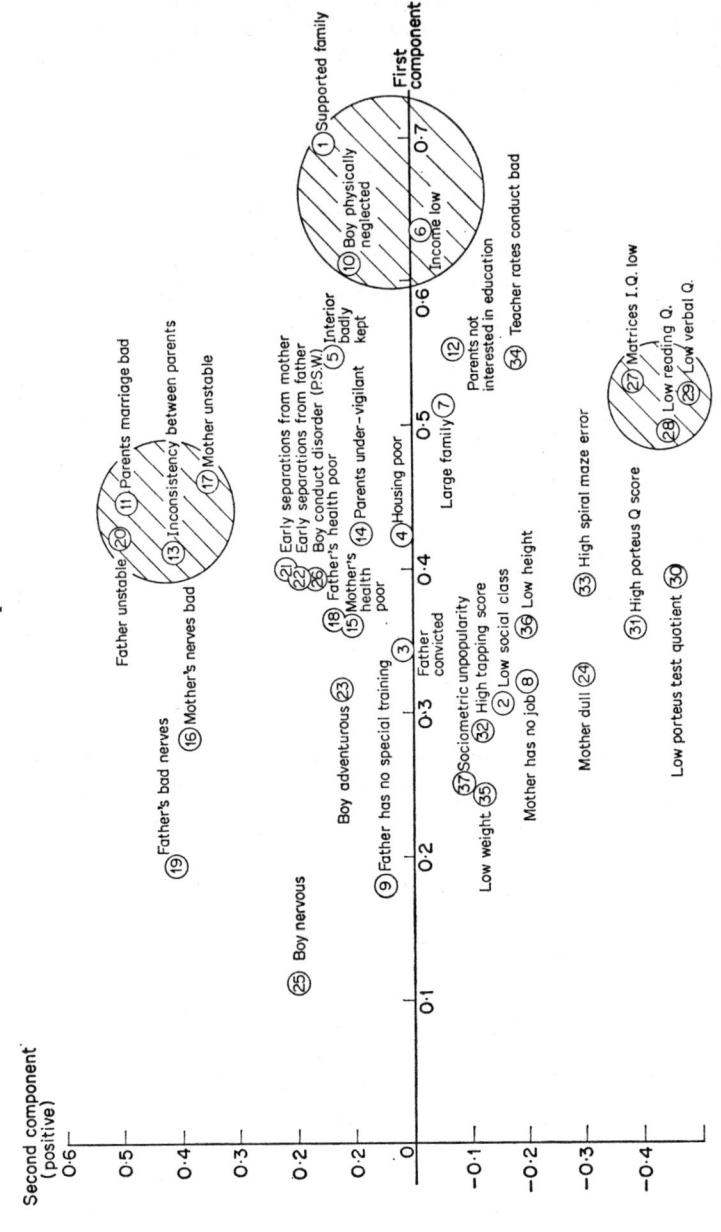

By definition, the second component is independent of, that is uncorrelated with, the first. It is consistent with this to find items 1 to 9, all of which are mainly related to social adversity, situated on the graph fairly close to the level of the horizontal axis, which means that they have small or insignificant loadings on the second component. The items with the largest positive loadings on the second component are 11 'disharmonious marriage' (·49), 20 'father unstable' (·51), 19 'father's nerves bad' (·41) and 13 'inconsistency between parents' (·41). Thus, whereas the first component may be thought to represent a general factor of social impoverishment, the second appears to correspond to a general factor of disturbance in family dynamics.

But the picture is not quite so simple as that. In Fig. VI (2), items with high positive loadings on both components appear at the top right. Four of these, items 11, 13, 20 and 17, are inside the top shaded circle. They represent bad marriage, parental inconsistency, unstable mothers and unstable fathers, which are all adverse parental features that are closely related both to general social handicap and to the P.S.Ws' perceptions of generally unfavourable family dynamics. Items 27, 28 and 29, which are within another of the shaded circles, appear grouped together at the bottom right of the graph, which means they are also strongly related to both components, positively to social adversity, but negatively to family dynamics. These items are all measures indicative of low intelligence and poor attainment of boys, and while it is reasonable that they should be correlated with social adversity it is most implausible that they should go with favourable family dynamics—which is what a negative loading on unfavourable dynamics would seem to imply. In other words, it would seem that *once the effect of social level has been accounted for*, the most disturbed families produce the more intelligent boys. Moreover, since item 34, teacher's rating of conduct poor, also has a negative loading on the second component, it would appear that the disturbed families produce the better behaved boys. A further apparent absurdity appears in item 24, 'mother dull', which also has a negative loading on the second component, implying that the duller the mother the less the chance of family disturbance.

The most reasonable interpretation of these curious results would seem to be that the second component represents family disturbance, not in an absolute sense, but family disturbance as communicated to the P.S.Ws. The dull mothers, who could be poor communicators, would reveal little, and hence would seem relatively favourable, while the more intelligent and forthcoming families would tend to perceive and enlarge upon their problems during interviews. If this is right, the second component represents a factor of 'complaining families' rather than of particularly disturbed families. The position of other items on the graph lends support to this interpretation. Items such as 7 'large family', 4 'poor housing', 35 'low weight of boy', 3 'father convicted', all of which are objective points established independently of parental communicativeness, have negligible loadings on the second component. Items concerned with poor showing at school, on psychomotor tests, on conduct reports, on intelligence tests, and on peer ratings all tend to appear below the horizontal axis, which means they are associated with under-complaining families. Items representing judgemental evaluations by P.S.Ws, particularly in regard to unfavourable parental behaviour and temperament, appear well above the horizontal axis, since these all reflect a tendency to communicate complaints. The striking exception, of course, was the P.S.Ws' assessment of an apparently 'dull mother'. Since this was associated with absence of expressed complaints it appeared well below the horizontal axis, on the same scale as the unfavourable measures which did not depend upon communication between parent and P.S.W.

The situation revealed by the principal component analysis may be summarized as follows. Social level or 'social handicap' was the one outstanding factor which effectively distinguished between groups of boys, on family dynamics no less than on conduct and performance in school. There was no doubt that individual and social handicaps marched together remarkably closely. Even allowing for possible bias due to over-critical assessments of the slum families, the general trend was too clear and consistent to be denied. It does not follow, of course, that because they are found together that personal maladjustment is caused by poverty; on the contrary, it could be argued that, under present day conditions, to be conspicuously poorer than one's neighbour is a consequence of personal inadequacy.

When further comparisons were made after allowing for the major factor of social level, it then appeared that certain of the more subjective interview ratings had yielded misleading impressions. Owing to their uncommunicativeness or resistance to inquiry, some of the duller and more disturbed families were put down as 'normal', in the absence of definite evidence to the contrary, while some of the more forthcoming families were rated too adversely because they had tended to enlarge upon their problems. The result was not altogether surprising. It had been foreshadowed in the previous analysis of the P.S.Ws' ratings of nervous tendency in boys, which were paradoxically associated with small families, inexperienced mothers and intelligent mothers, since these were the families most likely to notice and report symptoms. (See Appendix III (C).) But the importance of this element of bias within the total picture should not be exaggerated. The principal component identified with 'complaining' families accounted for a much smaller proportion of the variance than the social handicap component. Moreover, there was evidence that the effect of this bias was less in regard to the more extreme degrees of family disturbance. A positively identified item of serious disturbance was unlikely to be entirely unfounded, even though communication problems may have led to similar degrees of disturbance being over-looked or under-estimated in some other cases.

NOTES

[1] *N.B.* Only the scaled measures could be included. Groupings with no progressive rank order, such as the grouping of boys according to which school they belonged to, could not be used for correlational analysis.

[2] Owing to lack of information about some individuals in regard to certain items, the numbers of cases involved in these correlations differed slightly between one pair of variables and the next. For the most part correlations smaller than ± 0.1 can be regarded as of little or no statistical significance.

[3] For a more detailed explanation of the theory of this type of analysis see Moser and Scott (1961).

[4] The actual values of the loadings of all thirty-seven items on each of the first two principal components are listed in Appendix VI (A), Table VI A (2).

[5] Four further components were extracted from the matrix accounting for 5·0 per cent, 4·5 per cent, 4·4 per cent and 4·1 per cent of the total variance. This implies that the most important and meaningful part of the variance has already been accounted for by the first two components, so it would be pointless to enter into lengthy descriptions of these minor components. Suffice to say that on the third component only two items had large loadings, namely weight (·722) and height (·622). This third component, therefore, was mainly a matter of variation in physical size that remained after the first component of general social handicap had been accounted for.

VII
Pitfalls of Interpretation

1 *Differences between Raters*

If different interviewers, examining similar populations, report a substantially different incidence of any particular item, this means that they are not using the same rating standards, and therefore the measures cannot be reliable. In order to apply this test of reliability to the P.S.Ws' ratings in the present Study, the data were first classified into four groups. Class A consisted of all measures which were completely independent of interviewer judgement, such as psychological test scores, teachers' ratings and criminal records. Class B consisted of items of information, such as 'mother has had psychiatric treatment in hospital', which, though objective in themselves, might be recorded with varying exactness according to the P.S.Ws' success in eliciting the required particulars. Class C consisted of topics such as health, on which personal judgement had to be exercised in making a rating, but which might be guided a good deal by outside sources of information. Finally, Class D consisted of the measures which depended almost entirely upon the P.S.Ws' own judgement, including such assessments as parents' attitudes and personality and methods of discipline.

The boys had not been distributed at random between the three P.S.Ws, since P.S.W. B, who had no car, was given more of the nearby families, while P.S.W. C, who joined the Study later than the others, had more of the younger boys. However, apart from the variables of age and name of school, there were no significant differences in the score distributions of the Class A variables between the groups of boys allocated to each P.S.W. This strongly suggested that the P.S.Ws were in fact dealing with similar populations.

Of the twenty-two Class B variables, significant differences in rating between the three P.S.W. groups were found on only three measures. The most important was family income, on which P.S.W. A had a significantly smaller incidence of 'inadequate' income. In point of fact there was some independent evidence that by chance P.S.W. A had got a rather more affluent group, although it may also be true that her judgements of 'inadequate' income were more conservative.

Among the Class C variables, seven out of the total twenty-one were significantly different between one P.S.W. and another. One of the most noticeable differences was on the variable 'disturbance among siblings'. This was one of those difficult, over-inclusive ratings intended to include all cases in which one or more of the boy's siblings had some definite psychological or physical disturbance. P.S.W. B had a much greater proportion of 'disturbed siblings' than her two colleagues. Scrutiny of some of the other variables on which inter-rater differences occurred suggested that P.S.W. B had a tendency to record a variety of items of personal or social handicap rather more frequently than A or C.

On the variables in Class D there was a considerably greater degree of discordance between raters than in any of the other groups. Fourteen out of the thirty-six variables yielded significant rating differences, in a few cases so extreme that the assessments were unusable. A case in point was the rating of 'boy has few friends', which was found over twice as frequently by P.S.W. B as by P.S.W. A, and another the rating 'father has few social contacts', which was found twice as often by P.S.W. A as by P.S.W. B.

These observations show that, in spite of much preliminary discussion between raters, and a conscious effort to preserve similar standards, one cannot depend upon the reliability of interview judgements without a careful check. Even where the rating distribution is similar, one cannot be quite certain that the meaning attached to each point on the scale is the same for different raters. The ratings open to the most doubt are, naturally, those depending entirely upon interview judgements with no external check or guide.

This kind of unreliability was one of the chief difficulties in the way of making firm interpretations of the results of the social background inquiry. The difficulty was resolved to some extent by a drastic and very sad pruning of the interview ratings, whereby many interesting but suspect assessments were disregarded. The bulk of the analysis reported in this book (including the correlational matrix and principal component analysis), was restricted to a minority of the more important items which appeared to have some general validity regardless of which of the interviewers made the assessment. It has already been explained how, with certain particularly important items (such as the assessments of behaviour disturbance and nervous disturbance in boys) additional inquiries or adjustments were made before the ratings were made use of in the report.

2. *The Dangers of Contaminated Measures*

There is some truth in the criticism that social researchers like to wallow in a morass of meaningless correlations. In order to combat this tendency attention has been given throughout this report to a range of possible interpretations of the findings. One constantly recurring theme has been whether the immediately observable correlates of disturbed behaviour are important factors in themselves, or whether they are secondary to more fundamental factors, such as socio-economic circumstances. For instance, it was suggested that the apparent association between criminal fathers and the misbehaviour of their sons at school was due to the concentrated incidence of both these items among boys from the poorest social class. (See p. 102.)

An even more fundamental problem is how far the correlations observed represent true associations between independent measures, or whether they might not arise, at least in part, from contamination of one measure by another. For example, if the P.S.Ws viewed certain families with distrust, on account of a father being known or suspected to have a criminal record, they might tend to rate these families too harshly on the more subjective assessments of home background, and hence to produce spuriously exaggerated associations between bad background and paternal criminality. Some evidence that this kind of contamination actually took place was mentioned previously. (See p. 98, Note 8.)

Contamination effects occur mainly in connection with so-called 'soft' variables, that is assessments dependent upon human judgement, and therefore inevitably subject to all kinds of extraneous biassing influences. This was well illustrated by the outcome of an interesting analysis of the characteristics of boys whose fathers had a criminal conviction. Table VII (1) displays the nine items of a fairly factual nature which correlated most closely with paternal criminality, including, for example, low family income, large size of family, and a poor score by the boy on the verbal comprehension test. When the boys whose fathers had more than one conviction as an adult were compared with the rest of the sample (as in the right-hand column of the Table) the contrast was generally greater than when comparison was made between the larger group whose fathers had any sort of conviction and the remainder. This was reasonable, since having a father who had had just one isolated conviction, perhaps long ago when he was quite young, could not be of great social importance. To include such cases among those whose records were more persistent would tend to obscure the contrasts between the criminal and non-criminal segments of the sample.

A different picture is shown in Table VII (2), which displays some of the more subjective assessments involving complex judgements from interview material, such as parental 'under-vigiliance', 'laxness in rules', and 'paternal discipline erratic'. Here the greater contrasts

TABLE VII (1)

Associations between having a Convicted Father and certain Objective Variables

		A Father not convicted	B Father convicted[1] but not more than once as an adult	C Father convicted twice or more as an adult	Difference A/(B+C) χ^2	Difference (A+B)/C χ^2
Family supported by Social Agencies	Yes No	50 260	13 37	14 15	11·81*	14·13*
Father in lowest grade of socio-economic class	Yes No	44 266	7 43	10 19	2·03	6·91†
Family income inadequate	Yes No	57 246	14 34	13 15	8·90†	8·86‡
Family of over 5 children	Yes No	44 266	8 42	13 16	6·08‡	15·69*
Mother says she has no paid employment	Yes No	127 167	19 28	18 10	0·68	4·00‡
Parents rated as uninterested in their son's education	Yes No	43 251	7 39	11 17	3·35	9·60†
Father has a poor work record	Yes No	21 276	10 37	16 12	26·90*	25·79*
Boy of dull intelligence (Progressive Matrice test)	Yes No	60 250	11 39	12 17	3·02	6·27‡
Boy of dull verbal comprehension (N.F.E.R. test)	Yes No	101 197	24 25	19 10	10·92*	8·64†

* p<·001   † p<·01   ‡ p<·05

[1] *N.B.* This Table is based upon data available for punching and analysis in November 1964, and excludes 12 cases in which the father's identifying particulars were at that time incomplete.

TABLE VII (2)

Associations between having a Convicted Father and other Variables

Ratings by P.S.Ws:		A Father not convicted	B Father convicted[1] but not more than once as an adult	C Father convicted twice or more as an adult	Difference A/(B+C) χ^2	Difference (A+B)/C χ^2
Marriage rated as 'bad'	Yes No	62 234	17 29	8 19	5·04‡	0·29
Parents rated as 'under-vigilant' in care of their son	Yes No	29 267	10 36	4 23	4·14‡	0·05
Parents rated as 'lax in rules'	Yes No	46 245	14 32	6 19	5·05‡	0·26
Maternal discipline rated as 'erratic' against 'normal'	Yes No	79 140	22 19	11 11	4·77‡	0·64
Paternal discipline rated as 'erratic' against 'normal'	Yes No	32 151	18 15	6 9	20·16*	1·35
Boy rated as 'taking many risks'	Yes No	51 240	18 28	5 22	6·21‡	—

* p < ·001 ‡ p < ·05

This table is to be contrasted with Table IX (5). Here there is a positive association between the variables listed and some degree of criminality of father, but when the degree of *seriousness* of the father's criminal record is taken into account (as in the previous table) the association is rendered insignificant.

[1] *N.B.* This Table is based upon data available for punching and analysis in November 1964, and excludes 12 cases in which the father's identifying particulars were at that time incomplete.

were between the no conviction-any conviction groups. On the face of it, this suggests that unsatisfactory parental behaviour was more closely associated with mild paternal criminality than with serious paternal criminality. This implausible conclusion was almost certainly an anomaly due to rating bias. The known or suspected criminality of a deviant family doubtless cast a gloomy shadow upon the perceptions of the interviewers.[1] On the other hand, the actual seriousness of the criminal record would be for the most part unknown to the interviewers, being coded at a late stage on the basis of criminal record searches, and so could not have had the same influence upon their judgements.

3. *Negative Halo*

This is a particular variety of bias by contamination in which the presence of one notoriously adverse factor sensitizes the interviewer to the likelihood of other adverse factors being present as well, and results in exaggeratedly unfavourable ratings on a whole range of items. As has just been explained, the suspected presence of paternal criminality was one feature which appeared to cast a gloomy shadow or 'negative halo' upon a minority of boys.

Inspection of the inter-correlations displayed in Appendix VI (A) (and described in Chapter VI, p. 116 ff.) suggests the presence of a more important, because more generalized, negative halo whereby the defects of the poorer families at the lowest social level may have been in some respects exaggerated, at least in the more subjective of the ratings of family background. For instance, it will be seen that some of the ratings of parental characteristics, such as mother unstable, or parents' marriage disharmonious, correlated more highly with family income than did such objective items as low social class, poor housing or large family, which are logically a part of the poor family syndrome. This strongly suggests that, when a family appeared to be poor, the P.S.Ws had allowed this fact to influence their judgement on certain other matters. On marital relationships, for instance, the poorer mothers, with their unconcealed dissatisfactions, were probably rather too easily judged to have bad marriages.

The apparent associations between boys' misconduct and certain features of home background, may have been affected by this negative halo effect, whereby certain families become disfavoured on a whole series of ratings. For example, where P.S.Ws have judged a family to belong to the poor income class, or where they have received unfavourable impressions from social agencies, delinquency records, or school reports, these matters may have influenced their

FIG. VII (1)

Schematic Representation of some possible Interactions of various Sources of Information in Relation to assessments of Boys and Parents

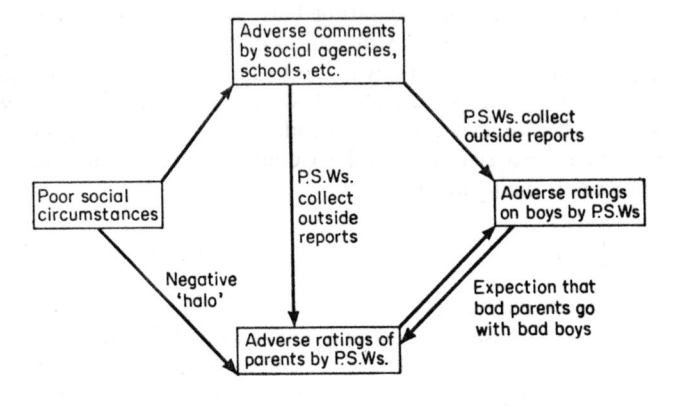

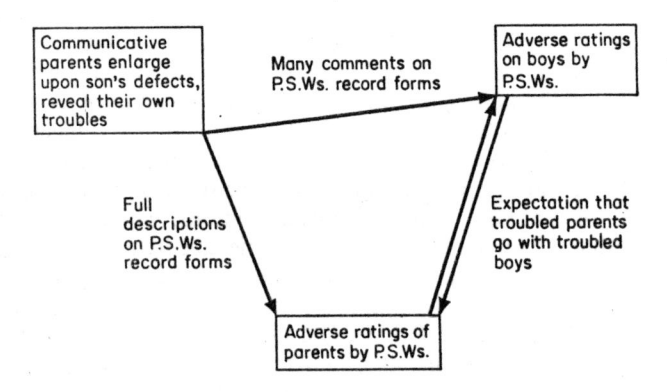

[Diagram — top section: "Poor social circumstances" → "Adverse comments by social agencies, schools, etc." → (P.S.Ws. collect outside reports) → "Adverse ratings on boys by P.S.Ws"; "Poor social circumstances" → (Negative 'halo') → "Adverse ratings of parents by P.S.Ws."; "Adverse comments by social agencies, schools, etc." → (P.S.Ws. collect outside reports) → "Adverse ratings of parents by P.S.Ws."; "Adverse ratings of parents by P.S.Ws." ↔ "Adverse ratings on boys by P.S.Ws" (Expection that bad parents go with bad boys).

Bottom section: "Communicative parents enlarge upon son's defects, reveal their own troubles" → (Many comments on P.S.Ws. record forms) → "Adverse ratings on boys by P.S.Ws."; → (Full descriptions on P.S.Ws. record forms) → "Adverse ratings of parents by P.S.Ws."; "Adverse ratings of parents by P.S.Ws." ↔ "Adverse ratings on boys by P.S.Ws." (Expectation that troubled parents go with troubled boys).]

impressions in an unfavourable direction on other things, including both parental mismanagement and boy's misconduct.

Some of the possible interactions which could contribute to a negative halo effect are illustrated in Fig. VII (1). The top section of the diagram refers to what one might call the slum halo, that is the expectation of finding family problems and bad behaviour wherever there is poverty. The bottom section refers to a different kind of halo, one already discussed in connection with ratings of nervousness in boys (see Appendix III (C)), and further amplified in the discussion of the results of the principal component analysis. (See p. 119 ff.) This was the tendency for the more intelligent and forthcoming to mention more difficulties, and hence to be rated more disturbed than they really are.

4. *Absence or Unreliability of Information in Particular Segments of the Sample*

In any survey of a non-captive population there are always difficulties in obtaining the required information on every individual. The boys in class did in fact constitute a more or less captive population, so that the data obtained from teachers' reports, and from some of the tests given at the schools, were virtually complete, but even here the position was not altogether satisfactory. In the case of persistent truants, it was sometimes necessary for the psychologist to return again and again before a particular boy could be tested. Moreover, at the commencement of the Study, the local education authority were still adhering to a rule that individual tests could not be given at the schools without prior parental consent in writing. The necessity to wait upon P.S.Ws visiting parents, and feeling the occasion ripe for presenting local authority consent forms, meant that the psychologist had to go to and from the schools many times, picking out certain boys for testing. Apart from the inconvenience to the schools, this could have affected the quality of the data. A group of children will accept nonchalantly a battery of tests given to all in class, but to pick out individuals a year after their class-mates have been tested creates a different situation, and some of these late-tested boys reacted badly to being singled out in this way. One might have demonstrated the extent of this effect by comparing the correlation between results of individual and group tests of intelligence among the early-tested and the late-tested boys respectively. If the latter gave less reliable results, the correlation should have been smaller. This was not possible, because the situation was further complicated by the late-tested boys including more school absentees and difficult characters, whose scores might have been expected to be less reliable at whatever time they were tested. Since many of the late-tested boys were not given individual tests between their eighth and ninth birthday, which was the age when the majority were tested, allowance for age had to be made in the scoring, and these were based on rather slender evidence about the regression of scores on age.

In the psychological test data, therefore, complete absence of information was less of a problem than a relative unreliability of the scores obtained from certain segments of the sample, in particular from the boys belonging to the more elusive and unco-operative families. The impossibility of obtaining valid results on a personality inventory from the least literate and least well motivated boys has already been sufficiently discussed (see pp. 44 and 166). A boy's performance, even on the non-verbal tests of intelligence, or on the psychomotor tasks, may sometimes be depressed by inattention and apathy rather than by genuine lack of ability. Fortunately, since this Study has the advantage of continuing observations over a period of years, and the boys were re-tested at age 11, anomalous results due to the special problems of testing the more difficult boys at an early age may be expected to be rectified later.

The quality and quantity of the information upon which the home background assessments were made varied with the particular parent's ability and willingness to relate intimate family matters to the visiting P.S.Ws. In the small minority of totally unco-operative families there was virtually no information whatsoever on a large proportion of home background variables. This would not have mattered so much if the missing cases had been no different from the rest of the sample, but there were indications that the incidence of adversity and maladjustment was higher among the boys whose parents would not or could not give the required information. For example, of the sixty-six boys whose parents were classed as either totally or partially unco-operative in giving interviews, 28·8 per cent were poorly behaved and only 6·1 per cent well behaved, according to teachers' ratings. Over the remainder of the sample, 23·5 per cent were rated poorly behaved and 23·8 per cent well behaved, which was a statistically significant difference. ($\chi^2 = 8·43$ with 2 d.f. $p < ·02$.) Owing to this selective omission, the incidence of such adverse background factors as unfavourable parental attitudes or methods of discipline, which are known to be associated with poor conduct in boys, have probably been slightly under-estimated. However, except in regard to the questionnaire sent to parents, where the response rate was very poor (see pp. 87, 93), complete absence of information was too rare to have had any great influence upon the picture of the sample as a whole.

More serious was the tendency for the assessments to vary in detail and accuracy between one segment of the sample and another, and especially between one social class and another. An example of this kind was the rating of mother's health, which was made in two parts, present health and health in the past. Present health was a matter of fairly direct report about facts of immediate concern, and was based upon observations during the whole period of contact up to the latest visit before the data counting in November 1964. In some cases it was supplemented by hospital records. Although mother's health in the past was defined as precisely as possible (by listing the various diseases and conditions likely to qualify for a positive rating) this inevitably depended more upon the mothers' recollections and admissions of past events. Now it is known that the lowest socio-economic class (Class V on the Registrar General's Scale) have more illnesses than those of the better classes (e.g. II or III non-manual). In fact, in Class V, mother's present health was rated poor in 37·1 per cent of cases compared with 18·2 per cent of cases in Classes II or III non-manual, a difference in accord with common-sense expectation. In contrast, the incidence of mother's past health being rated 'poor' was much the same in these different socio-economic groups, namely 32·2 per cent and 36·4 per cent, the better classes having slightly more ill-health. This was clearly an artefact of the under-reporting of the poorer families, so this rating of mother's past health was abandoned.

The influence of social level upon the quality of information obtainable was especially obvious in family background items where the availability of an independent opinion from father would be likely to lead to a more accurate assessment. The chances of a father being interviewed privately, or even being seen at all, were considerably smaller among the poorer families.[2] This goes some way to explain some oddities in the assessments which depended largely upon information from fathers themselves. For instance, where there was a rating on 'father's background adverse' (defined as lost one or both parents by death or desertion before age 16 and/or spent a substantial time in children's home or orphanage), 33·1 per cent of the higher Classes II and III non-manual were reported to have had adverse backgrounds compared with only 24 per cent of the Class V cases. This is obviously fallacious, and the origin of the fallacy is indicated even more clearly by the fact that 20 per cent of the Class V cases were not assessed at all on the variable 'father's background adverse', whereas all but 5·3 per cent of the top two classes were given a rating.

Another example was the variable 'inconsistency between parents', which was one of the items significantly correlated with poor conduct in boys. The likelihood of an adverse rating by the P.S.Ws was considerably decreased in those cases in which a father was never interviewed separately from mother, or never seen at all. In the inadequate income group, therefore, parental inconsistency, where present, had a lessened chance of being observed and positively rated by the P.S.Ws. In point of fact, the correlation between ratings of parental inconsistency and poor conduct was smaller in the sub-group of inadequate income than in the remainder of the sample; but quite likely the correlation would have been much the same had it been possible to assess the inadequate income group as thoroughly as the remainder of the sample.

Still another example of the influence of social level upon the judgements of family circumstances was the variable 'unsatisfactory housing'. In the low and average income group, this feature was, as expected, significantly correlated with bad conduct ratings of the boys. In the comfortable income group, however, the trend was exactly opposite, seventeen out of eighty-two boys in the best conduct categories (I or II on the combined ratings of teachers and P.S.Ws) were in unsatisfactory housing, compared with 0 out of 11 among the worst behaved boys (rated IV or V). Scrutiny of the written descriptions of housing on the actual case records suggested that these good boys from bad houses were not really worse housed than many others, but their mothers had complained a great deal about housing. It was the mothers who did not care or did not complain about bad housing who were likely to have the worst behaved sons.

This chapter had better conclude on one final note of caution. In deliberately picking out, for purposes of illustration, the most extreme examples of unreliability and bias, there is a danger of conveying the false impression that the family background ratings as a whole are totally unrealistic and misleading. While one may suppose that some instances of mild disturbance have been exaggerated and others have been missed, largely due to the varying levels of contact between mothers and P.S.Ws, there is reason to believe that for the most part the worst cases have been correctly identified. Moreover, as the accounts given in Chapter IV show, the ratings have been sufficiently realistic to reveal some definite associations between misconduct in boys and various anomalies of attitude and behaviour in parents. Since many of these associations were such as might have been predicted on theoretical grounds, and many were consistent throughout all three social class groupings, they are most unlikely to be all spurious.

NOTES

[1] It is interesting to see from Table VII (2) that 'Father's discipline erratic' produced the most extreme contrast. It has already been mentioned (see p. 98 footnote) that this was a particularly suspect assessment on other grounds.

[2] In the inadequate income group, the P.S.Ws interviewed separately the fathers of 20 per cent of the boys, interviewed the fathers jointly with mothers in 38 per cent, and failed to see father in 42 per cent. In the comfortable income group the corresponding percentages were 53 per cent, 34 per cent and 13 per cent. In the inadequate income group, where father was interviewed separately, 50 per cent rated as having 'inconsistent parents'. Where father was not seen at all, only 23·7 per cent were rated as having 'inconsistent parents', but 36·8 per cent were rated 'not known'. In the other income groups, the differences were smaller.

VIII

A Tentative Summing Up and Some Suggestions for Further Study

1. *The Incidence of Personal and Social Problems*

The present Report covers only the first phase of a long Study, namely the initial survey of the boys in their primary schools, and the investigation of their family circumstances when they were around 9 years of age. The relevance of the data collected at that time to the boys' subsequent behaviour remains to be seen, but the completion of this first stage of the inquiry calls for some kind of stocktaking. This can be done under two broad headings. First, one can say something about the methods of measuring personal and family disturbance of the kind commonly believed to foster delinquency, and one can come to some tentative conclusions about the incidence of such disturbances among urban schoolboys. In particular, one can see how far various items of disturbance are interrelated so as to produce an interlocking complex of adversities that weigh heavily upon the most vulnerable minority. Second, in the light of the relationships found to exist between personal background and current misbehaviour, it should be possible to clarify one's expectations about what factors are likely to prove most relevant to the genesis of delinquency in later years, and thus to formulate some hypotheses to be tested against the results of later stages of the Study.

Without attempting to repeat all the percentages and tabulations given in the body of the report, it may help to recapitulate some of the more striking findings concerning the incidence of certain basic adversities, bearing in mind at the same time that there is no reason to suppose the sample to be unusual for a working-class, urban neighbourhood. For instance, when the Study began, a half of the boys were living in homes without bathrooms. Compared with the national average, there were some three times as many with fathers in the lowest category of socio-economic status on the Registrar General's scale, and about twice as many belonging to large families with seven or more children. Their average height was significantly less than that of a normal population of boys of the same age. In intelligence potential, as measured by Raven's Matrices, they did not differ from the national average, but in reading attainment more than two-fifths were as retarded as the worst 10 per cent of the normal population. However, as subsequent data showed, the poor readers tended to catch up in later years.

The more subjective assessments of family dynamics could not be compared numerically with the population at large owing to the absence of standard scales of comparison. Nevertheless, on qualitative impressions, there was certainly a raised incidence of a great many unfavourable features, such as parents in serious marital disharmony, parents of unstable and deviant personality, and parents careless or perverse in their methods of child-rearing. This was scarcely surprising in view of the high concentration of these adverse characteristics at the lowest social level, coupled with the fact that families of low social level were much more frequent in this sample than in the population at large.

The social level of a family proved to be the most important single factor in discriminating the poorly behaved boys and the ineffectual parents from their peers and neighbours. The boys from backgrounds categorized by the investigators as socially handicapped to a severe degree (on the criteria of poor income, poor housing, large families, and a tendency to depend upon support from social agencies) constituted a very important segment of the Study population. Although they made up only one-eighth of the population numerically, they included a half of the boys with an 'unstable' mother, nearly a half of those whose parents were described as 'lax in rules', and over a quarter of those whose parents were in a state of marital disharmony. They included one-third of the boys placed in the worst category of conduct according to the combined assessments of teachers and P.S.Ws, and over one-fifth of the boys of below average intelligence on Raven's Matrices Test. The importance of social level as a concomitant of so many other features was confirmed by the principal component analysis of the inter-relationships between thirty-seven major variables. The first component yielded by the analysis turned out to be a factor of 'general social impoverishment'.

Social level is more easily defined than explained. Defects of the individual as well as defects of the environment may play a part. Dull, ineffectual and unstable persons may be expected to sink to the lowest level and hence to suffer from poor housing, low incomes and large unplanned families. They may also produce poorly socialized children who will carry the same features into the next generation (Robins, 1966, p. 304). It is a vicious circle. But explanation is one thing and prediction is another. From an actuarial point of view the most efficient way of identifying the potential problems of the future may be by means of a few easily registered and objective social facts. Indeed, in this Study the single item 'family income inadequate', which was assessed by the P.S.Ws, was remarkably effective in identifying a problem-prone minority. This may have been because the P.S.Ws did not use a rigid definition, but took account of the family's general style of living in the cases in which a precise figure of income was not ascertainable, thus giving some weight to poor management as well as poor income. It is interesting to note that the home background characteristics most typical of what has been called here the severely handicapped group, namely lax parental rules, unstable maternal personality and disharmonious and inconsistent parents, have much in common with the incohesive families, lax discipline and unsuitable style of maternal supervision which were identified by the Gluecks (Craig and Glueck, 1964) as the three factors most highly predictive of future delinquency among the wide range of background variables which they investigated.

The concentration of background adversities among an unfortunate minority was paralleled by the concentration of inadequacies of performance and behaviour among certain of the boys. This was quite apparent on crude inspection, as the names of certain notorious boys kept cropping up in social agencies, delinquency records, truancy reports and teachers' complaints. As has been explained, a half of the boys who were identified by the P.S.Ws as severely disordered in conduct, mainly on the basis of mothers' complaints, were also identified by the teachers as the most troublesome boys in the classroom. Among the 10 per cent of boys reported by the P.S.Ws to be suffering from a severe degree of nervous disturbance, two-thirds were seriously retarded readers, and two-fifths belonged to the relatively small category of troublesome 'acting-out' boys who were identified by a combination of conduct reports and psychological testing. In other words, the same boys tended to be picked out for unfavourable comment in a number of different contexts, such as nervous traits, classroom misconduct, educational retardation, unpopularity among class-mates and deviant scores on psychological tests.

The disturbed and deviant cases were more numerous in this Study than they would have been in a representative national sample, but this still left most of the boys healthy (using that word in the widest sense) and free from conspicuous social or individual adversity. Only about one in eight of the boys came from a background of 'severe social handicap', and only about one in four were identified as deviant on three or more of the measures of individual disturbance. Although the adverse features were largely concentrated among a readily identifiable disfavoured minority, by no means all of the boys who might have warranted special attention, such as remedial tuition, child guidance, or social supervision, were actually receiving aid or treatment. Of the seventy-seven boys categorized as 'acting-out' cases, most of whom were actual or potential social problems, less than half were in contact with relevant welfare agencies. Moreover, on qualitative impressions of severity of disturbance, it was not necessarily the worst cases who got official help.

2. *Reliability of Social Assessments*

Throughout the body of this report, and again in the special discussion in Chapter VII, a lot of attention has been given to examining the reliability and validity of the assessments, especially where these derived from subjective judgements rather than standard tests or strictly factual reports. No excuse need be offered for this. Indeed, one of the most important conclusions to have emerged from the research so far is the realization that assessments of the backgrounds of potential delinquents are much more difficult to obtain than is generally acknowledged in criminological publications. Many interesting points recorded on the P.S.Ws' interview schedules had to be discarded owing to the difficulty in achieving consistent standards and definitions between the different raters, or because of the impossibility of eliciting the relevant information in all cases.

Experience showed that simple questions about contemporary affairs generally yielded better information than retrospective inquiries or complex inferential judgements. For example, the ratings of mother's present health seemed more realistic than the ratings of mother's past health, which depended more upon the informant's ability to recall and was therefore much influenced by the informant's educational and social level. Likewise, the inquiry into separations of children from their parents during infancy ran into the difficulty that the number of separations recalled was very much a function of the persistence of the questioning and the communicativeness of the informant. The P.S.Ws' assessments of behaviour disorder among the boys became more consistent, and therefore probably more valid, when global judgements based upon a wide variety of items were abandoned in favour of a systematic count of a small number of basic points. Other assessments had to be left as they stood, in spite of evidence that they were not altogether free from bias. Such was the case in the assessment of nervous tendencies among boys based upon reports from mothers, where it was found that the younger and less experienced mothers, the more intelligent and communicative mothers, and those with small families, all tended to notice and report more symptoms. In other contexts it was the poorer families who attracted the unfavourable ratings. 'Physical neglect of boy' and 'parental lack of interest in boy's education' were almost entirely confined to the low income group, and marital disharmony was said to be more than twice as frequent among the low income group as in the rest of the sample. These suspiciously sharp contrasts between income groups, which were so much greater than the contrasts yielded by more objective measures or by assessments of the boys themselves, suggested that some of the impressions derived from interviews may have been subject to a contamination or 'halo' effect produced by the family's social circumstances.

The most serious difficulty encountered in the family background inquiry was the impossibility of obtaining information from a certain segment of the population. This was due to a variety of causes, such as refusal by parents to be interviewed, reluctance to speak frankly on certain topics, and communication difficulties in the case of foreign speaking or unintelligent informants. It was found that difficulty in obtaining information, indicated by such objective evidence as failure to secure interviews, failure to see father as well as mother, and failure to obtain completed parental questionnaires, was significantly correlated with many adverse features, including poor conduct and poor performance in boys and membership of the socially handicapped group. In short, information about some of the families of greatest criminological interest was neither so full nor so accurate as was available for the rest of the sample.

It is easy to see how these various sources of bias in the assessments of home backgrounds might yield spurious associations between family features and boys' misconduct. For this reason no firm conclusions have been drawn except when the associations were found to hold true within each of the three social levels taken separately. On the other hand, where there are clear-cut relations between conduct and background at all levels, it is unlikely that the 'halo' effect of social circumstances, or the relative difficulty of eliciting information about the lowest social group, could account for the results.

In sorting out these complications, and making due allowance for them, this Study has two great advantages. Being a longitudinal research, spread over a substantial period of years, the same boys and parents are being looked at on a number of different occasions using different techniques, so that there is a possibility of correcting some of the less accurate judgements. For example, in the assessment of classroom behaviour, it has been found helpful for certain purposes to combine the two sets of teachers' ratings obtained at age 8 and age 11 in order to arrive at a more accurate ranking of each individual. Another advantage is that the Study has covered a wide variety of items simultaneously. This policy is more or less forced upon any prospective survey, because the sample has to be large and tends to be expensive to recruit and maintain, so one feels obliged to collect as much information as possible to make the effort worthwhile. Having a wide range of data enables any particular assessment to be compared with many other measures, both objective and subjective, so that suspect or implausible findings can be identified and checked by further analysis or investigation. Another virtue of the comprehensive inquiry is that hasty conclusions drawn from correlations between a few factors considered in isolation are avoided.

3. *The Concomitants of Early Misconduct*

In so far as it is possible to describe any results at this stage of the inquiry, they concern what has been learned about the characteristics of those boys identified at an early age as troublesome individuals. The points that have emerged in this connection are worth summarizing in detail because it will be of great interest to see to what extent they will prove to foreshadow delinquency in later years.

Two methods of picking out the troublesome boys have been described. The main measure of misconduct used in the Study so far referred to behaviour at age 8 to 9 and was derived from two sources; class teachers, who were reporting on truancy, disciplinary problems, laziness, poor scholastic performance, aggressiveness, distractability, untidiness, etc., and assessments by P.S.Ws which were based upon reports by parents of lying, stealing, destructiveness, quarrelsomeness or defiance. It has already been demonstrated that the minority of boys identified as being particularly badly behaved according to the combined ratings of teachers and P.S.Ws, carried a greatly increased liability to juvenile court appearances at a tender age, that is to say under 14 years. It has also been shown that much the same segment of the sample as was identified as troublesome at the age of 8 was again picked out for unfavourable comment by a new set of teachers assessing the boys at the age of 11. With a further passage of time the position may change, for instance a substantial number of previously well-conducted boys may become delinquent during their last year at school, but observation so far strongly suggests that in this as in other studies a substantial proportion of persistently anti-social juveniles can be picked out by their behaviour well before the age of 10, when prosecutions begin.

Slightly more sophistication was introduced into the second measure of troublesomeness, the so-called 'acting-out' category. This was obtained by combining the behaviour ratings with some of the results of testing, namely low popularity scores on ratings by class-mates and scores indicative of neuroticism and extraversion on an Eysenckian type of personality test. It was hoped by this means to improve reliability, by combining information from a variety of sources, and perhaps to produce a more valid measure for predictive purposes, through tapping personality attributes that might have a more enduring quality than a boy's conduct of the moment. In the event, the acting-out group has not so far proved to be any worse as regards frequency of court appearances, or to be substantially different in other ways, from the boys identified by behavioural ratings alone. For this reason it will suffice to summarize the analysis of the poor conduct group, although it remains possible that in the long run the acting-out cases may yet prove to be the more persistently troublesome.

Troublesome conduct was found to be positively correlated with almost every adverse item, whether of the boy himself or his background. Thus poor conduct was significantly correlated with low scores on tests of intelligence and scholastic attainment, poor performance on psychomotor tests, unpopularity among class-mates, a tendency to neurotic-extraversion, and a tendency to heavy body build, as indicated by height/weight ratios. Poor conduct was also significantly correlated with a large number of home background items, including broken homes, temporary separation from parents, neglectful parents, unco-operative or uninformative parents, parents in marital conflict, parents lacking in vigilance, parents lax in rules, parents who were unloving or otherwise unsatisfactory in attitude to their boy, parents whose discipline was unsuitable, parents of unstable personality, and mothers of neurotic disposition. In fact, nearly every feature that had been incorporated in the inquiry on the basis of a presumptive connection with delinquency was in fact found to be correlated with behaviour problems detectable at age 9.

This was a gratifying result, in so far as it suggested that the chosen items were relevant, but it did not help much towards deciding the relative importance of different items. The size of a correlation was only a rough indication of the importance of an item, for the techniques of measurement were of very varied efficiency, and where the measures were comparatively crude (as for instance the personality inventory scores from 8-year-olds) the correlations would be reduced accordingly. Moreover, certain correlations were merely reflections of the basic factor of social level.

As an item on its own, the closest and most important concomitant of behaviour disturbance was found to be family income. It stood at the centre of a whole group of individual and social adversities and will probably outweigh in efficiency as a predictor of future delinquency all other measureable features of temperament, performance or parental background (1).[1] Certain adverse environmental features, notably criminality in fathers, appeared to have little importance except as part of the wider conglomeration of troubles common among low income families (2). This does not mean, of course, that low income causes delinquency in any simple, direct way. Income happens to be an easily registered statistic which acts as a signpost to a large number of factors, like ill-health and incompetence and social deviance, which are probably more fundamental.

The family backgrounds of the troublesome boys fell into line with the assumption that a wide variety of factors, from financial hardship to parental mismanagement, each contributed its quota to the totality of juvenile misconduct. For example, poor conduct ratings correlated significantly with belonging to a broken or anomalous parental home, with a history of separation from mother under the age of 6 years, and with indications of physical neglect. (See Table IV (1), p. 63.) In general, these, and almost all the other unfavourable features associated with bad behaviour in boys, were closely linked with the social level of the family. For example, the comment 'boy physically neglected' was largely restricted to those from the inadequate income group. In order to find out whether any given item of information added something to the likelihood of bad behaviour over and above what was already implied by the social level of the family, it was necessary to make comparisons between families of the same social group. For this purpose three levels of general social handicap were identified, using a combination of criteria such as income, housing, father's occupational grade, and size of family. It was found, for example, that there was some association between poor conduct and separations from mother at all three social levels. When similar and significant associations were found in all three segments of the sample, this not only suggested a specific connection independent of social class, it also went some way towards eliminating the possibility of the association being due to interviewers tending to rate the poorer families more unfavourably.

Some of the associations between poor conduct and other items were sufficiently close, and sufficiently marked at all social levels, to suggest a specific relationship calling for explanation. For example, the scarcity of well-behaved boys among those who performed badly on psychomotor tests was particularly noticeable. (See Table III (4), p. 51.) Whatever the reason for the poor performance, whether lack of motor skill or lack of motivation, these scores may well be found to provide a good means of identifying at least some of the probable future delinquents (3). The association between height/weight ratio and poor conduct was slight, but theoretically interesting, especially if one assumes that body-build is largely determined by heredity. These measurements having been repeated at intervals of several years, it should be possible to discover the ages at which body-build correlates most closely with the conduct measures recorded at different stages of the boys' lives (4). Of course, the boys who were heavy for their height may have become so as a consequence of dietary habits, for example excessive carbohydrate consumption, rather than because they were of naturally sturdy build. Repeat measurements taken at a later age included strength of grip, taken by means of a dynamometer, so it may be possible to distinguish between boys who are heavy through muscle development and those who are heavy from fat.

Of the measures concerned with the boys themselves, the ones which were found most closely related to behaviour disturbance were poor psychomotor performance, which has just been mentioned, unpopularity among class-mates, below average intelligence, and educational retardation. Unpopularity was very significantly associated with poor conduct at all social levels, and it seems likely that a boy's standing in the eyes of his peers will prove to be one of the better indices of persistent anti-social tendency (5). A preliminary analysis of the more refined sociometric ratings taken at age 11 suggests that boys of this age are able to identify with surprising clarity the more deviant and troublesome individuals (Gibson and Hanson, 1969). Boys given unfavourable ratings by both teachers and class-mates may be expected to be particularly vulnerable to delinquency (6), if only because, in general, combinations of measures tend to make more powerful predictors than isolated observations.

It was an unexpected finding that below average intelligence, as measured by a non-verbal test, the Raven's Matrices, was so closely related to poor conduct. The finding was not due to bias against the less able boys on the part of their teachers, since the P.S.Ws' assessments of behaviour showed a similar trend. Moreover, the finding was not due to the over-representation of duller children in the poorer classes, since the relationship held true at all social levels. Preliminary analyses of records of early delinquency have shown that low I.Q. on the Matrices Test is a significant predictor of liability to appearance at a juvenile court under the age of 13. In interpreting these results it needs to be kept in mind that test scores represent the outcome of two factors, actual intelligence potential, and the amount of effort made by the boy when taking the test. Since the matrices require subjects to persist with problems of increasing difficulty, the outcome must be influenced by motivation as well as ability. When the analysis of the more detailed tests at age 11 have been completed, it is hoped to be able to sort out these two factors and arrive at a clearer picture of the role of intelligence in delinquent behaviour. Even at this stage, however, it is possible to state that poor performance on the Matrices, whether at age 8 to 9, or at age 11, bears a very significant statistical relationship to the likelihood of appearing before a juvenile court at a tender age. Intelligence level and social level taken in conjunction appear to be very powerful predictors of early delinquency (7). Both of these factors need to be taken into account before the probable effect of other influences, such as parental attitudes and methods of discipline, can be adequately evaluated.

The educational retardation of the poorly behaved boys, as revealed in their relatively poor reading attainment scores, came as no surprise because this, more than lack of intelligence potential, has often been noted as a distinctive feature of juvenile delinquents (8). However, from the data collected at age 8, no support was found for the hypothesis that anti-social boys are characterized by a particularly wide gap between their intelligence potential and their actual educational performance (9).

A number of unfavourable parental characteristics were found to be associated with bad behaviour at all social levels. These included inconsistency between mother and father in the handling of the child (10), parental under-vigilance (i.e. lack of supervision, see p. 73 (11), and erratic maternal discipline (12) see p. 83. In other instances, however, the associations did not hold true at all social levels, or were even reversed. This was one of the most interesting and puzzling of the findings so far. One striking example was the assessment of marital disharmony of parents. This was generally associated, as expected, with increased likelihood of bad behaviour in boys, but at the lowest social level, where marital disharmony was reported as especially prevalent, there was no significant association. Two possible *ad hoc* explanations of this anomaly spring to mind. The P.S.Ws' ratings of the marriages of the poorer parents may have been unduly harsh, and hence ineffective. Alternatively, it may be that open marital disputes carry less emotional significance among poorer families, and thus have a less deleterious effect upon the children (13). A rather similar example was the assessment by the P.S.Ws of the quality of the mother's attitude to her boy, which was either 'loving normal' or else in one of the unfavourable categories called 'over-protective', 'cruel', 'passive' or 'neglecting'. Over the sample as a whole, having a 'loving normal' mother was associated with a lower incidence of bad behaviour, but among the socially handicapped minority this no longer held true. Once again, the anomaly could be due to the difficulty the P.S.Ws found in assessing the poorer families, or it could be due to a real difference in the family dynamics at different social levels. In the poorer group it was the anxious, over-protective mothers who more often had better behaved sons, perhaps because a certain level of anxiety may be beneficial where there are realistic social adversities to combat (14). Indeed it may be that the same item of parental behaviour has different effects in different social circumstances. A curious example of this kind was the apparently differing consequences of above average parental vigilance or above average parental interest in education. In the inadequate income group, both of these items were associated with better reading performance in boys, but in the rest of the sample neither item had any bearing upon reading performance (see p. 77). It is tempting to speculate that unusual concern on the part of parents may have a beneficial effect upon scholastic performance only if the social circumstances are especially adverse (15).

In interpreting the meaning of the associations between the conduct ratings and other items no assumptions about cause and effect are justified without careful consideration of alternative explanations. For instance, from the data collected by the P.S.Ws it appeared that maternal qualities were generally more closely correlated with boys' behaviour than paternal ones (16). This did not amount to proof that mothers have a greater influence than fathers, for contact with fathers was often only at second hand, so that the assessments of fathers may have been less effective. Contrary to what might have been expected from current beliefs, it was found that there were fewer badly behaved boys among the group whose mothers went out to work part-time, and fewer still whose mothers were working full-time (17) (see Table IV (2), p. 66). This result was in large part due to the fact that over-burdened mothers of very large families could not go out to work, and these were the mothers who produced the largest incidence of badly behaved sons. But that was not a complete explanation, for at each level of family size mothers who worked at least part-time had less badly behaved boys. In this neighbourhood, other things being equal, it was probably the less effectual mothers who elected to stay at home, which would account for the association between this item and poor conduct and other adverse features in boys.

The physical health of mothers and fathers, so far as this was investigated, appeared to have only slight bearing upon boys' behaviour (18), but mental health, particularly of mother, was distinctly relevant. Neurotic disturbance in mothers (both as assessed by a modified version of the Cornell Health Questionnaire and from assessments by P.S.Ws), correlated with bad behaviour in boys (19). Rather surprisingly, maternal neurotic tendency correlated only very slightly with nervous tendency among boys. Deviant or unstable personality in mother (defined by erratic behaviour, psychopathic traits, hysterical personality etc.) as identified by the P.S.Ws, was particularly closely linked with poor conduct in boys (20), but this was largely a social class phenomenon, since the P.S.Ws had rated over a half of the socially handicapped minority as 'mother unstable' compared with only 7 per cent among the rest of the sample. There was an almost equally extreme concentration of ratings 'father unstable' at the lowest social level, but even so this rating bore no significant relationship to poor conduct in boys.

The evidence that temporary separations from mother during infancy led to disturbed behaviour was interesting, but far from conclusive. The picture was confused by the variety of circumstances covered by the term separation, which included both unavoidable hospitalizations due to acute illness and unnecessary family breaks caused by parental negligence. It seemed unlikely that such different situations could be equally deleterious. Moreover, it was almost impossible to obtain adequate accounts by retrospective inquiry, since the number of separations recalled was in large part a function of the interest and intelligence of the mother and the persistence of the interviewer. No firm predictions about the relation between this item and future delinquency seem warranted. Complete and permanent disruptions of family life and chronically anomalous family situations, which result from illegitimacy, bereavement, desertion, divorce and fostering, will probably prove to be more relevant to juvenile delinquency than temporary separation (21).

An attempt to measure parental attitudes to child rearing by means of questionnaires, and to relate the scores to measures of boys' behaviour, produced very little result. This was largely due to the failure of a large proportion of parents to complete the forms. Nevertheless there was some slight tendency for maternal authoritarianism, as measured by questionnaire, to be associated with a higher incidence of poor conduct (22). In this, as in all the questionnaire inquiries addressed to parents, failure to complete the form proved to be the equivalent of a most unfavourable scoring category.

It has not been possible to come to any clear conclusions so far concerning the probable influence upon boys' future delinquency of the presence of other members of the family with convictions for offences. As regards the records of siblings, there was an obvious concentration of the item 'elder brother convicted' among the poorly behaved group of boys, but the explanation was obscure. Boys from large families ran an obviously greater risk of having a convicted brother, whereas eldest and only children ran no risk at all. The influence of a father's criminality was easier to assess, since nearly every boy had a father or father substitute. But even in this the boys were not all exposed to the same degree of risk, since the expectation of having a father with a criminal record is in part a function of father's age (see Table V A (1), p. 190). Over the sample as a whole the incidence of paternal convictions was significantly correlated with poor conduct, but within each social level there was no significant tendency for the worse behaved boys to have more convicted fathers. It appeared that paternal criminality was more closely tied to social level than to the individual boy's behaviour or to the individual family's characteristics (23). It may be, of course, that family criminality has a more direct bearing upon juvenile delinquency in later years than upon general misconduct at primary school age, but only time will tell (24). One point did stand out, namely the concentration of convictions in particular families. The fact of having a convicted mother increased the likelihood of having a convicted father three times.

The investigation of medical records of births gave no support to the theory that a significant contribution to troublesome behaviour can be traced to the widespread occurrence of sub-clinical brain damage caused by obstetric complications (25). In this Study only slight associations emerged between the incidence of mild abnormalities of birth or maternal pregnancy and the boys' conduct ratings. Such relationships as were discovered were easily accounted for by the operation of intervening variables, such as the varying incidence of both bad behaviour and obstetric complications with social class, size of family, position of the boy in the birth order, and likelihood of birth taking place in hospital.

Although they have not been dwelt upon very much, the better behaved and better functioning boys, especially if they come from adverse social or psychological environments, may teach us something about the factors that protect some individuals from delinquent developments. Above average intelligence, for example, was related to better behaviour in the lowest social group, but among the more affluent and socially favoured the fact of being intelligent was no protection against the development of anti-social tendencies (26). An attempt to isolate and investigate a group of well behaved boys from bad backgrounds was largely frustrated by the fact that there were so few of them, the socially handicapped group being largely comprised of boys with poor conduct ratings. The few exceptions were mostly boys whose social handicap was the result of accidental circumstances, such as father's death, rather than the usual conglomeration of parental shortcomings (27). At the opposite extreme, it was clear that many of the badly behaved boys from more affluent homes had been exposed to unfavourable psychological influences and were particularly liable to display a combination of nervous tendency and anti-social tendency (28).

As time passes, and the changes in status of individual boys as they grow older come to be charted, it should be possible to answer certain questions about the stages of development at which environmental factors show their effect. It appeared that up to the age of 10 no significant differences were observable between boys attending different local primary schools. When the inquiries at age 14 are completed, it should be possible to tell whether those boys lucky enough to have obtained grammar school places, or the equivalent, will have done better, in social behaviour and scholastic performance, than would have been expected from their previous history (29). It may be that as the boys grow older certain influences, such as the presence of a delinquent older brother (30), or the choice of friends of leisure pursuits, or the fact of parents migrating to improved housing, will assume greater importance as determinants of behaviour.

We do not yet know how accurately the characteristics of boys aged 8 or 9 will predict the behaviour of those same boys at adolescence. Most of the boys rated 'good' or 'bad' as to conduct by their teachers at age 8 were similarly categorized by different teachers three years later, but the ratings by teachers at age 14 are not yet available for comparison (31). On this and other items, such as popularity, psychomotor performance, and educational attainment, comparisons between the same individuals at different ages should not only show how far certain qualities remain constant, but should throw light on the processes of maturation. It will be of special interest to see whether the fact that an individual is improving or becoming more deviant in these respects has a bearing upon the chances of becoming delinquent (32).

Up till now, delinquency has been referred to as if it were some constant, homogeneous category of behaviour with much the same origins in different individuals. This would seem to be justified in relation to delinquency records at a very early age, which refer largely to minor thefts, but later on some method of classification according to type or seriousness of record will be necessary. In the analysis of paternal records, for example, it was shown that the presence of an isolated conviction had comparatively slight social significance, but the presence of two or more paternal convictions served to define a distinctive group of families with a high incidence of social adversities. In relation to the boys themselves, the identification of those with more serious delinquent tendencies may be considerably aided by the use of a technique of confidential questioning about undetected offences which is being applied at age 14. While the validity of such confessions is difficult to determine, it is relevant to note that it has been found that boys are surprisingly honest with reference to their actual court appearances, for which, of course, independent records are available. The seriousness of the delinquent acts which lead to court appearances depend in part upon the policy of local police, and how far they are ready to use informal cautioning or notifications to the Children's Department as alternatives to prosecution.

At first sight it may seem that already the findings of this Study in regard to the paramount importance of family income or social level in relation to boys' conduct and performance suggest that elementary and social and economic factors will outweigh the more subtle personal and psychological factors in the backgrounds of our future juvenile delinquents. For example, it was found that belonging to a socially handicapped family virtually ruled out the possibility of a boy obtaining the best conduct rating (see Table IV (3), p. 69). Moreover, in the socially handicapped group 76 per cent of boys were below average in intelligence according to the matrices scores, compared with only 42 per cent below average in the rest of the sample. For statistical purposes, therefore, basic social factors will undoubtedly prove the most effective predictors of delinquency, but cause and effect is another matter. This Study has also shown the remarkable concentration of parental pathology, in the shape of unsuitable discipline, unfortunate attitudes to children, personality deviation, etc., among the socially handicapped group. Personal inadequacies and external handicaps reinforce each other in these unfortunate families. Rather than trying to answer the conundrum 'Which comes first . . .?' it may be more useful to ask at what point to try to break the vicious circle.

These preliminary observations raise many questions. It is our pious hope that with the passage of time, and the opportunity to compile a sequel to this report, at least some answers will emerge.

NOTE

[1] In this section the numbers in brackets mark statements which can be readily put into the form of hypotheses to be tested against the findings of later stages of this Study.

APPENDIX I (A)

The Teachers' Ratings of Boys' Behaviour

The following questionnaire, based upon work by J. W. B. Douglas in the National Survey, was given to the class teachers of the boys in this Study when they were aged 8 to 9 years, and again when they were aged 10 to 11.

THE TEACHERS' QUESTIONNAIRE ABOUT BOYS IN CLASS   CONFIDENTIAL

How to fill in this Form
To reduce clerical work, this form is framed as a series of questions, many of which can be answered by one of several printed alternatives. Please put a circle round the number opposite the printed answer that most nearly describes your findings. If no alternative fits, please write the answer in the space directly under the question. We should also be most grateful for any further information you can give us to supplement these points.

Name of boy: .... Date of birth: ....

1. Is he in general
   - A very hard worker 1
   - A hard worker 2
   - An average worker 3
   - A poor worker 4
   - Lazy 5

2. Arithmetic. Please give a rating of his general arithmetical ability.
   - Good 1
   - Average 2
   - Poor 3

3. (*a*) Is there any subject(s) (including games and handwork as well as general school subjects) in which his performance is outstandingly GOOD?
   - Yes 1
   - No 0

   (if 'Yes')
3. (*b*) In which subject(s) is he outstandingly good?
   ....
   ....

4. (*a*) Is there any subject(s) (including games and handwork as well as general school subjects) in which his performance is outstandingly BAD?
   - Yes 1
   - No 0

   (if 'Yes')
4. (*b*) In which subject(s) is he outstandingly bad?
   ....
   ....
   ....

5. Do you think that he tries to be a credit to his parents?
   - Is very concerned 1
   - About average 2
   - Just doesn't care 3

6. Does he lack concentration, or is he restless in a way that seriously hinders his learning?
   - Yes 1
   - No 2

7. (a) Does he have difficulties in his relations with the other children in his class?
   Yes 1
   No......................................0
   (if 'Yes')
7. (b) What are these difficulties?
   ....
   ....

8. When he comes to school in the morning is he a clean and tidy boy (compared with others in his class)?
   Noticeably clean and tidy 1
   About average.....................2
   Noticeably below average 3

9. Is he difficult to discipline?
   Yes 1
   No......................................0

10. Attendance. Considering his record for the past year what does it show?
    Very regular attendance.........1
    Fair regularity....................2
    Rather a lot of absence 3
    Very poor attendance............4
    What is the reason for most of his absence (e.g. ill-health)?
    ....
    ....
    ....

11. Is there anything about this child you would like to comment on?
    ....
    ....
    ....
    ....
    ....

The following Table shows a comparison between teachers' ratings made on the boys in the Study and those made on a national sample. The comparison is based upon the sons of manual workers, since these were the closest in socio-economic status to the boys in this Study.

TABLE I A (1)
Percentage Frequencies of Teachers' use of Behavioural Categories

Behavioural Category		National Survey (N=821 boys from homes of manual workers) %	Present Study[1] (N=409 boys) %
Item 1.	Very hard worker	5·5	9·0*
	Hard worker	22·7	21·5
	Average worker	47·7	38·9
	Poor worker	19·2	21·0
	Lazy	4·9	9·6†
Item 6.	Poor concentration	27·0	33·7
Item 9.	Poor discipline	4·1	11·5‡

   * $p < ·05$ † $p < ·01$ ‡ $p < ·001$

[1] In other tables in this book, the two boys who did not have teachers' forms fully completed are rated 'average' on the basis of teachers' verbal reports.

APPENDIX I (B)

The Case Record Forms for recording Interviews with Parents

The first case record forms consisted of twenty-seven roneoed pages, with places for noting information on some hundreds of specified points. These varied from factual matters, such as nationality, full names, place and date of birth of parents, and full names and date of birth of siblings, to impressionistic ratings of the mother's personality, and her feelings for the boy. The points followed a logical sequence, similar to the method of setting out case histories customary in child guidance clinics, beginning with mother's own origin, family background and experience of school, work and marriage, then going on to the history of the boy's birth, infant characteristics, present temperament, behaviour and relations with his parents, and comparisons with his siblings. A considerable number of points concerned the mother's methods of child rearing, her modes of discipline, the degree of supervision and control exercised, and her own feelings about the boy.

A similar case record form on different-coloured paper was used for recording corresponding points from interviews with fathers; except that where reliable information was available from mother about the basic facts of family history and the child's birth and early development, or where father merely echoed the information mother had already given, these sections were omitted.

The actual content of the case records in relation to specific items will be dealt with under the topics concerned, but an example may help to explain the general system. Here is a sample page from a completed record form taken from the section recording the parents' marital situation, together with the corresponding sheet from the instruction guide.

Extract from the Record Form used by P.S.Ws for recording data and impressions from home interviews (showing a completed page).

G. PARENTS' MARRIAGE

COMMENTS

1. *Marital Relationship:* 1. 2. ③. 4.   Mother does not look happy and says she does not have much in common with father, and they have numerous rows, often in front of the children. She says he is not much company to her, and when he comes home he does not talk much but sits reading the paper or watching the television, cutting her out. I felt she was a lonely, dissatisfied woman.

2. *Sexual adjustment:*
    Satisfactory.   No intercourse.
    (Not enjoyed.) Disliked.

At the second visit mother told me that the marriage started off badly as they had to live with Paternal G.Ps for a while. This did not work out for her. As regard to the present she keeps on saying that she supposes it could be worse. When she compares her marriage with other people's she realizes she should be thankful. She appears bored and frustrated when she is talking about her husband.

3. *Birth control:*
    Coitus interruptus.

4. *Dominance:*

	Father		Mutual		Mother
Children:	2	1	(0)	1	2
General:	2	(1)	0	1	2

Generally father makes the decisions, particularly about money as she describes herself as a spendthrift, and says that father is able to save. What she really means is that he is mean. When it comes to other matters they are usually discussed between them.

5. *Age first married or cohabited:*
    M. 22   F. 24

Extract from the Corresponding Section of the Instruction Guide for the P.S.Ws Record Form.

PARENTS' MARRIAGE

1. *Marital Relationships:*
    These are interviewer's ratings:
    1. Harmonious = happy marriage, no more than occasional upsets or disagreements with no lasting differences.
    2. Evidence of some degree of conflict.
    3. Chronic tension or disagreement in many fields.
    4. Raging conflicts or completely estranged.

    (Q) I expect you and your husband have arguments from time to time, what happens?
    Do you or your husband get upset?
    How does it usually end?
    Can you have it out with each other or do either of you have to bottle up your feelings?
    When you or your husband get in a temper do you go for each other?
    Does he ever give you a hiding?

2. *Sex:*
    Satisfactory = no spontaneous complaint.
    Not enjoyed = mother may say it is something she has to put up with.

Disliked = would indicate a more serious aversion, and possibly frigidity in mother.

(Q) How is the physical side of marriage with you?
Do you worry in case you get pregnant?
Have you ever used birth control?
(Note if evidence that parents are sleeping in separate rooms.)

3. *Birth Control:*
Record methods used if any (C.I., abstinence, condom, cap, safe period), Why?

4. *Dominance:*
This section refers to who takes the lead in the organization of family life. The heading 'mutual' indicates that the parents discuss plans together, and work out a joint decision.
F2 or M2 = very little say left to partner.
F1 or M1 = other partner often excluded.
Children: this refers mainly to the choice of schools and future careers and discipline.

(Q) When it comes to things like:
(i) Holidays—who does the deciding over where to go (also weekend trips, etc.)?
(ii) I suppose you have your wages/housekeeping money from your husband, but when it comes to buying something special like a fridge or something on hire purchase, would your husband do that, or do you decide it together?

In this example the parents' marriage was rated as bad (i.e. 3), but not very bad (i.e. 4), sex was not enjoyed, and coitus interruptus was practised for birth control. Father was considered to be the more dominant partner in general decisions, whereas neither partner was dominant in decisions concerning children. The meaning of these ratings is enlarged upon in the descriptive comments recorded at the right of the page, which were written in at the first and subsequent visits.

In the process of analysis, some of these records had to be simplified or omitted. For instance, the item about birth control was so often missing, because the P.S.Ws had not felt they could put the question, that it could not be used in the analyses. The rating of 4 on marital relationships was so rarely used by the P.S.Ws that the few cases so marked were grouped together with those rated 3.

In using this complex recording form many decisions had to be taken concerning the rating of difficult or anomalous situations. For example, it had to be decided, in cases of broken homes or double marriages, who should be counted as 'mother' or 'father' for rating a particular item. Thus, on questions relating to the boy's birth, it was clearly the biological mother who was being considered, but on questions of discipline it was the person who was acting as mother at the time of intake who counted, or if there was none, the person who had so acted in the past, unless the child had had no mother figure since before the age of 3, in which case maternal discipline was rated 'not applicable'. In anomalous cases, the P.S.Ws were asked to indicate on the front page who was being counted as the 'operative' mother or father for the purpose of the majority of the ratings.

Among the sources of potential confusion in recording was the impossibility of obtaining the answers to certain questions in the case of some of the reluctant or evasive informants. Where information was not known, or perhaps not applicable, the P.S.Ws were asked to mark their forms accordingly, rather than simply leaving a blank, which might mean merely that the topic had been left over to a later interview. Where information from father or outside sources contradicted that given by mother, the P.S.Ws were asked to indicate which was the more trustworthy answer or rating. Where information from later interviews caused a modification of previously recorded ratings, the P.S.Ws were asked to alter the original ratings. (Owing to an oversight no convention was made to distinguish between alterations of clerical mistakes and changes of assessment.)

It has to be admitted that clinical workers do not take readily to the task of filling in forms for research purposes. The instructions were not in fact followed with complete reliability, but during the process of preliminary analysis the P.S.Ws co-operated in transcribing their ratings from the case record forms on to data lists, and during this process they were able to check their ratings and amend inconsistencies. The important questions of the accuracy and validity of ratings, and the comparability of ratings made by different interviewers, receives attention in later chapters. In addition to their comments on the form itself, the P.S.Ws compiled an on-going summary of every case, giving a pen-picture of the family history, and drawing attention to any salient peculiarities or difficulties.

APPENDIX II (A)

The Selection and Composition of the Sample

The total sample, consisting of 411 boys, was defined by age and attendance at selected primary schools. The size of the sample was pre-determined by staffing and budgetary considerations as well as scientific requirements, 400 being regarded as the maximum case-load for psychological tests and home visits, and the minimum number for statistical comparisons. The slight excess was due to the fact that the sample was incremented by whole classes and not by single individuals. Advantage was taken of the system of allocating children to classes by age to include whole classes of boys all of whom would be born within the same year. This aim could not be realized with complete perfection because a small minority of children were allocated to classes of a different age, and certain special classes were of mixed age. For this reason birth-date rather than class membership was made the final criterion of selection, so that the sample consisted of all boys on the attendance registers of the schools concerned who should have been in second year junior classes according to their age. All of the schools concerned had mixed classes, but only the boys were included. The schools were chosen on the basis of proximity, numbers and willingness to co-operate.

Since the number of boys was too large to allow of home visits and psychological tests on all of them to be completed within a single year, it was arranged to spread the intake over two years, and to include two successive classroom generations. The older and larger age cohort, amounting to 231 boys, was made up of all boys born between 1.9.52 and 31.8.53 who were attending the schools at the time the psychologist made contact for the purpose of administering tests in the classroom. This group was for the most part incorporated into the study during the academic year commencing September 1961. The younger age cohort was made up of 157 boys born between 1.9.53 and 31.8.54 who were for the most part admitted to the Study during the succeeding academic year, commencing September 1962. Two of the schools (D and E) were omitted from this further intake because numbers were sufficient without them. In addition, a small group of twenty-three boys, born between 1.9.51 and 31.8.52 constituting the oldest or pilot cohort, were taken from one class in school A, which was first approached before the others, during the summer of 1961. These boys have been included in all the counts, since they have received all the tests and observations given to the others, but they have been used as a pilot group for the purpose of trying out new tests in advance of the main sample.

Some slight exceptions to this order of intake were dictated by practical considerations. For example, the Church school (F) and the E.S.N.

school were not included until the second year of work, but nevertheless boys from both the main age cohorts were taken from these schools. The effect of these variations was to increase somewhat the age range of children at the time of testing, a point which had to be allowed for in some of the scoring. The E.S.N. school was the only one from which every boy on the register in the prescribed age range was not included. This was to avoid over-weighting the sample with E.S.N. boys. The twelve selected, who were dullards without gross physical abnormality, comprised 2·9 per cent of the sample, which was thought to be about the proportion of boys of primary school age to be found in special schools in a working-class area with a rather high incidence of social handicaps. The composition of the total sample, by age and school, is set out in Table II A (1).

TABLE II A (1)
Constitution of Sample by Age and School attended when admitted to the Study

Name of School	Pilot cohort born 1/9/51 to 31/8/52	First year cohort born 1/9/52 to 31/8/53	Second year cohort born 1/9/53 to 31/8/54	Totals
A	22	37	43	102
B	—	39	54	93
C	—	34	36	70
D	1*	60	—	61
E	—	45	1	46
F	—	11	16	27
ESN	—	5	7	12
TOTAL	23	231	157	411

* One boy, rightly belonging by age to the pilot cohort, was mistakenly included among those from D school, because he was working in a class younger than his age, and the fact that his birthday fell a month outside the defined age range had been overlooked.

The complete sample of 411 boys included fourteen pairs of brothers (of whom five pairs were twins), so that the total number of separate families was 397. Except where otherwise stated all counts have been based upon numbers of boys rather than numbers of parents.

Much more difficult than deciding who should be included in the sample was the actual recruitment of the 411 boys, since this depended upon the co-operation of the education department, the schools and the parents. At first, the education department made a ruling that group tests of intelligence and so forth, which could be administered simultaneously to the whole class, might be given provided only that the teachers were agreeable, but that anything which required taking children individually, one by one, could not be done without the written consent of parents given on a prescribed form. During the second year of work, this rule was relaxed, and a limited range of tests, which had to be approved by a psychologist representing the local authority, was permitted to be given to all the children. This involved re-visiting the schools to test children who had previously been left out, and meant that the children were not all of the same age at the time they were first tested. One extra school would have been included, but that the headmaster decided to withdraw not long after work had begun, and the boys and parents from that school who had been seen had to be eliminated from the Study. Apart from this, excellent co-operation was obtained from all of the schools, and certain basic information, such as ratings by class teachers, was obtained about every boy in the sample. Incompleteness in some of the measures taken at the schools arose from difficulties associated with the boys themselves, notably persistent absence from school, illiteracy and lack of verbal comprehension.

Enlistment of the parents' co-operation was not quite so successful. The local authority ruled that the home addresses of schoolchildren were confidential, and not to be revealed to investigators without written consent. It was therefore impossible simply to call upon parents to explain what was wanted. Instead, an official letter, partly composed by the local authority, and signed by headmasters, was dispatched to the parents with a request that they sign and post an enclosed form signifying their consent to be visited by someone from the Study. Predictably, in an area where standards of literacy were not very high, and reluctance to sign puzzling forms from headmasters was understandable, the response was poor. When a count was made in February 1962, out of 223 families approached, 40 per cent had either refused, or, much more often, failed to reply. Various expedients were tried to improve the situation, including reminders from headmasters, calls by co-operative parents upon their less co-operative neighbours, and the use of local welfare agencies to secure introductions. However, none of these methods proved really effective. During 1963 it was decided that the research team had been long enough in the neighbourhood, and had established sufficient contacts of their own, for the psychiatric social workers to call upon the mothers directly, without involving the education department. By meeting the mothers face to face, and explaining about the research in an informal way, the P.S.Ws were able to persuade most of them to agree to be visited and interviewed, from time to time. By May 1964, out of the total sample of 411 boys, a parent had been interviewed in 387 cases, leaving only 6 per cent whose parents refused altogether.

One consequence of the long delay in enlisting parental co-operation was that some homes were first visited when the boy was 10 years of age rather than 9, as first planned, and in a few instances not until he was turned 11.

All of the parents who were willing to open their doors to the P.S.Ws were not equally co-operative or forthcoming informants. At the time the situation was first analysed in November 1964, only 86·4 per cent of the 411 boys had parents classed as fully and continuing co-operative at interviews, 4·9 per cent were considered to have evasive or unforthcoming parents, 3·2 per cent had parents who tolerated visits at first but later withdrew consent to be interviewed further, and 5·6 per cent had parents who all along refused to agree to be interviewed. These graduations of cooperativeness were associated with corresponding variations in the extent and reliability of the background information collected by the P.S.Ws.

APPENDIX II (B)

Socio-Economic Class and Family Size among the Study Sample

TABLE II B (1)
Percentage of Families of Specified Size

Number of Children in Family	Study Sample (397 families) Number	Percentage	National Sample[1] (N=8,085) Number	Percentage
1	41	10·3	1,125	13·9
2	103	26·0	2,647	32·8
3	93	23·4	1,840	22·5
4	66	16·6	1,154	14·3
5	35	8·8	586	7·4
6	13	3·3	310	3·8
7 or more	46	11·6	423	5·3
TOTAL	397	100·0	8,085	100·0

[1] Taken from Douglas 1964, p. 168

TABLE II B (2)
Socio-Economic Class by Number of Children in Family
(Excluding only Children)

	Class II	Class III Non-Manual	Class III Manual	Class IV Non-Manual	Class IV Manual	Class V
Boys with 1–4 siblings	23 (95·8%)	26 (86·7%)	151 (78·3%)	13 (86·7%)	48 (80·0%)	42 (68·9%)
Boys with 5 or more siblings	1 (4·2%)	4 (13·3%)	29 (21·7%)	2 (13·3%)	12 (20·0%)	19 (31·1%)
TOTAL (N=370)	24 (100%)	30 (100%)	180 (100%)	15 (100%)	60 (100%)	61 (100%)

APPENDIX II (C)

Improvement in Reading Ability with Age

TABLE II C (1)
Reading Ability at Age 14½ compared with a National Sample[1]
(Based on Neale Analysis of Reading Ability)

Reading Age	Percentage of National Sample Chronological age 15 All types of school	Secondary Modern	Percentage of Study Sample Chronological age 14½ ($N=128$)
<9 years 'Semi-literate'	5·0	6·0	10·9
<12 years 'Backward'	17·0	23·0	21·1
12+years 'Average and above'	78·0	71·0	68·0
TOTAL	100	100	100

At age 14½ the bottom 10·9 per cent of the Study sample corresponded in reading performance to the bottom 5 or 6 per cent of the national sample of 1956. The excess was accounted for by the semi-literates. There was no complete illiterates, and no more moderately backward readers than the national average, considering the type of schools attended by most of the Study sample. This contrasts markedly with the findings at age 8 to 9 shown in Table II (2) p. 30.

[1] Ministry of Education (1957), *Standards in Reading*. H.M.S.O.

APPENDIX II (D)

Body-Build at Age 8 to 9 against Social Class and against Conduct Ratings

TABLE II D (1)
Socio-Economic Class by Height/Weight Ratio

	Socio-Economic Class on Registrar General's Classification			
	Upper Classes i.e. II or III		Lower Classes i.e. IV or V	
	No.	%	No.	%
'Heavily Built' Mesomorphic or Endomorphic	87	34·1	73	48·7
'Balanced'	108	42·4	56	37·3
'Lightly Built' Ectomorphic	60	23·5	21	14·0
TOTAL	255	100	150	100

$\chi^2 = 9.92$ with 2 d.f., $p < .01$

TABLE II D (2)
Boys' Conduct[1] (combined P.S.Ws' and Teachers' Ratings) against Body-Build

Body Build	Good				Conduct: Average		Bad			
	I		II		III		IV		V	
	No.	%	No.	%	No.	%	No.	%	No.	%
Heavy	18	26·1	64	40·0	34	36·1	28	52·8	15	51·7
Average	34	49·3	59	36·9	45	47·9	16	30·2	11	37·9
Light	17	24·6	37	23·1	15	16·0	9	17·0	3	10·3
TOTAL	69	100	160	100	94	100	53	100	29	100

There was a definite tendency which did not reach statistical significance for the less well behaved boys to be more often heavily built.

Boys of a heavy body-build were significantly commoner among the acting out group (*see* Table III (7), p. 57).

[1] See Table III A (1), p. 165 for an explanation of the rating scale of boys' conduct, which was derived from a combination of teachers' and P.S.Ws' assessments.

APPENDIX III (A)

Behaviour Disorder Ratings: Comparison between Ratings by three P.S.Ws

In the original method of rating by P.S.Ws, based upon a global impression of twelve items from the case record, boys rated *severely* behaviour disordered generally had at least three different items of undesirable behaviour recorded, and at least two in a pronounced degree. Those rated as behaviour disorder *absent* had none of the items present to any significant degree, those with *minimal* behaviour disorder had only one or two items to a significant degree. Of the 380 boys scored by the P.S.Ws on this rating, 251 had no behaviour disorder, 47 had severe disorder, 25 had moderate and 57 minimal disorder.

These assessments referred to the whole life history of the boys, and included a few whose behaviour disorder had subsided at the time of intake. As with all the P.S.Ws' assessments, they were primarily derived from reports by the parents, supplemented by occasional opportunity for direct observation in the home, but occasionally supplied by information from social agencies. Few ratings were made solely upon indirect sources of information.

Comparisons of the behaviour disorder ratings made by the three P.S.Ws showed such inconsistencies that it was clear they must have been using radically different criteria. Differences showed up in opposite trends in the correlations with independent variables. For example, the presence of behaviour disorder, in the rating of P.S.Ws B and C, correlated positively with scores of neuroticism ($r_{tet} = \cdot 26$ and $\cdot 27$) and with extraversion ($r_{tet} = \cdot 26$ and $\cdot 32$) as obtained from the personality inventory given in the schools. In the ratings of P.S.W. A, however, there was no correlation with neuroticism ($r_{tet} = \cdot 02$) and a negative association with extraversion ($r_{tet} = -\cdot 36$). Those rated as having behaviour disorder by P.S.Ws B and C had above average Porteus Q scores (as would have been expected since the Q score purports to measure a form of behaviour disorder) but the ratings of P.S.W. A showed no such association. Analysis of the correlations between the component items of the behaviour disorder assessments showed that it had been incorrect to assume that these items cluster together in a more or less homogeneous syndrome. Truancy and jealousy were in fact negatively correlated, the presence of one implying a likely absence of the other. Furthermore, the pattern of relationships between component items differed between raters. Lying and tempers were positively correlated in the behaviour disordered boys rated by P.S.W. A, negatively correlated among those rated by P.S.W. B.

Clearly, the items were too mixed, and the final judgement too complex and subjective to yield satisfactory ratings. A revised system was therefore introduced. The items under consideration were reduced to six (lying, stealing at home, stealing outside, destructiveness, quarrelsomeness, defiance), all of which were substantially and positively inter-correlated. Instead of asking the P.S.Ws to make a global judgement, the cases were graded on a points system, giving a number of points to each symptom according to severity, and totalling the score for each individual. Where information was incomplete on certain items, allocation was based on a modified scoring of the known items. The final rating was called Conduct Disorder; absent, moderate or severe. The initial and more intuitive rating, called Behaviour Disorder, was retained in the computer analysis. Even though it was less reliable, and less clearly defined, it might prove to have predictive value.

The two rating scales inter-correlated quite highly ($r = \cdot 71$)[1] but the final rating of conduct disorder was considered an improvement for several reasons. It reduced much of the inconsistencies between the ratings of the three P.S.Ws. It appeared to represent a more valid description of a natural cluster of behavioural items. It gave generally slightly higher correlations with other variables related to the boys themselves, and slightly smaller correlations with variables related to home and parents. This suggested that the initial behaviour disorder ratings may have been rather more contaminated by the P.S.Ws' perceptions of parents, and hence not such valid descriptions of the boys themselves.

One method of testing the validity of the P.S.Ws' assessments of Conduct Disorder is to see if they correlate significantly with variables having some logical connection with disturbed behaviour, which have been assessed independently by other people. The most obvious variable for the purpose, namely the teachers' ratings of misbehaviour in class, did in fact correlate significantly ($r = \cdot 29$), but this was not an entirely satisfactory test for the reason that the two sets of ratings were not made absolutely independently. The P.S.Ws had been given by the psychologist brief notes about some of the boys' performance at school to help them in establishing rapport with the mothers. Hence their judgements about conduct disorder could have been influenced by this, and although they considered any substantial bias of this sort unlikely, a quite small leakage could have produced a spurious statistical effect. For the same reason, the significant negative association between good intelligence (Matrices I.Q.) and Conduct Disorder ($r = -\cdot 12$) could not be used as evidence of validity. On the other hand, other psychological measures, on which the psychologist kept the scores to himself, could be used in this way. In particular the boys' psychomotor test results, which have a presumptive connection with behavioural disturbance, were found to correlate positively and significantly with the P.S.Ws' conduct disorder ratings (see Appendix VI (A) p. 197). The use of such comparisons does not imply that the psychological measures are necessarily more valid or effective descriptions of the boys than the interview ratings, but observations obtained by separate and independent techniques, if they agree, lend to each other mutual support.

In the main body of the Report, the chief measure of conduct disturbance was a five point scale combining the assessments of both teachers and

APPENDIX III (A)

P.S.Ws (see p. 42), which presumably afforded a more objective rating than either set of judgements taken separately. Table III A (1) shows how the points were allocated according to a boy's position on the two component scales:

TABLE III A (1)
Derivation of the Combined Scale of Boys' Conduct.
Relationship between Teachers' ratings of bad behaviour and P.S.Ws' ratings of Conduct Disorder

		Conduct Disorder rated by P.S.Ws:			
		Absent	Moderate	Severe	Not rated
Teachers' Ratings of conduct in class	Bad	(iii) 40	(iv) 22	(v) 30	(iv) 8
	Average	(ii) 153	(iii) 33	(iv) 23	(iii) 17
	Good	(i) 69	(ii) 7	(iii) 7	(ii) 2

(Figures in Roman numerals show the weightings which were allocated in forming a combined scale.)

NOTE

[1] Except where otherwise specified the correlations used in this report are product moment correlations, and the numbers involved are usually sufficient for any correlation higher than ± 0.1 to be statistically significant at the 5 per cent level.

APPENDIX III (B)

A New Test of Neuroticism-Extraversion

This personality inventory, presented as a card-sort test, consisted of forty-two cards in all, one-third of them being 'buffer' items, that is, items which bore no special emotional content. Besides making the task appear more like an ordinary reading test, the buffer items also provided some indication of whether the boy was responding meaningfully. Thus, if a card bore the legend 'He has red hair', accompanied by a picture of a red-headed boy, and the testee had hair of another colour, he would be expected to put it into the box labelled 'Not the same'. If he did not, the psychologist pointed out the error. By this means it was possible to see if the boy had grasped the principle of the test, and was following it correctly.

There are two main reasons why tests of this nature may be invalid in certain cases. First, the subject may guess the general purpose of the test, and not wish to give truthful answers. There is little that can be done about this. There was no lie scale for the identification of test-fakers incorporated in the present questionnaire. A second reason for invalid responses is that the subject may have difficulty in understanding many of the items, or may be unable to follow even the simplest instructions, in which case he tends to answer more or less at random. As explained above, when administering this test, the psychologist had some means of knowing if a boy constantly disregarded the test instruction. He noted that a substantial minority of the boys were answering largely at random. Usually these were boys of low verbal intelligence and reading ability. Because so many of the illiterates gave invalid responses on this test, the scores of any boy with a test quotient on either reading or verbal comprehension below 76 had to be excluded. A few Cypriots, whose English was too poor, were also discounted, and, for various reasons, some of the boys in the oldest pilot group could not be given the test at the time. Altogether 27 per cent of the sample had to be eliminated, so the self-reporting technique of personality assessment at this age was not entirely successful.

In order to assess the value of the responses to this *ad hoc* test, it was decided to intercorrelate all the items (excluding the buffer items) and to extract the principal components. A technical description of this analysis has been published elsewhere (Gibson, 1965). The test had been introduced as a measure of maladjustment. The results revealed two components which were largely independent of each other. According to the nature of the clusters of items which composed them, these components seemed to correspond to 'neuroticism' and 'extraversion' and the scoring scales derived from them have been so referred to in this Report.

Unfortunately, these traits may not be very stable or open to reliable assessment at this age. Of the boys who took this new test at age 8 to 9, 296 were also given the standard N.J.M.I. at age 11. The tetrachoric correlation between the 'neuroticism' scores on the two tests was quite low, only ·30, and between the 'extraversion' scores very slight, only ·09. The extraversion scores tended to identify the same boys on both occasions only in the case of individuals whose scores in this direction were fairly extreme when they were first tested. These disappointingly slight associations between two apparently similar measures serve to illustrate the instability of personality traits over time, as well as the difficulty of obtaining reliable assessments in the case of young and verbally unsophisticated subjects.

APPENDIX III (C)

Communication Difficulties in Interview Assessments of Nervous Disturbance in Boys

The P.S.Ws succeeded in arriving at a rating on the nervous condition of 382 of the boys, 10·7 per cent of whom they considered 'severely nervous', 13·3 per cent 'moderately nervous', 45·2 per cent with minimal disturbance and 51·6 per cent 'symptom free'. Unfortunately, the likelihood of a boy being rated 'nervous' was found to be in part a function of the degree of contact with a family. This was perhaps inevitable, since the P.S.Ws had to decide upon the significance of descriptions of symptoms provided by mothers of varying intelligence, perceptiveness and communicativeness. This resulted in the kind of effect illustrated in Table III C (1), which shows that, where parents could be interviewed separately, the likelihood of a boy being rated 'nervous' was increased accordingly. The proportion of cases in which parents were seen separately increases steadily as one progresses from the 'symptom free' to the most severely disturbed group.

TABLE III C (1)
P.S.Ws' Nervous Disturbance Ratings against Parents Interviewed Separately

Nervousness Rating	(1) Total boys in rating category	(2) Number of boys whose parents were seen separately	(3) Column (2) as a percentage of Column (1)
Symptom free	197	65	34·0
Minimal	93	42	45·2
Moderate	51	24	47·1
Severely nervous	41	21	51·2

The P.S.Ws recorded a rough impressionistic judgement as to which mothers seemed of bright intelligence and which seemed dull. As can be seen from Table III C (2), P.S.Ws A and B, who rated most of the sample, differed little in the overall proportion of nervous boys, but P.S.W. B had a singular reluctance to label as 'nervous' any boys whose mothers she considered dull. In marked contrast, P.S.W. C found almost a half of the boys of dull mothers to be 'nervous'. P.S.W. B must have been using the rating 'dull mother' or 'nervous boy' differently from her colleagues.

TABLE III C (2)
Incidence of Nervous Boys against P.S.Ws' Impression of Mothers' Intelligence

	Nervous Disturbance in Boys	Bright No.	Bright %	Average No.	Average %	Dull No.	Dull %
Rated by P.S.W. A	Nil or Minimal	35	81	77	75	14	78
	Moderate or Severe	8	19	26	25	4	22
	Total Rated	43	100	103	100	18	100
Rated by P.S.W. B	Nil or Minimal	30	70	69	73	27	96
	Moderate or Severe	13	30	26	27	1	4
	Total Rated	43	100	95	100	28	100
Rated by P.S.W. C	Nil or Minimal	8	73	18	82	8	53
	Moderate or Severe	3	27	4	18	7	47
	Total Rated	11	100	22	100	15	100

The measured ability of a boy probably gives a more valid clue to the intellectual level of a household than does an impressionistic judgement about his mother. It is interesting, therefore, to see from Table III C (3) that although, as one might expect on common-sense grounds, there was a relatively larger percentage of severely nervous boys among the poorer readers, there were also, and contrary to expectation, relatively larger proportions of minimally and moderately nervous boys among the better readers. It was in the less severe cases that the over-reporting of the intelligent and communicative families, and the under-reporting of the duller families, led to a difference in incidence of nervous symptoms that was almost certainly spurious.

TABLE III C (3)
P.S.Ws' Ratings of Nervous Disturbance in Boys against Boys' Reading Ability

Rating on Nervous Disturbance	Below 86 No.	Below 86 %	Above 105 No.	Above 105 %
No symptoms	100	53·5	32	47·8
Minimal	36	19·3	20	29·9
Moderate	24	12·8	12	17·9
Severe	27	14·4	3	4·5
TOTAL	187	100	67	100

A rating of 'severe' nervous disturbance might be expected to be more meaningful, and less dependent upon reporting bias than lesser degrees of disturbance, yet even here unexpected and anomalous findings emerged. For example, as can be seen from Table III C (4), very few boys from large families, and few who were youngest children, were rated as having a severe degree of nervous disturbance.

TABLE III C (4)

Incidence of Severe Nervous Disturbance of Boys in relation to some background Variables

Variable		Total 382 boys rated on 'nervousness'	Per cent rated 'severe nervous' disturbance	Level of p[1] of the difference
Family size	6 or more children	61	4·9	<·001
	Less than 6 children	321	11·8	
Ordinal position in family	Youngest	104	4·8	<·01
	Between	148	9·5	
	Eldest or only child	130	16·9	

[1] Values of p are based on χ^2 comparisons of the raw data.

These odd relationships are much more plausibly explained as a reflection of communication difficulties than as a genuinely reduced incidence of nervousness among youngest children or among the boys of large families. The low reporting of nervousness in large families might be due to the uncommunicativeness of busy, overburdened mothers. The reduced incidence of reported nervousness in youngest children might be due to their mothers being older and relatively more experienced in child-rearing, and hence less prone to dwell upon disturbances of little significance. This was confirmed by the observation that 19·0 per cent of the forty-two boys whose mothers fell into the youngest age category in the Study sample were rated 'severely nervous' compared with only 9·9 per cent of the remaining boys.

Clearly the difficulty of judging the significance of complicated descriptions given by mothers (and sometimes by fathers) of varying intelligence, perceptiveness and communicativeness had led to an uneven coverage of the sample. But apart from this, there was also some evidence of differences between the P.S.Ws in their interpretations of nervous disturbance. Whereas the nervous disturbance ratings produced by P.S.Ws B and C correlated positively and significantly with the psychological test scores of neuroticism. Both at age 8 and on re-test with the new form (Furneaux and Gibson, 1966) at age 11 ratings of P.S.W. A tended to go in the opposite direction, that is her 'nervous' boys were below average rather than above average on neuroticism. It would appear that P.S.W. A tended to rate as nervous a different type of boy from that described as nervous by the other two P.S.Ws.

Many penal administrators have to make decisions, and many investigators reach conclusions, on the basis of interview impressions much less carefully considered than the ones used in this Study. The complications experienced with these ratings are of some general interest, since they suggest the need for much greater caution than is at present customary in using interview impressions for purposes of social administration and research.

APPENDIX IV (A)

P.S.W. Assessments of Boy Physically Neglected

TABLE IV A (1)
Correlations between P.S.Ws' Ratings of Boy Physically Neglected with certain other Variables of Adversity

Calculations made separately for three sub-divisions of the sample according to which P.S.W. made the assessment

	Boys rated physically neglected by:		
	P.S.W. A r_{tet}	P.S.W. B r_{tet}	P.S.W. C r_{tet}
Housing very unsatisfactory	·74	·53	·71
Accommodation very neglected	·95	·88	·85
Income inadequate	·77	·63	·88
Large family (6 or more children)	·74	·77	·93
Disharmonious marriage	·82	·54	·76
Parents lax in rules	·84	·92	·87
Parents uninterested in boy's education	·77	·53	·68
Father has poor work record	·69	·63	·55
Mother has unstable personality	·66	·69	·87
Boy's conduct in class rated poor by teacher	·61	·64	·44
Parents 'under-vigilant'	·50	·73	·84
Low I.Q. on Matrices	·24	·48	·06
Bad Porteus Q score	·21	·54	·41
Unhealthy child	·26	·29	·45

For P.S.Ws A and B all coefficients > ·50 are significant at the ·01 level or beyond. For P.S.W. C the number rated as physically neglected was only seven, so probability levels have not been calculated.

APPENDIX IV (B)

Parental Behaviour worse at lower Socio-Economic Level

TABLE IV B (1)
Association between Parental Child-Rearing Methods and Inadequate Income

Parental Rating		No. of boys rated	Per cent rated as having inadequate income	Significance[1] of difference
Physical neglect	Absent	342	16·7	p < ·001
	Present	49	67·3	
Interest in Education	Interested	315	16·5	p < ·001
	Uninterested	62	54·8	
Inconsistency	Absent	258	15·9	p < ·001
	Present	99	34·3	
Under-vigilance	Absent	336	19·6	p < ·001
	Present	42	47·6	
Rules	Not lax	306	15·4	p < ·001
	Lax	66	53·0	
Praise of boy	Praised	326	21·2	p < ·05
	Not praised	43	34·9	

[1] Significance based on χ^2 comparison of the raw figures.

APPENDIX IV (C)

Illustrations of Relationships Varying with Social Level

FIG. IV C (1)
Relationships between Parental Vigilance and Mean Reading Quotient of Boys, in three sub-samples of Different Income Level

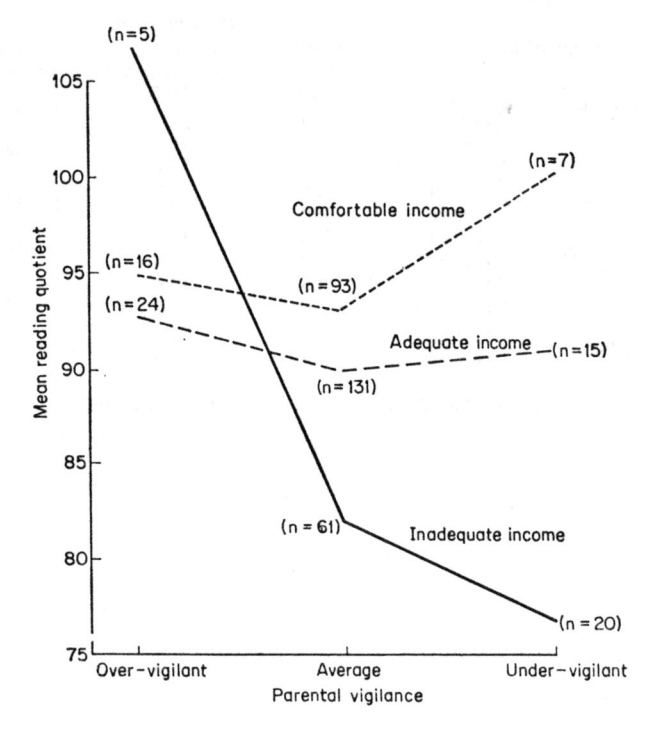

Among the comfortable and adequate income groups, which represent the bulk of the sample, there is no tendency for the boys of under-vigilant parents to be backward readers. In the sub-sample of boys of inadequate income families there is a statistically significant tendency for boys with under-vigilant parents to have reading quotients below eighty-six.

$$(\chi^2 = 9.60 \text{ with 2 d.f., } p < .01)$$

FIG. IV C (2)
Relationships between Parental Interest in Education and Mean Reading Quotients in Boys, in three sub-samples of Different Income Level

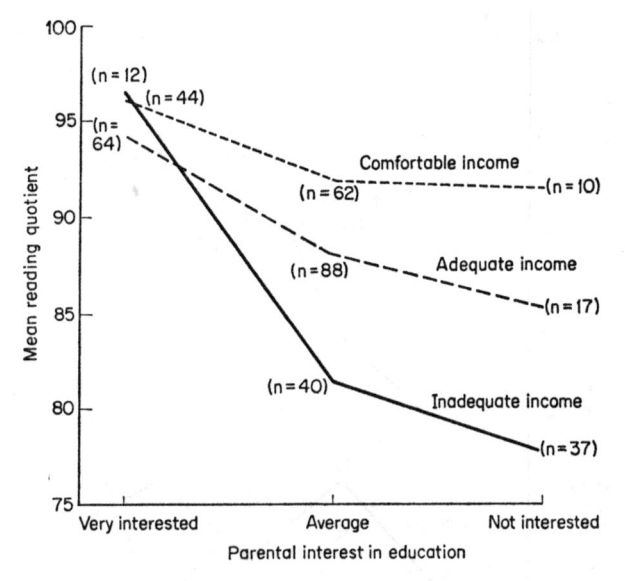

The only statistically significant relationship between parental interest in education and boys' reading ability was in the sub-group of inadequate income.

FIG. IV C (3)
Parents Uninterested in Boy's Education against Boy's Conduct at three Levels of Income

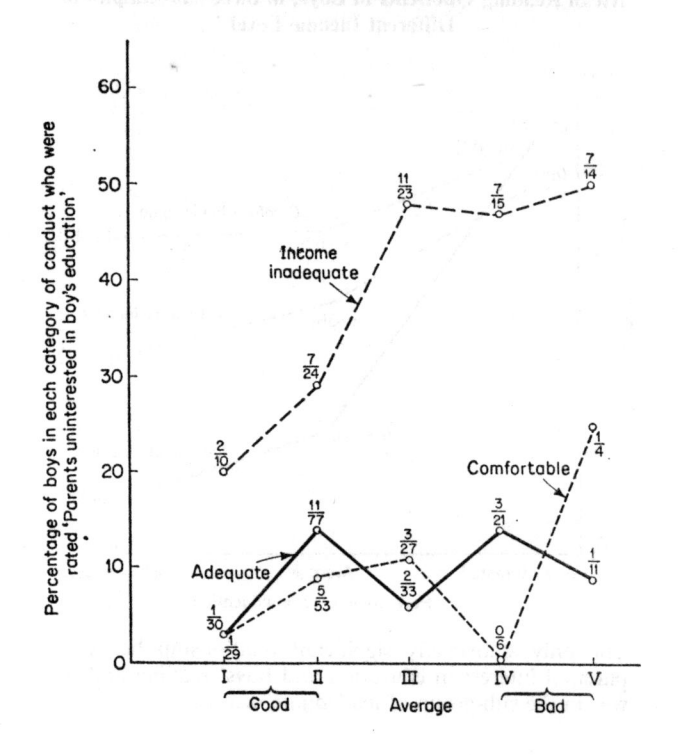

Boys' conduct (ratings by teachers and P.S.Ws. combined)

APPENDIX IV (D)

Categories of Parental Behaviour associated with differing incidences of Troublesome Boys according to the Social Level of the Family

TABLE IV D (1)
Acting Out Tendency in Boys related to Parental Attitude and Discipline at three Levels of Family Income

Family Background Variable:		Comfortable No. Rated	% rated Acting-Out	Adequate No. Rated	% rated Acting-Out	Inadequate No. Rated	% rated Acting-Out
Paternal attitude	Loving normal	70	7·1	96	13·5 ⎫	55	38·2
	Loving anxious or over-protective	34	14·7	61	21·3 ⎬ *	19	21·1
	Cruel passive or neglecting	15	13·3	14	42·9 ⎭	13	46·2
Maternal attitude	Warm	103	9·7	139	15·8	42	35·7
	Not warm (i.e. passive, cruel, neglecting)	15	13·3	23	30·4	30	43·3
	Absent or dead	—	—	8	12·5	16	18·8
Paternal discipline	Normal	73	4·1 ⎫ †	72	12·5 ⎫ †	31	29·0
	Erratic	25	24·0 ⎭	52	32·7 ⎭	35	45·7
	Lax	1	—	7	28·6	8	37·5
	Strict or very strict	19	10·5	37	10·8	13	23·1
Maternal discipline	Normal	59	5·1 ⎫ *	90	13·3	27	33·3
	Lax	14	35·7 ⎭	16	25·0	11	63·6
	Erratic	13	7·7	21	28·6	22	36·4
	Strict or very strict	32	9·4	39	15·4	15	20·0

Significance levels of the difference in incidence of 'acting-out' are based upon comparisons of the raw figures by the χ^2 test

* $p < ·01$
† $p < ·02$

APPENDIX IV (E)

Development of the Parental Attitude Inventories

According to psychological literature, excessively authoritarian parents, characterized by rigidly disciplinarian attitudes and over-strict control, tend to produce children who are altogether too passive, conventional and rule-bound, whereas a more democratic approach produces better adjusted personalities (Baldwin, 1948). Likewise, maternal under-concern or rejection has been identified with aggressive, undisciplined and delinquent children, whereas, at the opposite extreme, maternal over-concern or over-protective 'smothering' has been held to lead to timid, withdrawn, neurotic children (Hewitt and Jenkins, 1946).

These concepts had their origins in clinical impressions based upon pathologically extreme cases, but the existence of the two fundamental dimensions of parental attitude has been validated by more recent questionnaire studies of normal populations (Schaefer and Bell, 1958). In particular, computer analyses, intercorrelating the responses to every item, and identifying meaningful clusters or patterns of response by means of factor or principal component analyses, have shown that the two factors authoritarianism-permissiveness and over-concern under-concern do appear to represent major and universal components of parental attitudes.

For the purpose of this Study, H. B. Gibson constructed a new attitude inventory. Items were taken from the questionnaires used by A. N. Oppenheim in some unpublished work in 1956, and by Shoben (1949). The wording of the items was shortened and simplified to suit the kind of population being dealt with. Further items were devised with the help of the P.S.Ws, who were able to quote expressions actually used by parents in the district when discussing their boys.

In a pilot survey, four separate versions of the draft inventory were prepared, two for fathers, and two for mothers. Approximately one hundred of each of these forms were completed by parents not belonging to the main Study. The four forms were analysed separately by the method of principal components, and on the basis of the results items were selected for inclusion in the two final versions of the form. Each of the items chosen had a high loading on the components representing 'authoritarianism' or, in the case of the maternal form, 'under-concern'. Items on which more than 95 per cent of the respondents all either agreed or disagreed were excluded.

In the first instance, the inventories were dispatched to the parents (that is to say to all of the parents except a small minority of adamantly unco-operative individuals) by post, together with an accompanying letter asking both mother and father to complete their own form, and enclosing a stamped addressed envelope. Because of the very slow rate of return by these forms, a principal component analysis was undertaken when only 188 of the mothers' forms and 173 of the fathers' forms had been received. This analysis again revealed satisfactory components identified as representing authoritarianism-permissiveness and under-concern over-concern. A scoring system was devised using those items which had the highest loadings on these components.[1] This scoring system was then applied to all the forms that were eventually received by April, 1966. Further details of the development of this questionnaire are to be found in a paper by H. B. Gibson (1968).

The final versions of the inventories, as used in the present Study, are shown below:

Parental Attitude Inventories used for Mothers and Fathers respectively

(1) MOTHER'S FORM

Please read each item and: if you agree put a ring round (Agree)

or if you *don't* agree put a ring round (Disagree)

Don't miss any please: your opinion is wanted on *all* these questions.

1. You must expect a real boy to get into fights ...... Agree Disagree
2. Parents should decide the sort of work their children are to do .... Agree Disagree
3. A mother needs to get right away from her children sometimes .... Agree Disagree
4. Bedwetting cannot be cured by punishing the child Agree Disagree
5. Small children must learn to do without their mothers sometimes .... Agree Disagree
6. If a boy has got a bit of spirit he *won't* always do as you say .... Agree Disagree
7. It is most important for a mother to see who her boy plays with .... Agree Disagree
8. It is not right to worry children at home about their school lessons.. Agree Disagree
9. Too much mothering will make a boy a 'softie' ... Agree Disagree
10. Troublesome teenagers often come from harsh homes .... Agree Disagree
11. 'Mother knows best', is still true today .... Agree Disagree
12. It doesn't matter if boys get to know about sex when they are little .... Agree Disagree
13. No child is really bad if you take enough trouble with him .... Agree Disagree
14. Keep boys down young and they won't get into trouble later .... Agree Disagree
15. It's the *school's* job to teach the child—not the parents' .... Agree Disagree

16. There is no harm in boys playing with dolls or at girlish games .... Agree Disagree
17. Parents should not let their children take up all their time.. Agree Disagree
18. Boys should fight their own battles and not run to mother... Agree Disagree
19. We needn't expect our children to look after us when we are old.. Agree Disagree
20. Children should have a fixed bed-time and never sit up later .... Agree Disagree
21. School dinners make a welcome break for mother Agree Disagree
22. There should be more discipline in schools today Agree Disagree
23. A child should never keep a secret from his mother Agree Disagree
24. There's little thanks or pleasure in bringing up children .... Agree Disagree
25. Children will respect you more if they are a bit afraid sometimes .... Agree Disagree
26. It's sad to see boys grow up because then they don't seem to need you .... Agree Disagree
27. Though he *says* he's poorly at schooltime he should go just the same... Agree Disagree
28. Mothers must learn to mind their own business when a boy is growing up .... Agree Disagree
29. Strict discipline develops a good strong character in children .... Agree Disagree
30. Sometimes children are more of a nuisance than a blessing .... Agree Disagree
31. A mother must always know just what her children are doing... Agree Disagree
32. If there's trouble at school, mothers should *always* see the teacher .... Agree Disagree
33. Old-fashioned parents were far too strict .... Agree Disagree

(2) FATHER'S FORM

Please read each item and: if you agree put a ring round (Agree)

or if you *don't* agree put a ring round (Disagree)

Don't miss any please: your opinion is wanted on *all* these questions.

1. Older boys and girls should be taught together at school .... Agree Disagree
2. Punishing a boy is *father's* job........................... Agree Disagree
3. Children have a right to choose their own jobs ... Agree Disagree
4. The 11+ exam in schools is not fair to many children .... Agree Disagree

5. Boys should just do as they are told without any argument .... Agree Disagree
6. Immunization against polio should be compulsory   Agree Disagree
7. Strict discipline develops a good strong character in children .... Agree Disagree
8. It doesn't matter if boys sit up a bit late sometimes watching TV .... Agree Disagree
9. Old-fashioned parents were far too strict .... Agree Disagree
10. Children should be able to leave school before the age of 15 .... Agree Disagree
11. You should never make a child afraid of you ...... Agree Disagree
12. Troublesome teenagers often have parents who were too soft .... Agree Disagree
13. Caning in schools should be abolished .... Agree Disagree
14. It's better for a boy to be obedient than clever ...... Agree Disagree
15. Flats and housing estates should all have special playgrounds .... Agree Disagree
16. Most mothers nag at their children too much ...... Agree Disagree
17. There is no harm in boys playing with dolls or at girlish games .... Agree Disagree
18. You won't get children to obey unless you can tell them why .... Agree Disagree
19. Most boys need a good hiding sometimes .... Agree Disagree
20. In a good home *father's* word is law .... Agree Disagree
21. *Women* schoolteachers are just as good for boys as men are .... Agree Disagree
22. The saying 'Children should be seen and not heard', is just silly .... Agree Disagree
23. If parents stand no nonsense, bedwetting can soon be cured .... Agree Disagree
24. Children should have a fixed bedtime and never stay up later .... Agree Disagree
25. The discipline of the army is a fine training for boys .... Agree Disagree
26. Children get more freedom nowadays, and a good thing too .... Agree Disagree
27. More public money should be spent on providing children's playgrounds .... Agree Disagree
28. Boys grow up without spirit if they're kept down young .... Agree Disagree
29. There should be more discipline in schools today ... Agree Disagree
30. Children won't work at school unless you keep on at them .... Agree Disagree
31. Children learn to behave best if their parents are patient with them .... Agree Disagree
32. Mothers are generally too soft with their sons ...... Agree Disagree
33. Children who are made to obey will thank their parents later .... Agree Disagree

TABLE IV E (1)
Numbers of Completed Parental Attitude Inventories against Socio-Educational Status of Mother

Mother's socio-educational status[a]		Total Boys	Maternal Inventories Returned No.	%	Paternal Inventories Returned No.	%
High	1	64	57	89·1	49	76·6
	2	118	92	78·0	78	66·1
	3	40	31	77·5	27	67·5
	4	54	36	66·6	26	48·1
Low	5	135	75	54·8	52	38·5
	TOTAL	411	291	70·8	232	57·7

For the maternal inventory: $\chi^2 = 33·1$ with 4 d.f. $p < ·001$

For the paternal inventory: $\chi^2 = 36·2$ with 4 d.f. $p < ·001$

TABLE IV E (2)
Questionnaire Scores of Maternal Authoritarianism against P.S.W. Ratings of Maternal Discipline

Questionnaire Score on Maternal Authoritarianism	Normal No.	%	Erratic No.	%	Strict or very strict No.	%	Total
Low	31	67·3	14	41·1	11	44·0	56
High	15	32·7	20	58·9	14	56·0	49
TOTAL	46	100	34	100	25	100	105

$\chi^2 = 6·53$ with 2 d.f. $p < ·05$

TABLE IV E (3)
Questionnaire Scores of Maternal Over-concern and Under-concern against P.S.W. Ratings of Maternal Attitude, Quality of Discipline and Vigilance

P.S.W. Ratings of Mother:	Maternal Attitude by Questionnaire: Very over-concerned (score ≤ 6)	Very under-concerned (score ≥ 11)	Total
Mother Cruel, Neglecting harsh or disinterested	5	10	15
All other categories of mother	32	29	61
Mother over-vigilant but not cruel, etc.	11	4	15
TOTAL	48	43	91

$\chi^2 = 4·81$ with 2 d.f. $p < ·10$

APPENDIX IV (E)

TABLE IV E (4)
Questionnaire Scores of Fathers' Authoritarianism against P.S.W. Ratings of Fathers' Discipline

	Inventory Scores on Father's Authoritarianism:			
P.S.W. Rating of Father's Discipline	Low (Score ≤ 6)		High (Score ≥ 13)	
	No.	%	No.	%
Strict or very strict	7	17·5	19	34·5
Other categories	33	82·5	36	65·5
TOTAL	40	100	55	100

The trend towards higher authoritarianism among stricter fathers is in the expected direction, but numbers are too small for statistical significance. ($\chi^2 = 2·59$ with 1 d.f.)

N.B. P.S.W. ratings on fathers' attitude and quality of discipline had no significant association with inventory scores of fathers' authoritarianism.

NOTES

[1] In the case of the mothers' inventories, the components labelled authoritarianism and under-concern accounted for 8·4 and 6·8 per cent of the variance respectively, and the items used for scoring had mean loadings of ·42 and ·33 on these two components respectively. In the case of the fathers' inventories, the major component, representing 10·4 per cent of the variance, appeared to correspond to authoritarianism, and the twenty items used in scoring had a mean loading of ·38 on this component. There was no significant association between the scale of maternal under-concern and authoritarianism on either the maternal or paternal scales.

[2] This scale was based upon a questionnaire given by the social workers to the mothers in the Study during 1965, supplemented by previous records. It combined mother's social class on the Registrar General's Scale (according to the highest status employment she had ever had) with a question about whether she has had any education or training after the statutory earliest age for leaving school.

APPENDIX IV (F)

The Health Questionnaire

(A Modified and Shortened Version of the Cornell Medical Index)
The form of the health questionnaire given to mothers in this Study is shown below:

HEALTH QUESTIONNAIRE FOR MOTHERS

If you can answer YES to the question asked, put a circle round the
(YES)
If you have to answer NO to the question asked, put a circle round the (NO)
Please answer *all* the questions.

1. Do you need glasses to read? .... Yes No
2. Do your eyes continually blink or water? .... Yes No
3. Do you often have bad pains in your eyes? .... Yes No
4. Are your eyes often red or inflamed? .... Yes No
5. Do you have to clear your throat frequently? .... Yes No
6. Do you often feel a choking lump in your throat? .... Yes No
7. Is your nose continually stuffed up? .... Yes No
8. Have you at times had bad nose bleeds? .... Yes No
9. Do you often catch severe colds? .... Yes No
10. Do you frequently suffer from heavy chest colds? .... Yes No
11. Do frequent colds keep you miserable all winter? .... Yes No
12. Do you get hay fever? .... Yes No
13. Do you sometimes have severe soaking sweats at night?... Yes No
14. Do you have pains in the heart or chest? .... Yes No
15. Are you often bothered by thumping of the heart? .... Yes No
16. Does your heart often race like mad? .... Yes No
17. Do you often have difficulty in breathing? .... Yes No
18. Do you get out of breath long before anyone else? ...... Yes No
19. Do you sometimes get out of breath just sitting still?... Yes No
20. Are your ankles often badly swollen? .... Yes No
21. Do cold hands or feet trouble you even in hot weather? ... Yes No
22. Do you suffer from frequent cramps in your legs? ...... Yes No
23. Does heart trouble run in your family? .... Yes No
24. Are you troubled by bleeding gums? .... Yes No
25. Have you often had severe toothaches? .... Yes No
26. Is your tongue usually badly coated? .... Yes No
27. Is your appetite always poor? .... Yes No
28. Do you usually eat sweets or other food between meals? Yes No
29. Do you always gulp your food in a hurry? .... Yes No

30. Do you often suffer from an upset stomach? .... Yes No
31. Do you usually feel bloated after eating? .... Yes No
32. Do you usually belch a lot after eating? .... Yes No
33. Are you often sick in your stomach? .... Yes No
34. Do you suffer from indigestion? .... Yes No
35. Do you constantly suffer from bad constipation? .... Yes No
36. Have you ever had piles (rectal haemorrhoids)? .... Yes No
37. Does rheumatism (arthritis) run in your family? .... Yes No
38. Do pains in the back make it hard for you to keep up with your work? .... Yes No
39. Does your face often get badly flushed? .... Yes No
40. Do you sweat a great deal even in cold weather? ...... Yes No
41. Are you often bothered by severe itching? .... Yes No
42. Do you suffer badly from frequent severe headaches? ... Yes No
43. Does pressure or pain in the head often make life miserable? .... Yes No
44. Are headaches common in your family? .... Yes No
45. Do you have hot or cold spells? .... Yes No
46. Do you often have spells of severe dizziness? .... Yes No
47. Do you frequently feel faint? .... Yes No
48. Have you fainted more than twice in your life? .... Yes No
49. Do you have constant numbness or tingling in any part of your body? .... Yes No
50. Have you at times had a twitching of the face, head or shoulders? .... Yes No
51. Have you often felt weak or sick with your periods? ... Yes No
52. Have you often had to lie down when your periods came on? .... Yes No
53. Have you ever had constant severe hot flushes and sweats? Yes No
54. Do you have to get up every night and urinate? .... Yes No
55. During the day, do you usually have to urinate frequently? Yes No
56. Do you often get spells of complete exhaustion or fatigue? Yes No
57. Does working tire you out completely? .... Yes No
58. Do you usually get up tired and exhausted in the morning? Yes No
59. Does every little effort wear you out? .... Yes No
60. Are you constantly too tired and exhausted even to eat? Yes No
61. Do you suffer from severe nervous exhaustion? .... Yes No
62. Are you always in poor health? .... Yes No
63. Does severe pains and aches make it impossible for you to do your work? .... Yes No
64. Do you wear yourself out worrying about your health? ... Yes No
65. Are you always ill and unhappy? .... Yes No
66. Are you constantly made miserable by poor health? ... Yes No
67. Did you ever have scarlet fever? .... Yes No
68. As a child, did you have rheumatic fever or growing pains? Yes No
69. Are you definitely *under* weight? .... Yes No
70. Did a doctor ever say you had varicose veins (swollen veins) in your legs? .... Yes No

71. Did you ever have a serious operation?........................ Yes No
72. Do you usually have great difficulty in falling asleep or
    staying asleep? .... Yes No
73. Do you find it impossible to take a regular rest period each
    day?... Yes No
74. Do you find it impossible to take regular daily exercise?... Yes No
75. Do you drink more than six cups of coffee or tea a day?... Yes No

In the above questionnaire the following item numbers were not used for scoring because pilot work had shown them to be insufficiently discriminative:

8, 12, 24, 25, 28, 32, 35, 36, 67, 70, 75.

In Table IV F (1) and Fig. IV F (1) P.S.W. ratings of 'mothers' nervous tendency' and 'mother has had psychiatric treatment' are matched against the health questionnaire scores. It appears that, of the boys whose mothers gave high scores (i.e. in the top quartile of rank order), 23·5 per cent had 'very nervous' mothers, whereas of those whose mothers produced low scores only 3·5 per cent were judged to have 'very nervous' mothers. Similarly, whereas in 31·4 per cent of the highest scoring group mother had had psychiatric treatment, in the lowest scoring group only 5·3 per cent had had treatment. Furthermore, the percentage with unstable mothers in the highest scoring group was 17·1 per cent compared with only 3·5 per cent in the lowest scoring group. It was noteworthy that among the group who had no questionnaire returned, the percentages with 'nervous', 'treated' and 'unstable' mothers were all significantly higher than in the sample as a whole—a clear indication, once again, that non-response or non-co-operation was associated with a high incidence of abnormality or deviance.

TABLE IV F (1)

Mothers' Neuroticism, according to Health Questionnaire Scores, against Mothers' Nervous Tendency, according to P.S.Ws' Ratings

Mothers' Nervous Tendency as Rated by P.S.Ws:	\multicolumn{8}{c}{Health Questionnaire Scores ranked in (approximate) quartiles:}	Question- naires not completed	Total Boys
	1 (Low)		2		3		4 (High)			
	No.	%	No.	%	No.	%	No.	%	No. %	
Very Nervous	2	3·5	6	7·9	14	18·4	20	28·6	31 23·5	73
Moderately Nervous	8	14·0	28	36·8	31	40·8	29	41·4	32 24·2	128
No symptoms	47	82·4	41	54·0	30	39·5	20	28·6	44 33·3	182
Not rated	—	—	1	1·3	1	1·3	1	1·4	25 18·9	28
TOTAL	57	100	76	100	76	100	70	100	132 100	411

Counting only the cells with both questionnaire and P.S.W. ratings, $\chi^2 = 45.99$ with 6 d.f., $p < .001$.

FIG. IV F (1)

Mothers' Neuroticism, according to Health Questionnaire Scores, against "Mother has had Psychiatric Treatment"

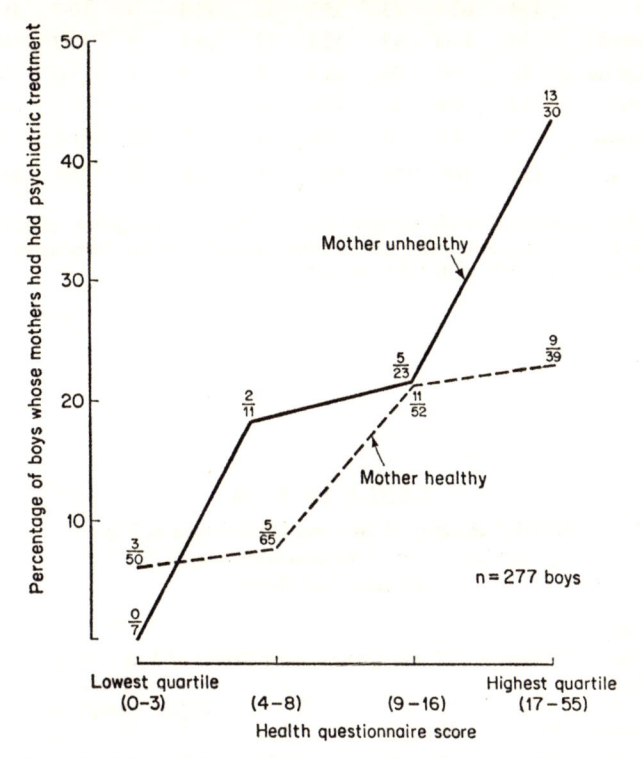

Since the unhealthy mothers start at a disadvantage on this questionnaire (some of their responses being due to organic rather than neurotic complaints) those rated 'unhealthy' by the P.S.Ws are shown separately. The trend is actually stronger in the unhealthy group.

TABLE IV F (2)
P.S.Ws' Ratings of Nervous Disturbance in Boys against P.S.Ws' Ratings of Nervousness in Mothers

P.S.W. Ratings of Nervous Disturbance in Boys:	Nil No.	%	Moderate No.	%	Severe No.	%	Not known or Not applicable No.	%	Total
Nil	114	62·6	45	35·2	35	48·0	3	10·7	197
Minimal	36	19·8	42	32·8	12	16·4	3	10·7	93
Moderate	18	9·9	24	18·8	8	11·0	1	3·6	51
Severe	12	6·6	14	10·9	14	19·2	1	3·6	41
Not rated	2	1·1	3	2·3	4	5·5	20	71·4	29
TOTAL	182	100	128	100	73	100	28	100	411

N.B. Mothers rated severely nervous have the highest proportion of severely nervous boys. Comparing cells representing 'severe' nervous disturbance with the remainder, $\chi^2 = 6·91$ with 1 d.f., $p < ·01$

TABLE IV F (3)
P.S.Ws' Ratings of Nervous Disturbance in Boys against Health Questionnaire Scores of Neuroticism in Mothers

P.S.W. Ratings of Boys' Nervous Disturbance:	1 (Low) No.	%	2 No.	%	3 No.	%	4 (High) No.	%	Form not completed No.	%	Total Boys
Nil	29	50·9	38	50·0	34	44·7	35	50·0	61	46·2	197
Minimal	13	22·8	25	32·9	20	26·3	12	17·1	23	17·4	93
Moderate	8	14·0	7	9·2	12	15·8	13	18·6	11	8·3	51
Severe	7	12·3	5	6·6	9	11·8	9	12·9	11	8·3	41
Not rated	—	—	1	1·3	1	1·3	1	1·4	26	19·7	29
TOTAL	57	100	76	100	76	100	70	100	132	100	411

N.B. The Table shows a very slight trend. Of the boys whose mothers gave scores in the top half of the neuroticism scale 30·0 per cent were rated moderately or severely nervous; whereas only 20·3 per cent of the boys with mothers in the lower half of the neuroticism scale were so rated.

TABLE IV F (4)
Neuroticism of Mother, assessed by Health Questionnaire Scores against Boy's Conduct, on the Ratings of P.S.Ws and Teachers combined

Boy's Conduct Category:		1 (Low) No.	%	2 No.	%	3 No.	%	4 (High) No.	%	No form completed No.	%	Total
Good	(I or II)	46	80·7	54	71·1	41	53·9	30	42·9	60	45·4	231
Average	(III)	5	8·8	11	14·5	24	31·6	19	27·2	38	28·8	97
Bad	(IV or V)	6	10·6	11	14·5	11	14·5	21	30·0	34	25·8	83
TOTAL		57	100	76	100	76	100	70	100	132	100	411

Counting the cells representing completed health questionnaires, $\chi^2 = 28·67$ with 6 d.f. $p < ·001$. The tendency for a higher percentage of badly behaved boys to be associated with high maternal neuroticism scores held true at all three levels of social handicap.

APPENDIX V (A)

The Effect of Age and Generation on Paternal Conviction Rate

TABLE V A (1)
Variation in Proportion of Boys with a Convicted Father according to Father's Date of Birth

No. of Boys with Father:	Born before 1915	Born 1915–1929	Born After 1929
Not convicted	60 (75·9%)	229 (82·4%)	28 (66·7%)
Convicted, but not more than once as an adult	12 (15·2%)	29 (10·4%)	11 (26·2%)
Convicted more than once as an adult	7 (8·9%)	20 (7·2%)	3 (7·1%)
TOTAL	79 (100%)	278 (100%)	42 (100%)

(Not known or not applicable in 12 cases)

Comparing frequencies of all categories: $\chi^2 = 8·75$ with 4 d.f. (N.S.).

Comparing no conviction/any conviction: $\chi^2 = 6·31$ with 2 d.f., $p < ·05$.

APPENDIX V (B)

Low Intelligence Correlated with Poor Conduct at all Social Levels

The association between Matrices I.Q. and the combined ratings of boys' conduct was statistically highly significant. The four points of the Matrices scale tabulated against the five points of the conduct scale made a 20 cell contingency table yielding a x^2 of 38·4 with 12 d.f., $p < ·001$. Contingency coefficient = 0·3. The relationships within each social level are illustrated in Fig. V B (1).

FIG. V B (1)

Boys' Intelligence Below Average (i.e. Matrices I.Q. −100 N=193) against Combined Ratings of Conduct at three Levels of Social Handicap

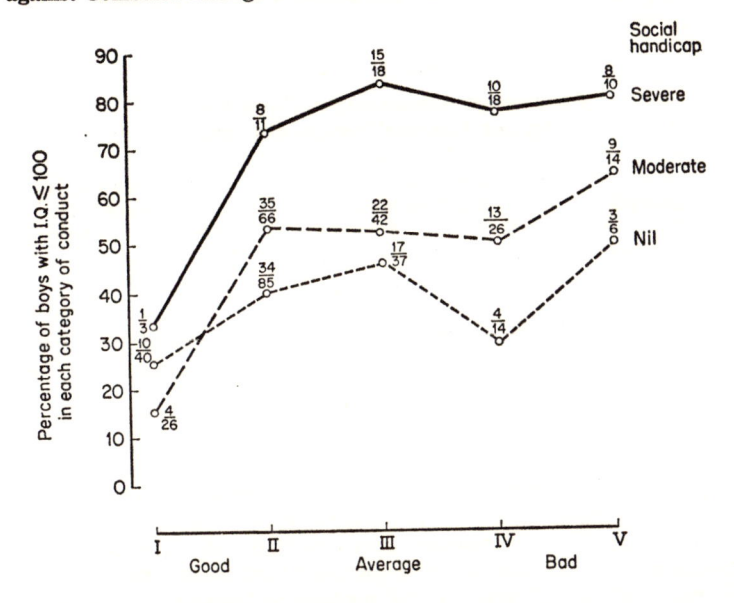

Boys' conduct (combined ratings of P.S.Ws. and teachers)

APPENDIX V (C)

Anomalous Relationships between Conduct and Birth History According to Birth Order and Social Level

As can be seen from Table V C (1), in the case of the later-born sample, the proportion of badly behaved boys was higher among those who had had abnormal confinements. This trend, though slight, and not amounting to statistical significance, was nevertheless in conformity with expectation on the brain damage hypothesis. In the sub-sample of first-born boys, however, the trend was just the reverse, and against expectation.

TABLE V C (1)
Confinement Abnormality in Hospital Births Against Teachers' Ratings of Conduct

Teachers' Rating of Conduct	Confinements of 125 first-born boys				Confinements of 146 later-born boys			
	Normal		Abnormal		Normal		Abnormal	
	No.	%	No.	%	No.	%	No.	%
Good	11	16·7	18	30·5	21	21·7	8	16·3
Average	38	57·6	32	54·2	56	57·7	23	46·9
Bad	17	25·7	9	15·3	20	20·6	18	36·8
TOTAL	66	100	59	100	97	100	49	100

A clue to the probable explanation of this anomaly was discovered by dividing the sample of hospital births according to whether the boys were from 'adequate' or 'inadequate' social backgrounds. The criterion of 'inadequate' was a combination of low social class membership (Registrar General's III M, IV and V) and inadequate housing conditions. (Of course this was only very rough, since the ratings had been made when the boys were aged 9 rather than at birth.) The obstetric histories of the socially adequate and inadequate groups were significantly different in several respects. For example, among the socially adequate, the first-borns had a significantly higher incidence of abnormality of confinement, but this was not true of the socially inadequate group. (See Table V C (2)).

TABLE V C (2)
Social Circumstances, Birth Order and Abnormality of Confinement in Hospital Births

Confinement	Boys from socially 'adequate' background				Boys from socially 'inadequate' background			
	First-born		All others		First-born		All others	
	No.	%	No.	%	No.	%	No.	%
Normal	29	44·6	53	73·6	37	61·6	44	59·5
Abnormal	36	55·4	19	26·4	23	38·4	30	40·5
Total	65	100	72	100	60	100	74	100

$\chi^2 = 10.79$ with 1 d.f., $p < .01$ χ^2 insignificant

The same feature was found in regard to abnormalities of pregnancy, which were fewer in later-born than first-born boys in the socially adequate and sub-sample, but, if anything, more frequent in the later-born boys of the socially inadequate group.

The Figure V (C) 1, p. 194, relates the three variables, birth order, teachers' conduct rating and percentage of confinement abnormality in the two sub-samples of socially adequate and socially inadequate backgrounds.

The numbers are too small for statistical tests of significance level, but a suggestive pattern can be seen. In both sub-samples, but particularly in the sub-sample of inadequate social background, the percentages of abnormal confinement histories, in the case of the later-born children, increases with the teachers' conduct rating from good, through average to bad which is just as it should be on the brain damage theory. However, among first-born boys, the order is reversed, and the worst behaved boys have the fewest obstetric abnormalities. The explanation of this anomaly may possibly lie in the selective admission to hospital for childbirths.

Suppose, hypothetically, that mothers of first-born children usually elect to have their babies in hospital, because that is accepted custom, but that a certain minority from good homes elect to have their babies outside unless there is some medical reason to anticipate a difficult confinement. Suppose further that nearly all women from inadequate social backgrounds have their first baby in hospital because they have little choice; what would be the effect? The hospital population would be weighted by a group of socially inadequate mothers of normal obstetric history likely to produce badly-behaved boys because of the nature of their background, and another group of mothers from favoured backgrounds, but with obstetric complications, who might nevertheless be expected to bring up well-behaved boys. The net result might well be (as here observed) a reversal of the expected association between bad confinement and subsequent bad behaviour. But why should the same considerations cease to apply to later-born boys? Suppose that mothers from socially inadequate backgrounds run greater risk of obstetric abnormalities in connection with their later-born children,[1] and are also much more likely to have their later-born children in hospital (and there is evidence to support both these statements from the present data), the net result would be a clustering together of bad conduct and obstetric complications in this segment of the sample, which is what was actually observed.

FIG. V C (1)
Percentage of Abnormal Births among Boys born in Hospital

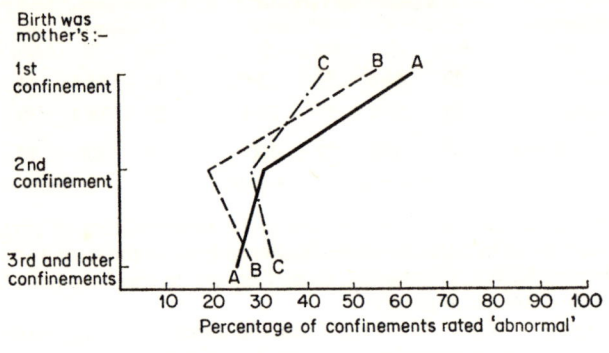

(a) Sample from adequate social background

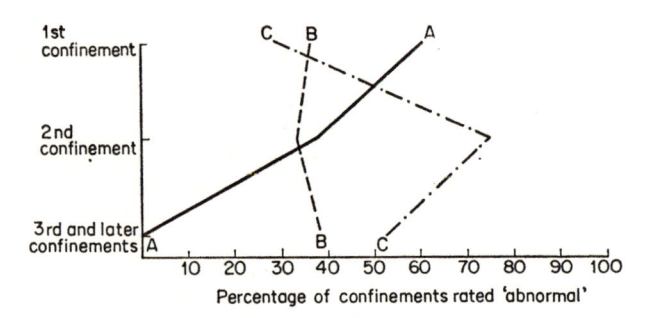

(b) Sample from inadequate social background

Subdivided into first-born, second-born or later-born children, and also grouped according to teachers' ratings of conduct, i.e. A good, B average, C bad. The samples from adequate and inadequate social backgrounds analysed separately.

This *ad hoc* explanation is not put forward as a serious, definitive interpretation of the data, but merely by way of illustration of possible reasons for the somewhat anomalous results obtained. It is less important to arrive at an exact interpretation than to see how selection processes and intervening variables may produce non-causal correlations, or may even mask a genuine relationship.

NOTE

[1] See Table V C (2), above

APPENDIX VI (A)

Correlational Analysis

APPENDIX VI (A) Correlational Analysis

TABLE VI A (1) Intercorrelational Matrix of 37 Major Variables
(Figures in each cell are product moment correlations × 100)

Variable	1	2	3	4	5	6	7	8	9	10	11	12	13	14	15	16	17	18	19	20	21	22	23	24	25	26	27	28	29	30	31	32	33	34	35	36	37
Family supported by social agencies 1		23	21	27	37	53	37	15	17	45	31	34	19	27	30	25	33	32	15	37	28	29	18	13	08	21	32	19	30	24	13	13	17	31	09	16	14
Low social class 2			11	09	16	31	11	12	20	08	11	11	08	03	07	01	05	11	03	06	05	02	-02	18	04	02	22	15	19	16	07	04	21	17	-02	09	11
Father convicted 3				18	09	12	17	05	08	20	10	17	02	10	16	16	20	07	04	24	07	16	09	06	02	08	18	16	21	12	06	17	08	15	06	12	12
Housing poor 4					39	31	18	14	02	30	10	15	08	13	11	02	22	11	00	16	16	24	13	09	-02	18	19	17	14	12	17	11	13	18	04	08	02
Interior badly kept 5						35	28	17	06	59	22	24	27	19	19	12	34	22	05	24	08	12	14	04	01	13	15	14	16	16	14	12	19	27	05	10	12
Income low 6							31	30	12	37	30	28	19	18	26	15	27	28	06	25	22	22	08	23	02	09	31	25	28	24	17	09	25	29	10	12	15
Large family 7								22	08	38	12	34	14	25	23	04	21	16	03	20	18	21	17	10	-11	06	16	20	30	18	15	14	04	18	18	25	03
Mother has no job 8									04	17	04	11	07	01	08	05	11	06	07	00	03	03	-01	25	13	08	08	15	18	15	19	10	24	17	11	15	16
Father has no special training 9										10	04	08	00	04	01	09	13	13	03	04	06	09	04	07	05	08	05	09	05	00	-03	02	02	14	-05	05	03
Boy physically neglected 10											23	33	26	30	19	13	36	23	10	26	10	06	19	06	04	18	20	21	20	19	23	07	23	30	05	16	10
Parents' marriage bad 11												21	48	16	13	32	29	22	28	46	18	15	08	10	09	24	10	07	04	-02	03	06	08	14	05	07	06
Parents not interested in education 12													20	27	20	09	22	20	08	18	18	14	14	34	-05	19	26	29	32	18	12	10	20	25	09	22	15
Inconsistency between parents 13														22	09	24	30	09	22	33	16	12	12	14	25	29	08	06	04	03	06	17	12	15	04	10	05
Parents undervigilant 14															15	06	24	15	13	08	11	14	38	11	-09	25	21	14	18	10	10	11	07	20	09	14	02
Mother's health poor 15																25	20	15	09	13	13	09	12	11	-01	08	10	12	14	10	01	06	12	13	02	-03	16
Mother's nerves bad 16																	18	14	12	18	16	12	12	05	19	20	08	02	05	-01	-10	-02	-01	13	03	01	07

#	Variable	Correlations
19	Father's nerves bad	23 15 11 14 09 10 -05 08 15 13 11 07 09 -04 07 09 10 07 04
20	Father unstable	35 13 14 03 -02 14 11 05 02 00 -09 -07 02 01 03 02 01 06
21	Early separations from Mother	29 31 09 -02 14 05 07 06 05 -03 01 11 02 06 09 10 08
22	Early separations from Father	65 12 00 07 20 19 14 11 03 11 05 08 23 14 14 07
23	Boy adventurous	11 01 03 09 16 16 13 05 09 15 03 17 12 13 10
24	Mother dull	03 -05 34 12 06 03 09 07 12 04 18 15 17 -02
25	Boy nervous	-02 05 23 24 32 13 07 08 17 21 11 16 07
26	Boy conduct disorder	27 06 05 -03 03 05 -01 06 13 -01 -05 04
27	Low I.Q. on Matrices	12 12 15 11 07 17 15 29 11 18 06
28	Low Reading quotient	49 49 40 30 17 25 30 10 17 18
29	Low Verbal quotient	67 26 28 15 20 32 12 22 16
30	Low Porteus T.Q.	32 20 15 25 29 15 22 06
31	High Porteus Q score	44 19 28 26 09 06 05
32	High Tapping score	25 33 25 01 15 09
33	High Spiral Maze Error	10 13 04 11 17
34	Teacher rates conduct bad	28 05 16 11
35	Low Weight	10 18 29
36	Low Height	72 -07
37	Unpopular on peer-rating	09

TABLE VI A (2)
Loadings of the 37 Major Variables on the two Principal Components of the Correlational Matrix

Item	Component I (17·7% of the variance)	Component II (7·3% of the variance)
1. Supported family	0·6950	0·1592
2. Low social class	0·3045	−0·1642
3. Father convicted	0·3452	0·0107
4. Housing poor	0·4270	0·0081
5. Interior badly kept	0·5471	0·1371
6. Income low	0·6379	−0·0087
7. Large family	0·5138	−0·0351
8. Mother has no job	0·3223	−0·1988
9. Father has no special training	0·1800	0·0481
10. Boy physically neglected	0·6161	0·1100
11. Parents marriage bad	0·4364	0·4915
12. Parents not interested in education	0·5544	−0·0687
13. Inconsistency between parents	0·4116	0·4087
14. Parents under-vigilant	0·4273	0·0874
15. Mother's health poor	0·3621	0·1230
16. Mother's nerves bad	0·2818	0·3870
17. Mother unstable	0·4605	0·3567
18. Father's health poor	0·3676	0·1513
19. Father's nerves bad	0·1953	0·4101
20. Father unstable	0·4207	0·5067
21. Early separations from mother	0·4014	0·2175
22. Early separation from father	0·3952	0·1969
23. Boy adventurous	0·3162	0·1256
24. Mother dull	0·3234	−0·2950
25. Boy nervous	0·1115	0·1970
26. Boy conduct disorder (P.S.W.)	0·3954	0·1697
27. Matrices I.Q. Low	0·5329	−0·3837
28. Low reading Q.	0·5006	−0·4500
29. Low verbal Q.	0·5253	−0·4828
30. Low Porteus T.Q.	0·3900	−0·4592
31. High Porteus Q. score	0·3613	−0·3924
32. High Tapping score	0·2908	−0·1189
33. High Spiral Maze Error	0·3928	−0·2991
34. Teacher rates conduct bad	0·5496	−0·1800
35. Low weight	0·2426	−0·1191
36. Low Height	0·3626	−0·2018
37. Peer Rating (unpopularity)	0·2526	−0·0848

List of References

AINSWORTH, Mary D. (1965), 'Further research into the adverse effects of maternal deprivation' in Bowlby, J., *Child Care and the Growth of Love*, London, Penguin: p. 65.

ANDRY, R. G. (1960), *Delinquency and Parental Pathology*, London, Methuen: p. 95.

ANTHONY, H. Sylvia (1960), 'Anxiety as a function of psychomotor and social behaviour,' *British Journal of Educational Psychology*, 51, 141–52: p. 48.

BALDWIN, A. L. (1948), 'Socialisation and parent-child relationships,' *Child Development*, 19, 127–36: p. 178.

BENNETT, Ivy (1960), *Delinquent and Neurotic Children: a comparative study*, London, Tavistock: pp. 48, 96.

BIZE, P. R. et al. (1964) 1965), 'Etude comparative de la psychomotricité,' *Annales de Vaucresson*, 2, 3–56; 3, 81–96, Paris, Cujas: p. 48.

BUTLER, N. R. & BONHAM, D. G. (1963), *Perinatal Mortality*, London and Edinburgh, Livingstone: p. 111.

CONGER, J. J. & MILLER, W. C. (1966), *Personality, Social Class and Delinquency*, New York, John Wiley: p. 105.

CRAIG, Maude M. & GLUECK, Selma J. (1964), *A Manual of Procedures for the Application of the Glueck Prediction Table*, New York City Youth Board: p. 137.

CROFT, I. J. & GRYGIER, T. G. (1956), 'Social relationships of truants and juvenile delinquents,' *Human Relations*, 9, 439–66: p. 52.

DOCTER, R. F. & WINDER, C. L. (1954), 'Delinquent vs nondelinquent performance on the Porteus Qualitative Maze Test,' *Journal of Consulting Psychology*, 18, 71–3: p. 49.

DOUGLAS, J. W. B. (1960), ' "Premature" children at Primary Schools,' *British Medical Journal*, 1, 1008–13: p. 109.

DOUGLAS, J. W. B. (1964), *The Home and the School*, London, MacGibbon & Kee: pp. 7, 29, 39, 40, 77, 160.

DOUGLAS, J. W. B. (1966), 'The school progress of nervous and troublesome children,' *British Journal of Psychiatry*, 112, 1115–16: p. 36.

DRILLIEN, C. M. (1964), *The Growth and Development of the Prematurely Born Infant*, London, Livingstone: p. 110.

EILENBERG, M. D. (1961), 'Remand Home Boys: 1930–1955,' *British Journal of Criminology*, 2, 111–31: p. 102.

EYSENCK, H. J. (1964), *Crime and Personality*, Routledge: p. 44.

FOULDS, G. A. (1961), 'Scatter of tapping among mental patients,' *Journal of Clinical Pathology*, 17, 168–9: p. 50.

FURNEAUX, W. D. & GIBSON, H. B. (1961), 'A children's personality test designed to measure neuroticism and extraversion,' *British Journal of Educational Psychology*, 31, 204–7: p. 44.

FURNEAUX, W. D. & GIBSON, H. B. (1966), *Manual of the New Junior Maudsley Inventory*, London, University of London Press: p. 170.

GIBBENS, T. C. N. (1963), *Psychiatric Studies of Borstal Lads*, London, Oxford University Press: p. 34.

GIBSON, H. B. (1964), 'The Spiral Maze. A psychomotor test with implications for the study of delinquency,' *British Journal of Psychology*, 55, 219–25: p. 50.

GIBSON, H. B. (1965), 'A new personality test for boys,' *British Journal of Educational Psychology*, 35, 244–8: p. 166.

GIBSON, H. B. (1965), *Manual of the Gibson Spiral Maze Test*, London, University of London Press: p. 49.

GIBSON, H. B., HANSON, Ruth & WEST, D. J. (1967), 'A questionnaire measure of neuroticism using a shortened scale derived from the Cornell Medical Index,' *British Journal of social and clinical Psychology*, 6, 129–36: p. 92.

GIBSON, H. B. (1968), 'The measurement of parental attitudes and their relation to boys' behaviour,' *British Journal of Educational Psychology*, 38, 233–9: p. 179.

GIBSON, H. B. & HANSON, Ruth (1969), Peer ratings as predictors of school behaviour and delinquency (unpublished study): p. 143.

GLUECK, S. & GLUECK, Eleanor T. (1950), *Unravelling Juvenile Delinquency*, New York, The Commonwealth Fund: pp. 7, 39.

GLUECK, S. & GLUECK, Eleanor T. (1956), *Physique and Delinquency*, New York, Harper: p. 34.

GLUECK, Sheldon & GLUECK, Eleanor T. (1962), *Family Environment and Delinquency*, London, Kegan Paul: p. 78.

HARGREAVES, D. H. (1967), *Social Relations in a Secondary School*, London, Routledge: p. 52.

HARPER, D. (1965), *Some Correlates of Sociometric Status among Adolescent Boys*, Report to the Study Group on Research Methods in Child Development, London School of Economics: p. 52.

HARTSHORNE, H. & MAY, M. A. (1928), *Studies in Deceit*, New York, Macmillan: p. 40.

HATHAWAY, S. R. & MONACHESI, E. D. (1953), *Analysing and*

LIST OF REFERENCES

Predicting Juvenile Delinquency with the M.M.P.I., Minneapolis, Univ. of Minesota Press: p. 38.
HEWITT, L. F. & JENKINS, R. L. (1946), *Fundamental Patterns of Maladjustment*, Illinois, D. H. Green: p. 178.
HIMMELWEIT, H. T. & PETRIE, A. (1946), 'An experimental investigation of neuroticism,' *Journal of Personality*, **15**, 173–96: p. 50.
HOTELLING, E. (1933), 'Analysis of a complex of statistical variables into principal components,' *Journal Educational Psychology*, **24**, 417–41, 498–520: p. 118.
JENSEN, A. R. (1964), 'The Rorschach Technique: a re-evaluation,' *Acta Psychologica*, **22**, 60–77: p. 10.
JONSSON, G. (1967), *Delinquent Boys, their Parents and Grandparents*, Copenhagen, Munksgaard: p. 65.
KELLMER PRINGLE, M. L., BUTLER, N. R., DAVIE, R. (1966), *11,000 Seven-Year-Olds*, London, Longmans: pp. 31, 69, 77.
KHLIEF, B. B. (1964), 'Teachers as predictors of juvenile delinquency and psychiatric disturbance,' *Social Problems*, **11**, 270–282: p. 39.
KLEIN, Josephine (1965), *Samples from English Cultures*, London, Routledge: p. 25.
KVARACEUS, W. C. (1961), 'Forecasting juvenile delinquency,' *Exceptional Children*, **27**, 429–35: p. 38.
LAWLEY, D. N. & MAXWELL, A. E. (1963), *Factor Analysis as a Statistical Method*, London, Butterworth: p. 118.
McCORD, W., McCORD, Joan & ZOLA, I. K. (1959), *Origins of Crime*, New York, Columbia University Press: pp. 7, 14, 78.
MACFARLANE, J. W. *et al.* (1954), *Behaviour Problems of Normal Children*, University California Press: p. 14, 58.
MEEHL, P. (1965), 'Seer over sign: the first good example,' *Journal experimental Research Personality*, **1**, 27–32: p. 10.
MINISTRY OF EDUCATION (1957), *Standards in Reading*, H.M.S.O.: p. 161.
MOSER, C. A. & SCOTT, W. (1961), *British Towns*, London, Oliver and Boyd: p. 123.
PANETH, Marie (1944), *Branch Street*, London, Allen and Unwin: p. 25.
PARNELL, R. W. (1958), *Behaviour and Physique*, London, Edward Arnold: p. 34.
PASAMANICK, B. *et al.* (1956), 'Pregnancy experience and the development of behaviour disorders in children,' *American Journal of Psychiatry*, **112**, 613–17: p. 109.
PORTEUS, S. D. (1942), *Qualitative Performance in the Maze Test*, Vineland, N. J. Smith Printing House: pp. 49, 59.

PORTEUS, S. D. (1959), *The Maze Test and Clinical Pathology*, Pacific Books, California: p. 32.

POWER, M. J. (1967), 'Epidemiological studies of delinquency,' *Journal of the Medical Womens' Federation*, **49**, 196–9: p. 36.

RADZINOWICZ, L. (1966), *Ideology and Crime*, London, Heinemann Educational Books: p. 99.

RAVEN, J. C. (1956), *The Standard Progressive Matrices*, Cambridge Univ. Press: p. 29.

REISS, A. J. (1951), 'Delinquency as the failure of personal and social controls,' *American Sociological Review*, **15**, 196–207: p. 38.

ROBINS, Lee N. (1966), *Deviant Children Grown Up*, Baltimore, Williams and Wilins: pp. 7, 95, 136.

RUTTER, M. (1966), *Children of Sick Parents*, London, Oxford University Press: p. 97.

RUTTER, M. & GRAHAM, P. (1966), 'Psychiatric disorder in 10- and 11-year-old children,' *Proceedings of the Royal Society of Medicine*, **59**, 382–7: p. 47, 88.

RYLE, A. (1967), *Neurosis in the Ordinary Family*, London, Tavistock Publications: pp. 65, 89.

SANDERSON, M. H. (1945), 'Performance of fifth, eighth and eleventh grade children on the Porteus Qualitative Maze Test,' *Journal of Genetic Psychology*, **67**, 57–65: pp. 49, 59.

SCHAEFER, E. S. & BELL, E. Q. (1958), 'Development of the parental attitude research instrument,' *Child Development*, **29**, 339–61: p. 178.

SCOTT, J. A. (1961), *Report on the Heights and Weights of School Pupils in the County of London in 1959*, London County Council: p. 33.

SHELDON, W. H. (1949), *Varieties of Delinquent Youth*, New York, Harper: p. 34.

SHOBEN, E. J. (1949), 'The assessment of parental attitudes in relation to child adjustment,' *Genetic Psychological Monographs*, **39**, 101–48: p. 178.

SPROTT, W. J. H. (1954), *The Social Background of Delinquency*, Nottingham University Press: p. 25.

STOTT, D. H. (1964), 'Sociological and psychological explanations of delinquency,' *International Journal of Social Psychiatry* (Congress Ed. No. 4), 35–43: p. 39.

SUGARMAN, B. (1968), 'Social norms in teenage boys' peer groups,' *Human Relations*, **21**, 41–58: p. 52.

TANNER, J. M. (1961), *Education and Physical Growth*, London, University of London Press: p. 34.

TRASLER, G. D. (1962), *The Explanation of Criminality*, London, Routledge: p. 45.

LIST OF REFERENCES

TRENAMAN, J. (1952), *Out of Step*, London and New York: p. 100.
VERNON, P. E. (1965), 'Environmental handicaps and intellectual development,' *British Journal Educational Psychology*, 35, 1–22: p. 32.
WATTS, H. F. (1958), *The Sentence Reading Test 1*, National Foundation for Educational Research, London: p. 30.
WILLETT, T. C. (1964), *Criminal on the Road*, London, Tavistock Publications: p. 48.
WILLMOTT, P. & YOUNG, M. (1957), *Family and Kinship in East London*, London, Routledge and Kegan Paul: p. 25.
WOLFF, Sula (1967), 'The contribution of obstetric complications to the etiology of behaviour disorders in childhood,' *Journal Child Psychology and Psychiatry*, 8, 57–66: p. 113.
ZWEIG, F. (1961), *The Workers in an Affluent Society*, London, Heinemann: p. 26.

Index

Acting-out, 54–8, 69, 86, 103, 138, 140–1, 177
Age cohorts, 15, 156–7
Age at earliest conviction, 36, 37, 55, 105, 106
at time of study, 3, 15, 87, 97
and reading ability, 161

Behaviour disorder, *see* Acting-out, Conduct assessments, Delinquency of early onset
Birth injury, 108–15, 147, 192–4
Body sway test, 50, 59
Brain damage, 108–10, 147, 193
Broken homes, 60, 63, 142

Case examples, 23, 42–3, 46, 56–7, 60–1, 64–5, 68, 72, 80–2, 90–1, 94–5, 101–2, 107–8
Case records forms, 12–14, 138, 152–5
Child welfare needs, 47, 57–8, 138
Conduct assessments, *see also* Teachers' assessments, 37, 41–4, 45, 47, 51–3, 58, 63, 66, 67, 69–72, 75, 76, 85–6, 88, 94–8, 103–8, 112–13, 121, 136–7, 140–9, 162–5, 189
Conduct, bad from good background, 107–8, 148
good from poor background, 107, 147

Co-operation, levels of, 55–6, 63–5, 87–8, 96, 122, 131–3, 146, 158–9, 166
Correlational matrix, 53, 66, 115, 116–17, 123, 141, 165, 196–197

Delinquency of early onset, 27, 35–6, 41, 55, 88, 105–6, 143, 148, 164
self-reported, 149
Discipline, *see* Father, Mother

Educational attainment, 30–2, 35, 102–5, 136, 144, 161, 174–5
Educational subnormality, 35, 54, 157
Ethnic origin, 24

Father, adverse background of, 133
age of, 101, 147, 190
attitudes of, 79–85, 106
Attitude Inventory, 146, 178–183
criminal convictions of, 57, 98, 99–102, 105–6, 114, 126–9, 134, 142, 147, 190
cruel, passive or neglecting, 79–84, 177
death of, 60–1
discipline by, 82–4, 86, 98, 128, 134, 177
health of, 90–5, 97, 98, 145
interviews with, 13, 85, 97, 133–4, 145

Father, occupation of, 17–18, 21, 119, 160, 162
  socio-educational status of, 87
  unstable, 57, 90–1, 95

Gibson Spiral Maze, 49–50

Halo effect, 98, 129–31, 139
Housing problems, 21–4, 134, 135

Illegitimacy, 60, 97
Illiteracy, 31, 35, 37, 44, 161, 166
Income, *see also* Social handicap, 17–19, 44, 67–9, 76–7, 95, 129, 137, 141–2, 173–7
Information absent, 63–4, 88, 131–3
Intelligence, 29–33, 58, 102–6, 121, 136, 143–4, 147
Interview assessments, reliability of, 47, 61–2, 93, 98, 121–3, 124–34, 138–40, 145, 168–171
Interview methods, 11–14, 152–155, 168
Inventories, *see* Mother, attitude inventory; Neuroticism

Lying, 41, 140, 163–4

Migration, 24
Mother, age of, 170
  attitudes of, 78–86
  Attitude Inventory, 87–9, 146, 178–83
  criminal convictions of, 100–102, 147
  cruel, passive or neglecting, 79–81, 86, 177
  death of, 60
  discipline by, 82–3, 128, 144, 177
  'dull', 121–2
  health of, 89–95, 97, 98, 112, 132, 145–6, 184–9
  influence of predominant, 85, 95, 145
  socio-educational status of, 87, 182–3
  unstable, 57, 90–1, 94–5, 96, 146
  working, 19, 65–6, 145
  separation from, 60–3, 65, 142, 146

Neighbourhood characteristics, 15–17, 19–26
Neurotic tendency in boys, 44–8, 58, 94, 95, 119, 137, 148, 166–7, 168–71, 188
Neuroticism Inventory for boys, 44–5, 166–7
Neuroticism Inventory for mothers, 92–3, 97, 184–9

Parents, *see also* Father, Interview, Mother
  biological or acting, 100, 154–155
  inconsistency between, 73, 75, 96, 133–4
  interest of, in education, 75, 76, 173, 175–6
  marital adjustment of, 70–2, 105–6, 153
  no praise from, 74–5
  physical neglect by, 62–3, 66, 67, 73, 75, 76, 96, 119, 142, 172
  psychopathic traits, 90, 95
  rules made by, 74, 76–7, 105–6, 128
  vigilence of, 73, 75, 77, 105–6, 128, 144, 173–4
Peer rating, *see* Popularity
Physique, 33–4, 135, 143, 162
Pilot group, 15, 157

INDEX

Pilot work, 92, 166–7, 178–9
Popularity, 51–3
Porteus Maze Test, 32–3, 48–9, 59
Prediction of delinquency, 3, 38–9, 54–6, 137, 140, 143, 144, 148–9
Principal component analysis, 114, 117–23, 179, 196–8
Prospective studies, 3–6, 140
Psychiatric social workers, 12–14, 61–2, 93, 98, 124–34, 138–9, 163–5, 172
Psychomotor performance, 48–51, 53, 59

Refusal of parents, *see* Cooperation
Religion, 24, 37
Retrospective bias, 4, 61, 132–3
Roman Catholics, 24, 36, 37

Sample selection, 15, 156–9
Schools in the study, 26–9, 36, 54, 148, 156–7
Siblings, birth order of, 170, 192–4

delinquency among, 99–101, 146–7
numbers of, 19, 37, 57, 157, 160, 170
Social agencies, 11
amenities, 20–1
handicap, *see also* Income, 67–70, 83–4, 87, 93, 102, 104–8, 119, 122, 136, 149
handicap, relationships varying with level of, 70–1, 75–8, 85–6, 96, 97, 137, 174–7, 192–4

Tapping test, 50, 59
Teachers' assessments, *see also* Conduct assessments, 11, 38–41, 45, 47, 54, 58, 75, 88, 139, 150–1, 165
Topics studied, 7–8
Twins and brothers, 157

Verbal attainment, 30–2, 35, 37, 103, 161, 174–5

Working mothers, 19, 65–6, 145

Finding Meaning in an Uncertain World

Finding Meaning
in an
Uncertain World

Second Edition

With an Adult Ministry Study Guide

LeRoy H. Aden

CASCADE *Books* • Eugene, Oregon

FINDING MEANING IN AN UNCERTAIN WORLD,
SECOND EDITION
With an Adult Ministry Study Guide

Copyright © 2015 LeRoy H. Aden. All rights reserved. Except for brief quotations in critical publications or reviews, no part of this book may be reproduced in any manner without prior written permission from the publisher. Write: Permissions, Wipf and Stock Publishers, 199 W. 8th Ave., Suite 3, Eugene, OR 97401.

New Revised Standard Version Bible, copyright 1989. Division of Christian Education of the National Council of the Churches of Christ in the United State of America. Used by permission. All rights reserved.

Cascade Books
An Imprint of Wipf and Stock Publishers
199 W. 8th Ave., Suite 3
Eugene, OR 97401

www.wipfandstock.com

ISBN: 978-1-4982-3325-5

Cataloguing-in-Publication data:

Aden, LeRoy H.

Finding Meaning in an Uncertain World / LeRoy H. Aden.

xii + 94 pp. ; 23 cm. Includes bibliographical references.

ISBN 13: 978-1-4982-3325-5

1. Meaning—Psychology. 2. Meaning—Religious aspects—Christianity. I. Title.

BF778 A35 2013

Manufactured in the U.S.A.

To Ruth and to Beth and David,
who have been a great source of meaning
and encouragement in my life.

Contents

Introduction ix

1 Meaning and Meaninglessness 1

Part 1: Sources of Meaning

2 Meaning and Relationships 11

3 Meaning and the Self 25

4 Meaning and the Family 32

5 Treasure Chests of Meaning 40

Part 2: Challenges to Meaning

6 Meaning and Suffering 51

7 Meaning and Old Age 59

8 Meaning and Death 72

Part 3: A Christian Approach to Meaning

9 God's Plan for Us 83

10 God's Gift of Meaning in an Uncertain World 86

Bibliography 93

An Adult Ministry Study Guide 95

Introduction

ALL OF US HAVE a drive, a will to survive, not just in the simple sense of existing but in the more profound sense of living with purpose and meaning. Our desire to survive is resolute, even if we must go against and overcome the people or the circumstances that would diminish or destroy us.

The creation of a meaningful world is not an automatic or sure thing. We have been given the power (the ability) to deliberate and to decide, and we are required to shape, or at least to discover, what is meaningful to us. There are obstacles (sometimes major obstacles) in the path, but the mandate is ours. The challenge is to make the right decisions and to do the right things to bring about a life that is realistic and meaningful, even in an uncertain world.

In many ways, the world in which we live is stable and predictable. The sun rises and sets at a predictable time. We rely on most of our friends to behave in expected ways. And what we find meaningful yesterday is meaningful to us today.

At the same time, the world we live in is uncertain and unpredictable. The friend we haven't seen for a decade now bears the marks of aging, and we do not share the same interests that we once did. Even the church we knew in our younger years may not feel like "our church" anymore. And

Finding Meaning in an Uncertain World

the things we found meaningful in our younger years may not be meaningful to our mid-life crisis.

The uncertainty of the world means that our search for meaning is constant. As our world changes we are required to find meaning within it. This is the theme, and major concern, of the present book. More specifically, I want to discuss some of the factors involved in pursuing and finding a meaningful life in an uncertain world. My interest is not a theoretical one, though theory is involved, but I want to illuminate the human side of meaning by addressing personal issues or dimensions involved in our pursuit of meaning.

In a previous book, I dealt with our search for fulfillment. That search and the search for meaning have many things in common. A fulfilled life deals with moments when things come together, when we experience a sense of unity and wholeness. In contrast, a meaningful life examines fulfillment from the viewpoint of intention and significance, from the viewpoint of purpose and meaning. "Is my life going anywhere? Do I mean anything to anyone? What do I amount to in the larger scheme of things?"

The lives of all of us revolve around meaning and being meaningful. We go to the movies and derive meaning from them; we visit friends who we have not seen for years and find meaning in the things that we share in common; we give ourselves to other people or we exchange gifts with loved ones and derive meaning from the giving. We are insatiable meaning-seeking creatures.

Recently, I was at a meeting where the speaker said, "I hope my comments are meaningful to you." The speaker could have also said, "I hope my comments mean something to you." We have an intuitive sense of what she is saying. She hopes to connect with us and to communicate ideas or thoughts that are relevant and important to us.

Introduction

Generally, we could say that we derive meaning from anything or anyone that addresses us and that elicits a response from us. In this sense, there are degrees of meaning that stretch, on a rough and experiential scale, from "means little or nothing to me" to "is very meaningful to me." What a stranger thinks of me is much less meaningful to me than what a dear friend thinks of me. In addition, how I assess an event depends on how deeply it touches me or how close it is to the center of my being.

Given the life-giving quality of meaning, we are dismayed to learn that some people feel meaningful only when they are undercutting the work and the worth of other people. The goal of their lives, it seems, is to discredit the lives of others and to question the value of their accomplishments. Only in this very negative way can they experience a sense of meaning.

There are better and more positive approaches to meaning. We seldom find a shortcut to a meaningful life, but a consideration of some of the challenges and obstacles that stand in the way can put us on the path to a fuller life.

In chapter one, I deal with meaning and meaninglessness, not as two separate entities in life but as two possibilities that can exist side by side. We can feel both meaningful and meaningless. I use the life and the findings of Viktor Frankl[1] to concretize the struggle. Frankl was an astute observer and an insightful theoretician in terms of our search for meaning. I conclude the chapter with a list of Frankl-like guidelines that help us find meaning in life. The sequence of nine chapters that follows can be divided into three sections. The first section, chapters two through five, forms a quadruplet: Chapter two deals with the role of relationships in the formation of meaning. I find that relationships are the baseline of

1. Frankl, *Man's Search for Meaning.* See also Frankl, *The Will to Meaning.*

living with meaning, primarily because they meet our need to be affirmed by someone who means something to us. Chapter three deals with the role of the self in the exercise of meaning. The self serves as a monitor of meaning—to our detriment if it leads us in self-centered directions, to our enhancement if it fills our life with authentic meaning. Chapter four deals with the role of the family in the development of meaning. Our family of origin is the world in which we first experience meaning, and it may be the most lasting impression that we have of ourselves and of other people. Chapter five deals with treasure chests of meaning. Special times and places, nodal events, and other depositories become storehouses of memories and meanings. The next section, chapters six through eight, forms a trilogy: Chapter six deals with suffering as a threat to meaning. Chapter seven deals with old age as a threat to meaning, and chapter eight deals with death as a threat to meaning. The third and final section, chapters nine and ten, turns our attention from the human side of meaning and looks at meaning from the vantage point of the Christian faith. What is our meaning in God's world? Or more fully, what do we mean to God and how does our relationship with God impact our existence in a world that is constantly changing?

Chapter 1

Meaning and Meaninglessness

VIKTOR FRANKL WAS A thirty-five-year-old psychiatrist who was of Jewish decent in Hitler's Nazi Germany, during World War II. From 1942–1945, he was imprisoned in a series of concentration camps, the worst being Kaufering (affiliated with Dachau). He spent five months there as a slave laborer. He was reduced to a skeleton and carried on a daily struggle to survive. He was surrounded by suffering and despair of all kinds and was stripped of all dignity and strength. To go on living seemed masochistic and even ridiculous.

More than once, Frankl asked himself, "Does all this suffering and dying have a meaning? In fact, does life under any circumstance have a purpose, a reason to be?"[1] Frankl was not asking an academic question. He was looking for a reason to go on living. He found that reason in what he considered a uniquely human gift. We may be robbed of all freedom and hope but one thing cannot be taken from us—the ability to stand above tragedy and to choose how we relate to it. With our ability to take a stand against emptiness and despair, our lives take on renewed meaning, and we have a reason to go on living and striving.

1. Paraphrased from Frankl, *Man's Search for Meaning*.

Meaning and Meaninglessness

Frankl found clinical support for his belief by observing the fate of his fellow inmates. The inmates who looked forward to a time when they would be released from captivity, and the inmates who were invested in long-term projects of some sort, were the ones who lived through the suffering and the despair. In a word, they had the will to survive, and many of them did.

The Importance of Meaning

Frankl was liberated in April of 1945 and went on to develop a new approach to life and to therapy.[2] He came to believe that the search for meaning is the primary motive in our lives. He used one of Friedrich Nietzsche's more positive insights to summarize the point: "He who has a why to live can bear with almost any how."[3]

Frankl's life is a remarkable testimony to the belief that meaninglessness can be surmounted and meaning can be found, even in situations of great suffering. His struggle with meaninglessness prompted him to live a life filled with purpose and meaning. Shortly after being released from captivity, he wrote about his life as a prisoner and shared his belief that we are basically motivated by a search for meaning rather than by a pursuit of pleasure or power. His book, *The Search for Meaning*, became a bestseller and laid the foundation for what Frankl called logotherapy, a therapy designed to help individuals find meaning in life, no matter what their situation might be. He brought a ray of hope to persons who at the time were paralyzed by a widespread sense of emptiness and aimlessness.

2. Ibid.
3. Boeree, "Viktor Frankl 1915–1997."

Meaning and Meaninglessness

During his captivity, Frankl also found that no one could hand him, or even instill in him, a sense of meaning. Neither could anyone fabricate an imaginary world of meaning that had no basis in fact. On the contrary, the person had to discover the meaning that was present or possible in the turbulent world in which he lived.

Frankl was convinced that meaning is an individual thing, unique to a person's life and not necessarily given in society's tendency to promote particular meanings in and through proscribed codes of conduct. He suggested that we can get in touch with major meanings that are embedded in our lives by attending to three areas of life.[4] The first area is the relationships we value, especially our relationships of love. The second area is the things we create or accomplish, including the ways in which we grow and fulfill ourselves. The third area is invested in our being compassionate or courageous or having a good sense of humor, but finding meaning in and through suffering is the most challenging and basic part of Frank's third area of meaning.[5] Frankl came to see that it is the job of therapists and physicians "to help people find and fulfill their own unique meanings."[6]

Frankl's conclusions are not limited to the meaninglessness of a concentration camp. In the years after imprisonment, he reflected on life in America and concluded that we are living in a milieu of meaninglessness, in a world of uncertainties. He maintained that we have undergone a series of changes, all of which contribute to the demise of meaning. We have emptied life of absolute values and given priority to relative values or no values at all. We have given up long-term loyalties and have settled on what or who is relevant to our immediate needs (wants). We have

4. Ibid., 9–10.
5. Ibid., 10.
6. Ibid., 6.

Meaning and Meaninglessness

narrowed life down to the present moment, to the "now" and have forsaken the treasures of the past and the future. And we have reduced our spiritual needs to psychological reactions. In a word, we have divested life of everything that gives substantial meaning to it, and in this "existential vacuum" we live in a void, an empty world. If Frankl is right, our struggle means that we must rise above a society, indeed a world, that favors emptiness and meaninglessness. Frankl laments, "More people today have the means to live, but no meaning to live for."[7]

Frankl is not the only one who has recognized the meaninglessness of life. The Preacher in the Old Testament book of Ecclesiastes was an inquisitive person who was also a very serious person. He made up his mind to experience all aspects of life. He acquired great wisdom, got to know folly and to taste pleasure, he built houses and planted vineyards until he "surpassed all who were in Jerusalem." Then he reflected on all that he had done and decided that it was meaningless or, in his words, "all was vanity and a chasing after wind, and there was nothing to be gained under the sun."[8]

Frankl's struggle is our struggle. Hopefully, we will not wrestle with meaninglessness to the depth that Frankl did, but neither do we escape our own sense of emptiness and lack of meaning. Our struggle with meaning is often reflected in the TV programs that companies sponsor. Not long ago quiz shows addressed, and supplied an answer to, the values and hopes of many Americans. They chose a winner by various means and rewarded the winner with huge amounts of money or with other material benefits. The winners were ecstatic. They jumped up and down and embraced the nearest person with obvious joy. The message was clear. Money is

7. Frankl, *Man's Search for Meaning*, 142.
8. Eccl 2:11.

Meaning and Meaninglessness

power and success and can bring a great sense of meaning and well-being to the lives of those who have it.

Sports, like money, is of key importance in our society. It attracts hordes of people and seems to be used to fill gaps in a relatively mundane existence. People, especially men, pick their favorite sport and their favorite team or player and live life through them. Sports has the advantage of being a true-to-life drama. It has leaders and followers, players and spectators, people who are in and those who are out, good days and bad days, gifted and not-so-gifted players, successes and defeats, reality and fantasy, individual performance versus teamwork. It has all the ingredients necessary to make life meaningful in a world of empty spaces.[9]

Guidelines to Meaning

From Frankl's struggle with meaninglessness we can draw up a series of practical guidelines that help us find meaning in life.

1. At any one time, the meaning of life for us should be specific and concrete. Abstract or generalized goals will not do, and goals for the whole human race will not necessarily fill our lives with meaning. On the contrary, what gives us meaning must be a personal mandate or activity, something that comes out of our particular situation. In Frankl's case, it was to survive the day and be helpful to his fellow prisoners. In a larger sense, it was his tireless attempt to to be helpful to the disillusioned and the depressed. When asked by an editor of *Who's Who in America* to summarize his life in a few lines, Frankl responded, "I have seen the

---

9. Hear Harry Chapin's "Vacancy" for a musical description of modern man's emptiness.

Meaning and Meaninglessness

meaning of my life in helping others to see in their lives a meaning."[10]

2. The meaning of our life is most meaningful when it is "our thing to do," our purpose to fulfill. It may be a very humble and unpretentious thing, but it is ours to do, and no one else can do it in quite the same way that we can. The grandmother who loves and cares for a grandchild in her own unique way may gain a great sense of meaning and purpose in an otherwise drab and empty world.

3. No person can tell another person what the purpose of his or her life should be. We can help other persons find and clarify their particular purpose, but in the end they must own it as their own and must accept responsibility for what they make of it.

4. What is meaningful to us or what bestows meaning on us may change as our circumstances change. This is also true as we move from one stage of development to another stage. What is meaningful to us as a teenager may not be meaningful to us as an older person. The quest for meaning, then, is an ongoing process that builds on the past but lives in the present and reaches into, and helps to shape, the future.

5. Life is full of threats to meaning, and in most cases the greatest threat is death. Death threatens life with futility and meaninglessness, because as an extinction it casts doubt on life and appears to be the end of all meaning. "As for man, his days are like grass; he flourishes like a flower of the field; the wind passes over it, and it is gone."[11] My cousin's husband Darrell was

---

10. Frankl, *The Will to Meaning*, 160.
11. Ps 103:15.

a foreman for a utility company. He was standing on the shoulder of a country road, supervising the installation of a transformer on an electric pole. The transformer swung free and out of control and hit Darrell directly in the head. In a moment, he was gone and left a thirty-five-year-old wife and four daughters ranging from five to thirteen to make it on their own.

6. Our search for, or pursuit of, meaning must be anchored in a higher, more absolute (lasting) purpose or meaning. In the midst of despair, Frankl concluded that we strive to obtain a higher and more lasting meaning in our lives. As he and other prisoners stumbled forward on a dark and treacherous road, Frankl found that higher, life-giving force in the boundless and caring love of his wife. He held her love in memory (she was in another concentration camp), and her love gave meaning to his shattered and meaningless life.

I will have occasion to return to some of these points later in the book. Meanwhile, Frankl's struggle has laid bare the heart of our concern. How can we find meaning in a life that confronts us, potentially if not actually, with meaninglessness? Or more generally, what lies ahead of us on the road to a meaningful life?

Part 1

Sources of Meaning

Chapter 2

Meaning and Relationships

WE HUMANS ARE NOT a tabula rasa, a blank tablet, when we are born, but neither are we given a world filled with meaning. We must discover our own meaning, that is, what life means to us and what we mean to ourselves and others. We do not address these issues in a vacuum, but find answers to them as we interact with the world around us. Specifically, both relationships and affirmations are at the base of life and are primary in the birth of meaning.

The Birth of Meaning

There is an endless variety of relationships and they are central in every stage of life, beginning with the fetus's attachment to the mother and ending with our last breath on earth. I want to focus our discussion on the role of relationships in our adult years.

Sometimes when I am out in public and observing people, especially couples, I ask myself, "What attracted those two people to each other?" In some cases, I can point to external factors that may have drawn them together. One

Part 1: Sources of Meaning

of them may stand out in a special way or one person may seem especially attentive to the other person.

Usually, though, I quickly run out of possibilities and am left with the unanswered question: "How did these two people ever get together?" To be honest, I don't have a clue. I have no idea what each person saw in the other person, or, if they are an older couple, why they have stayed together for years. In other words, I am confronted by a mystery, by a relationship whose deeper dynamics are hidden from view. As a matter of fact, the couple themselves may not know what they saw, or continue to see, in each other.

The complexity of relationships is a witness to their importance and priority. Relationships can be disjunctive or even destructive, but ideally (hopefully) they build up and establish the self. Erick Erickson,[1] a developmental psychologist, helps us to understand why they are crucial to our sense of meaning.

Erickson maintains that adolescents must be confirmed in order to emerge as persons in their own right. By confirmed, Erikson is not talking about the religious rite of confirmation. He is talking about a communal validation, a societal (interpersonal) affirmation. He says that adolescents must be confirmed by those who mean most to them, confirmed by receiving a genuine indication that what they do and who they are makes sense to persons who are close to them. In other words, adolescents must be meaningful to those who are meaningful to them. If they aren't confirmed, they may seek out groups, even counterculture groups, that do affirm them.

While the need for confirmation (I prefer the term "affirmation") may come to an apex in adolescence, I think the need exists in all of us. We must make sense to people around us. Our lives become meaningful only as we mean

1. Erickson, *Identity and the Life Cycle.*

Meaning and Relationships

something to people who are meaningful to us. Andras Angyal says that we come to life "by being acknowledged and understood by someone. Otherwise [our] existence has no [more] meaning . . . than an inscription on a rock on an uninhabited planet."[2]

I was reminded of the importance of being affirmed by an incident that happened recently in our family. When my latest book came out, I autographed a copy of it and sent it to my granddaughter Britta. In the autograph, I thanked her for her love of learning and for her passion for living life. A week later, when my granddaughter had received the book, I got a call from her. What I wrote to her touched her deeply. She felt affirmed and accepted for who she was, and she was overjoyed. Because her life was meaningful to me, she became more meaningful and acceptable to herself.

We feel affirmed when we receive positive strokes from others. What is not so obvious is that we can affirm, or be affirmed, by negative reactions, by being confronted or faced with demands or criticisms. By confronting us the person acknowledges our existence and implies that we are worthy of a response. What negates us or wipes us out is when people who mean something to us completely ignore us, when they treat us as though we don't exist or are of no relevance or importance. Have you ever been in a group where a close friend looks past you and pays attention to everyone else? Or have you yourself ever used the silent treatment on someone who has offended you or embarrassed you? If you have, you know that apathy or neglect robs us of all meaning, except the feeling that we are of little or no meaning.

To affirm a person in a complete sense means three things. First it means that we affirm the person's existence, that we grant his or her right to live as an autonomous and

2. Angyal, "A Theoretical Model for Personality Studies," 18.

Part 1: Sources of Meaning

viable human being who deserves our respect and validation. Second, it means that we acknowledge the person's presence, not just his or her physical presence but his or her presence in Martin Buber's sense of person relating to person, of an "I" relating to a "Thou."[3] Third, it means that we affirm the person's importance and relevance to us and to our lives.

As long as we are embedded in fairly stable relationships, we tend to feel that we mean something to someone. But if our relationships or circumstances change in any notable way, we may find ourselves questioning how much we really mean to people. Since we cannot live comfortably without a sense of purpose and meaning, we may make a special effort to overcome the discomfort, to test the threat. We may try to gauge how likeable, if not important, we are to people around us, but they may pay little or no attention to us. We may reach out to communicate, if not to influence, other people, but they may seem unaware of our presence or disinterested in our sage advice. At such moments, the threat of emptiness looms large and we feel like Miss J, a friend who saw herself as a "void center, whirling around itself." Destitute of meaning, we search for reassurance and affirmation.

In our search for meaning, we basically want to be recognized and respected as a person, as a human being. Our thirst, though, may run deeper. We may want to be special to those who are special to us. Deeper still, we may want to be, as Ernest Becker says, of immortal value, of "cosmic significance" in a network of relationships.[4]

Our discussion to this point has put great emphasis on the other person's contribution to our sense of meaning. However true, we must also recognize that we have to be able to affirm ourselves in spite of the times when we let

3. Buber, *I and Thou*.
4. Paraphrased from Becker, *The Denial of Death*, 3.

Meaning and Relationships

ourselves down. The 2012 summer Olympics in London provides us with concrete material. The Olympics is about performance, about being the world's best in a chosen sport. But it is also a very personal and touching story. With great commitment and sometimes with great sacrifice, young men and women choose to focus their lives and energy (resources) on becoming the very best. If you listen to their stories, you know that their efforts often transcend self-aggrandizement and have to do with promoting a cause, a country, or a loved one.

Feelings of success run high when the athlete stands on the podium and bends forward to receive a gold Olympian medal while his or her national anthem is being played. It is tolerable if an athlete walks away with a silver or a bronze medal. But the world comes crashing down when a person fails to qualify for the games or falls short of achieving the goal. There may be any number of reasons for the failure. The athlete may do the best he or she can, but it isn't enough. The person may have a bad day and not perform at peak efficiency. The athlete may stumble and have to drop out of the race. The judges may have scored the performance incorrectly. The person may not have trained as faithfully as he or she should have. The athlete may be drained after three days of competition. And, heaven forbid, the goddess of athletics may have other plans for the athlete. Whatever the reason, the athlete falls short of being the best in the world, and sooner or later he or she has to be able to accept the loss and affirm himself or herself as a person of worth, actually as a person who is far more than a race or a medal.

Affirming the self comes with its own temptations. Like the rest of us, athletes can think either too little or too much of themselves. If they think too highly of themselves, they may experience blame but aim it at everyone but themselves. They engage in what is called self-justification

Part 1: Sources of Meaning

and see themselves as innocent victims of everyone else's faults or mistakes. If they think too little of themselves, they berate (castigate) themselves and see their performance as another indication of how inadequate they are or how they can never succeed at anything. In either case, they have used self-affirmation to reinforce what they already think of themselves instead of gaining a fuller and more balanced perception of themselves, of their weaknesses and their strengths. They have failed to learn from the situation or to use it as an opportunity to improve their performance the next time. Affirming oneself serves a positive purpose if individuals gain a fuller and more balanced perception (understanding) of themselves and use it to evaluate how their perception of themselves may be contributing to their success or failure.

In my earlier years, I was an avid tennis player. My enthusiasm for the game did not determine (guarantee) how good I was or how well I was going to play. It was obvious to me that my attitude in terms of how I was doing was important, sometimes decisive, in how well I did. My intuition was put into words by a book entitled *The Inner Game of Tennis*, in which the author (whose name I forget) maintains that we can either defeat or encourage ourselves by the attitude we take toward ourselves and our playing.

Unfortunately, the book did not prevent me from getting on my case when I did poorly, but it certainly made me aware of what I was doing to myself. I simply could not accept myself when I did not measure up to my inner expectations, whereas my challenger, when he was behind, became more determined and went on to win the game.

Meaning and Relationships

A Further Word about Meaning

The professional career of Tiger Woods[5] can teach us additional things about affirmation and meaning. Woods's biography reads like an impossible dream.

As an amateur golfer, he stood out as an outstanding athlete. He won the Junior World Championship in golf six times, which includes four consecutive wins. At the age of eight, he shot under eighty and became the youngest-ever winner of the US Junior Amateur Championship. In 1991, at the age of sixteen, he was chosen as Southern California Amateur Player of the Year, and *Golf Digest*, *Golf World*, and *Golf Week* followed suit by naming him Player of the Year.

Woods became a professional golfer in August of 1996 and stood on the threshold of one of the most impressive records in the history of golf. In 1997 he won the Masters tournament and set a record for his rapid rise to the Number 1 spot. He occupied that spot for 264 consecutive weeks in 1999 to 2004 and for 281 weeks in June, 2005 to October, 2010. In 1996, *Sports Illustrated* named him "Sportsman of the Year" and the PGA Tour called him "The Rookie of the Year." Woods hit a temporary slump following the death of his father in May, 2006, but he recovered after a nine-week reprieve and went on to end the season by winning six consecutive tour events. "With fifty-four tour wins and twelve major wins, Woods [broke] the tour records for both total wins and total major wins over eleven seasons."[6]

Woods's achievements on the golf course are enhanced by his activity in the larger world of golf. In 1997, Woods launched his own website in order to stay in touch with his fans around the world and to provide them with a personal blog, with video highlights of recent tournaments

---

5. Woods, "About Woods."
6. "Tiger Woods," Wikipedia.

Part 1: Sources of Meaning

(games), and with breaking news and announcements. He added a Facebook page that serves 2.2 million followers and a Twitter account that serves 1.5 million followers. Through the Tiger Woods Foundation, Woods reaches out to "underserved youth in all stages of their academic life" while the Tiger Woods Learning Centers provide hands-on help in science, technology, mathematics, etc. Woods also established the Earl Woods Scholarship Program, which attempts to help young people who are going through college or vocational careers (stress). Finally, Tiger Woods uses his experience and his many gifts to design "amazing golf courses around the world."[7]

Woods teaches us several things about affirmation and meaning. First, he reinforces the idea that we gain greater meaning from an activity if it is our thing to do. Golf was at the center of Woods's life and was for him the essence of living with purpose and meaning. His gift for golf manifested itself early in life. At the impossible age of two, he appeared on the Mike Douglas Show and putted against Bob Hope. By the age of three, he scored forty-eight in nine holes at the Cypress Navy course and by five he was featured in *Golf Digest* and appeared in "That's Incredible." Woods would have been far less satisfied and fulfilled if he had pursued a career as a professional basketball player.

Second, success and meaning were not handed to Woods on a silver platter. Success came through discipline and hard work; meaning, no doubt, came to him as he discovered and pursued what was meaningful to him and what was not.

Third, Woods reminds us that the search for meaning is an ongoing endeavor. A win in one tournament is the

---

7. "The mission of the Tiger Woods Design program is to make golf an enjoyable and unique experience for every level of skill." See "About Tiger Woods," 2.

Meaning and Relationships

beginning, not the end, of Woods's search. He has to prove himself each time he enters a tournament, and every win or loss contributes to, or takes away from, his overall sense of meaning. His search for meaning also extended beyond the game of golf. As meaningful as golf was to Woods, it did not exhaust the breadth of his search. He found meaning not only in the game itself but by interacting with and helping other people, especially young kids.

Meaning is born and nurtured in the cradle of relationships. And like relationships, meaning can be related to a relatively simple truth about ourselves ("A good night's sleep is meaningful to me") to basic and central truths about who we are and what we are about ("I feel fulfilled when I have contributed to the welfare of the human race").

The Disruption of Meaning

Relationships are stable and enduring. That is more wish than fact. In actuality, relationships change or are given up, and in the process meanings are disrupted, if not destroyed. The world that we once knew, the world that we relied on to define who we are and what we mean, is no more, at least not in a sense that gives us security and identity.

Jane and Joe were going on forty-four years of marriage. They had two gifted children and were at a pinnacle in Joe's career. Joe was invited to a large southern church to give lectures to laypersons, and he did his usual splendid job—so much so that the secretary of the church got many requests for Joe's presentations, and the local paper ran a special article on his series.

Joe had no trouble getting to sleep, but his usual need for eight hours of sleep was interrupted by pain in his back and lower abdomen. He took Tylenol to relieve the pain but soon that was not enough. The pain grew so intense that Joe

Part 1: Sources of Meaning

gave up his longstanding resolve to avoid doctors at all costs, and he agreed to see one as soon as they returned home.

The doctor altered his overloaded schedule to see Joe in two days. He listened to Joe's symptoms and urged him to see a specialist and to undergo any tests that were recommended. The tests confirmed the doctor's worst fears. They indicated that Joe may have prostate cancer. Later tests showed that the cancer had spread beyond the prostate to become a growth on the spine. Joe went through chemotherapy and radiation treatments, and even participated for a short time in an experimental drug program. The treatments gave him five years of fairly good health, but on an ordinary day in November Joe's fight came to an end.

Jane thought that her husband's extended struggle had prepared her for the inevitable, but his loss (death) sent her into a tailspin. Everywhere she turned she ran into a black hole, and it confronted her when she was least prepared to deal with it—when she set the breakfast table and poured two cups of coffee instead of one, when she was searching for a note that she had left herself and ran across a photo that was taken on a recent trip, when she went to church and an awkward silence came between a close friend and her. But the most difficult moments were when she was with a group of married friends, and she did not fit in anymore.

The usual approach to Jane's loss is through the dynamics of grief. Kenneth Mitchell and Herbert Anderson are helpful here.[8] They did a study of losses and griefs and came up with five components that make up the landscape of grief. First, we experience numbness. We go into shock and become numb to feelings. When feelings return, we experience a cluster of emotions: We tend to feel empty inside, lonely in a world of people, and isolated from friends and loved ones. We may also experience anxiety about

8. Mitchell and Anderson, *All Our Losses, All Our Griefs*, 64–82.

Meaning and Relationships

being abandoned and fear about the uncertain future that lies ahead. Along the way, we become aware of things done or left undone when the deceased was still living and experience grief as guilt or shame. Anger is a natural, though often an irrational, part of grief, and it attacks various objects, depending on the circumstances surrounding the loss. God is a likely target, because God is easily blamed for not stalling death or for not making it less painful. Finally, there is sadness and even despair, and if one or more of these emotions are hard to express directly, any one of them may be expressed non-verbally through the body.

This approach to loss and grief has clinical evidence to support it, and therefore it serves us well in dealing with mourners. But I do not think that it exhausts the full impact of loss and grief. Take, for example, Jane and Joe. When Joe died, Jane did not just lose a single strand of meaning but a whole network of interrelated meanings. She lost what Joe meant to her, what she meant to Joe, what the relationship between them meant to each other, and, near the end of Joe's life, what it meant to Jane to take care of Joe, and what it meant to Joe to be taken care of. Some of these losses may come to mind when we announce that Joe has died, but they are so vital or central to our lives that they ought to be recognized explicitly. The family will remember, and share stories about, Joe as a son, a husband, a father, and a grandfather, and these memories are much more about Joe's meaning to us and our meaning to him than the clinical observation that Joe has died.

The Rebirth of Purpose and Meaning

What the loss of relationships tears down, grief work, the process of working through loss, is expected to rebuild, to repair. Normally, it involves two tasks: to help us let go of

Part 1: Sources of Meaning

former relationships and to help us accept new ones. We can stall the process at any point, but generally grief is demanding enough or persistent enough to get something done.

As long as we hold on to former, now extinct, relationships, we continue to live as though the world has not changed. We do not give up familiar or fulfilling relationships easily and, besides, grief is a tortuous process. The survivor who keeps the room of the deceased just as it was when the deceased person died indicates a desire not necessarily to honor the deceased but to keep "things just as they were."

From the outside, grief work looks like a negative and fruitless process, but in helping the survivor to let go, it serves a very necessary and positive purpose. It must be achieved in some form before the second task, to accept new relationships, has a chance to succeed. The acceptance of new relationships, not the re-establishment of old ones but the creation of new relationships, becomes the cradle for the birth of new meaning. And this birth is as important, if not more important than the original birth of meaning.

The process of birth and rebirth is not a once-for-all achievement. In fact, with the continued loss of relationships, the process is constantly repeated in some form throughout our lives. Thus the world of meaning that we lived by at one time may not resemble the world of meaning that we live by as adults or older people.

And, in any case, the loss of meaning is not the end of the process. Death, and the loss of relationships, does more than disrupt meaning, especially if the loss involves the death of a spouse or some other significant person. With the loss of meaning comes the loss of purpose, the loss of either a reason to live or a desire to live. This is the real challenge of lost relationships. The survivor's life may be so tied in with the deceased that there seems to be no reason to live. Or the survivor may feel that the purpose of his or her

Meaning and Relationships

life has been achieved, e.g., raising children and equipping them to survive in the world, that there is no reason to go on. "I am ready to go. And I want to die and be with so and so in heaven."

Grace, the mother of two young adults, bids "goodbye" to the one remaining child at home and turns to face an "empty nest." For years, the children gave meaning to her life, but now suddenly they are gone. Grace faces more than loneliness. She is stripped of a reason to live. She must go through a tortuous process of redefining her life or live with the emptiness of lost relationships.

A similar struggle with meaning, or the lack of it, marks Steven's retirement as a pharmacist. For years, Steve looked forward to the time when he would not have to work ten to twelve hours a day. Now he sits in the sun porch in front of the TV and recalls some of the customers who looked to him for advice or guidance. His life is bereft of meaning, and his plight is exaggerated by a society that favors those who actively contribute to the social and economic welfare of the community.

Meaning and purpose often go hand in hand. In *The Purpose-Driven Life,* Rick Warren ties the two together by building a whole structure on the idea that we are created by God for a particular purpose—God's purpose—and that fulfilling that purpose gives meaning—lasting meaning—to our lives. Warren elaborates his thought in fine detail and with convincing evidence. I think the relation can flow in the opposite direction, that is, experiencing meaning in our lives can give us a reason to live, a purpose to strive for. When Grace begins to re-establish meaningful relationships with other people, she will also experience a renewed reason to keep on living. Or as Steve adjusts to retirement and finds meaning in it, he will also recover or discover a purpose in retirement. In the end, it does not matter which

Part 1: Sources of Meaning

way the relation flows. It is more important to realize that meaning and purpose go together, and often we need the one to experience the other. Purpose without meaning is motive (motion) without significance and meaning without purpose is significance without motion (direction).

Chapter 3

Meaning and the Self

WHAT DO WE MEAN to ourselves? Or more fully, what role does the self play in the search for meaning, in the pursuit of a meaningful life? There are no obvious or simple answers, but there are important considerations.

In an interview with *Good Housekeeping*'s Rosemary Ellis, Meredith Vieira,[1] former co-anchor on the *Today* show, was asked to reflect on her decision to leave the show. She readily admits that part of why she left was the demands that the show were putting on her and her family relationships. She was so preoccupied with being prepared that she got up at a ridiculously early hour and that put undue hardship and stress on her husband and the children. But Mereith was also concerned about what the show was doing to her. She suffered from sleep deprivation and was paying a hefty price for it. She did not feel well most of the time. She struggled with gaining weight, and she experienced moments of depression and anxiety. While she did not define herself by fame and fortune, by the high profile job she had, or by the impressive salary she was earning, she felt a need to reclaim her life in order to find out who she

1. Veira, "Happy at Home."

Part 1: Sources of Meaning

was "at the core." She had lost an essential part of who she was, and she needed to find out what that meant.

After deciding to leave the show, she experienced a new set of worries. She did not know what she would be or do without her TV family, and she was unsure what the loss of income would mean to her.

Nevertheless, she left the show. What is remarkable about her decision was that she could listen to her inner self and know that it was time to leave in spite of all the forces and advantages that would urge her to continue. She gave up a life that was meaningful to pursue a life that seemed to offer more meaning by giving her a chance to get reacquainted with herself and her family.

As Meredith implies, the question of whether we make sense to ourselves and to others is constantly with us. We seldom ask the question explicitly, but we have a feel for how we are doing. We can live with ourselves if the answer is positive, but any serious doubt puts us between a sense of OKness and not OKness, between meaning and uncertainty. Mereith's situation raises a related concern, and it can be expressed succinctly by the phrase "doing versus being" or by "what I do versus who I am." In each case, we see ourselves differently and experience meaning in a different way.

My sister Lee was diagnosed with cancer in the liver and went downhill rapidly. Shortly before her death, she said, "My whole life has been wrong." I do not know exactly what she was referring to, but I took her comment to be an admission that she now felt that her priorities and values were faulty and that what was meaningful to her earlier in life was not meaningful to her in the face of death. She had invested heavily in what she did and in what she accomplished. She accumulated an impressive array of clothes and jewelry, and money, but she sacrificed relationships and was

Meaning and the Self

known as a driven and controlling person—all in the name of living by what she did or how she performed.

My sister did not arrive at this point all by herself. She had the backing of a society that puts great weight on performing or doing. One of the first things we may ask a person who we have just met is, "What do you do? What is your vocation?" We may never get to know who the person is, because what the person does is all we want to know or all we need to know in order to relate to him or her.

To define ourselves by what we do, not only minimizes, or negates, who we are but it also means that we are living by a relatively small part of our total being. Our job, our accomplishments, or whatever else, becomes the criterion by which we are judged or prized The emphasis on doing may be a secular equivalent of theology's belief that often we live by our own supposed goodness, by what we deserve. Theology sees this attempt as a state of bondage, not a state of freedom.

We are more than our job or any other thing we might strive to do. It is this more, this personhood, or as we will say shortly this being fully human, that is left unrecognized and undeveloped if we live by doing. And when we lose our job or our energy fades, we experience the emptiness, the void of being half a person. We may find ourselves resonating with the middle-aged woman who sighed, "I am a bunch of talents and activities, but I have no idea who I am. Somewhere along the line, I have lost me."

I have cast living by our deeds in a harsh and negative light, and it is deserved if we center ourselves in doing to the exclusion of being. But the fault is in us, not necessarily in doing. We are endowed with the ability to do a great number of things, and our world is richly blessed by our ability to build buildings and bridges, to design cars and planes, to write books and to compose symphonies. These achievements have been used to express and to enhance who we are, and in the process doing is a worthy partner in the actualization of being.

We can advance our discussion of the self and its role in finding meaning by noting that there is a difference between being self-centered and being a centered self. Actually, there is a wide world between them. To be self-centered means that we relate everything to the self, actually to the aggrandizement of the self, making ourselves a pivotal center of life. We may even think of the self as the source of meaning. In distinction, being a centered self means that we are focused; we have a nucleus, a core around which we are organized into an integrated and clearly defined whole. The two "selves" react differently to the same statement, "Your act of kindness was very meaningful to me." Self-centered people tend to take the comment personally and believe that they have once again proven how good they are and how people appreciate their goodness. In distinction, the centered self does not have to feed the ego but sees the act of kindness as a natural expression of its concern for others.

Being Fully Human

The concept of the centered self can be put in another way. We are to become fully human, that is, we are to achieve a fair balance between our two given natures. On the one hand, we have a physical body, or better we are a body. Like other animals, we are part of the created world, which means that we are mortal and finite creatures who live with definite limitations. We are subject to the necessities and vicissitudes of life and live with the prospect of eventual death. As an example, we are required to get a certain amount of sleep, if not last night than certainly tonight. Or from a different angle, I often get irritated when my body

Meaning and the Self

calls for a trip to the bathroom and interrupts my mind's struggle with a profound and promising insight.

On the other hand, being human means that we are transcendent beings, or as Reinhold Niebuhr puts it, we are children of the spirit.[2] We can stand above ourselves and the world and make them objects of our attention and concern. If I ask you, "Can you remember what you did last Wednesday," your mind can immediately shift its attention from what you are reading now to what you did last week. Our capacity to transcend ourselves also gives us the power of self-determination. Within limits, we can choose our own goals and determine the way in which we are going to achieve them. We cannot eliminate our limitations completely, and in fact some of them are beyond our control, but we can determine what we are going to do with them or how we are going to live with them. In this sense, we are "created a little lower than the angels" and can enjoy the benefits of finite freedom.

As we have said, we are under the mandate to relate to our two "natures" and form them in some kind of fair and balanced unity, but often that is only "a consummation devoutly to be wished."[3] We can and do favor one of the parts over the other part and in this way we try to avoid the tension between them. We can accentuate our creaturely limitations and can become less than we are and find security or excuses in our finite existence. All of us do that to some degree. We live in a mundane world, a world that Heidegger calls the "everyday" and lose ourselves in the popular or enjoyable thing to do. Or, we can deny our limitations and accentuate our possibilities. We can stand above our creatureliness and live as spiritual beings. In its

2. Niebuhr, *The Self and the Dramas of History*, 99.
3. Shakespeare, *The Tragedy of Hamlet*, 63.

Part 1: Sources of Meaning

extreme form we center life around ourselves and try to become like God.

Both options miss the mark. God created us to be human, both finite and infinite, both bound and free, both creature and transcendent. We are to live between heaven and earth and to find meaning in both of them.

To be fully human enables us to see and to honor the humanity of the other person, so that we are equally concerned about our fulfillment and the fulfillment of the other person. We become a rich source of meaning in an uncertain world. Instead of diminishing or destroying life, we align ourselves with St. Paul's call to build up the fellowship.

Marian and Jack Smith are amazing people. Marian suffers from the ill effects of macular degeneration and is legally blind, and in recent years Jack has been impaired by peripheral neuropathy. I would expect them to be bitter and even resentful, but instead they have come to accept their limitations, and in gratitude give of themselves to serve others. They are thankful for the gift of life and for the purpose and meaning that goes with it.

As I have elaborated it, the role of the self stands over against two other approaches to the topic. It differs from Rick Warren's belief[4] that we are created by God to serve a specific and predetermined purpose. Instead we believe that God endowed us with the gift of choice and of self-determination and that it is our responsibility to find purpose and meaning in the life that is given to us and in the life that is shaped by us. Our approach also stands against psychologists who call for the actualization of the self, which means that we are to achieve fulfillment by developing our own innate potentialities. Our paradox of finiteness and infinity is more complex and more demanding than that. We are to become both bound and free creatures.

4. Warren, *The Purpose-Driven Life*, 22–25.

Meaning and the Self

A final point needs to be made about the role of the self in the search for meaning. The self is the arbitrator of meaning. It finds meaning in a wide variety of encounters. Anyone, or anything, that educates or entertains, comforts or confronts, confirms or reproves, addresses and enhances us can be seen as meaningful and therefore as desirable. For example, we may find a lecture especially meaningful, because it addresses our love of learning. Or again, we may find a get well card from a friend meaningful, because it indicates that someone is thinking of us. The self, then, functions on the frontier of our uncertain world and satisfies, or at least addresses, our hunger for a meaningful existence.

Chapter 4

Meaning and the Family

OUR FAMILY OF ORIGIN gives us the first, and maybe the most enduring, impression that we have of life. It is the crucible in which we form our understanding of the world and in which we begin to clarify what we mean to self and others. It is vital, therefore, to know some of the factors that operate in the family and to understand how they equip us, or fail to equip us, for the years ahead.

I will use an intergenerational family perspective to make sense of the operation of key dynamics in a family. In an attempt to domesticate a complex system, I will focus on major concepts and ideas, the first of which is called relational justice.

One of the primary transactions that takes place in the family is illustrated by a brother's comment to his younger sibling, "Your cookie is bigger than mine." Or again, Tommy Smothers of the Smothers Brothers always drew an empathic laugh when he complained: "Mom always liked you better." In a different vein, Job of the Old Testament said, "The Lord gave and the Lord has taken away"[1] but unlike Job we often

---

1. Job 1:21.

Meaning and the Family

get upset not only with what the Lord has taken away but with what the Lord has given in the first place.

The Balance between Give and Receive

There is a serious issue at stake here, and it is a concern to children as much as it is to adults. It refers to the balance between what we give and what we receive in family interactions (in a family). What we give should be reciprocated by what we receive, not in a quid pro quo way but in a qualitative way.

When Lewis, age forty-eight, reflects back on his life, he is aware of a certain void that scars his childhood and adolescent years. He has felt excluded from the family for a long time, especially from the close and exclusive relationship between his wife and oldest daughter. He feels close to his youngest daughter, but that relationship does not compensate for his exclusion from the rest of the family. Recently, he found out that the oldest daughter was dating a young man who he neither liked nor trusted. His wife knew of the relationship but kept it from him. His resentment and sadness grew when he was told that the daughter became pregnant by the young man, but that she decided to terminate the pregnancy.

Lewis admits that he has looked for solace outside the family. He spends an inordinate amount of time at his job and takes pride in the recognition that he gets from his coworkers. Still, Lewis longs for respect and care from his wife and daughter. And when he does not get it for a long time, he becomes morbid and occasionally verbally abusive. It is difficult for him to live in a situation where he means little or nothing to anyone.

Lewis knows that what we give and receive at any one time is often difficult to determine, sometimes because it is

Part 1: Sources of Meaning

difficult to know what is just and fair between family members and sometimes because it is subject to change in our day-to-day transactions within the family. Nevertheless, some kind of equality must be achieved between what we give others and what we receive from them. In the case of Lewis, there seems to be a great imbalance between give and receive. In fact, there doesn't seem to be any serious attempt to achieve a balance in Lewis's family, even if we can grant that Lewis's view of the family may be skewed. The wife and oldest daughter give very little, if any, consideration to other members of the family, and in fact they seem to dismiss Lewis completely by simply ignoring him.

When we look back, we may tend to think that our experience with our family was mostly positive, but in actual fact family life for most of us is frequently ambivalent. It affirms and negates, loves and rejects, supports and undercuts, agrees and disagrees, gives freedom and takes it away. In a word, family life is full of contradictions, but it remains the crucible in which our understanding of life is shaped (formed) and what we mean to ourselves and to others is clarified.

Sometimes children are especially sensitive to unfairness in various relationships within the family. Though they may not be able to articulate the disparity, they know intuitively if there is an imbalance between parents or between siblings or between a parent and siblings. This sensitivity to fairness is a testimony to the pervasive and decisive role that relational justice plays in the family.

If a child emerges from childhood with the feeling that he or she has been cheated of proper care, out of relational justice, he or she may spend a lifetime trying to compensate for the deficit. The child, now an adult, may hold a spouse or some other significant person hostage to the deficit. He or she expects someone to make up for the emptiness. After

Meaning and the Family

all, it is a matter justice. Generally, though, a deficit experienced in one relationship cannot be satisfied in or worked through in another relationship.

The situation with Lewis is not just his problem. It is the family's problem. A great gap has been created in the family, one that makes Lewis feel rejected and not an accepted part of the family. He is cheated of his just due and in the process other members of the family are cheated of a functional family, whether they are aware of it or not. The youngest daughter probably takes the brunt of the family's dysfunction. Though Lewis feels relatively close to her, he is so depleted by neglect that he is fixated on what he is not receiving rather than on what he could or should be giving.

The whole situation takes away from what the family should mean to Lewis, to the youngest daughter, and yes to the wife and oldest daughter. Instead everyone is decimated by the imbalance between giving and receiving, and each member of the family experiences a measure of emptiness and even meaninglessness. Lewis feels undesirable and rejected; the youngest daughter feels abandoned; and the wife and oldest daughter must feel isolated and insecure. Lewis, and other members of the family, do not mean much to themselves if they mean very little to others in the family. Unfortunately, the family's plight is not solved easily. It requires a shake up in the whole system, a renegotiation of relational justice in a very stuck situation.

And as we noted earlier, the family's dysfunction does not end with the break-up of the family. Each person's sense of being cheated becomes an important issue in the relationships that they establish with persons outside the family, and the trouble is transmitted to the next generation unless there is a major change in the family's dynamics.

I have sketched the pessimistic side of familial dysfunction, but intergenerational therapy is more inclusive

Part 1: Sources of Meaning

and positive. Underneath all the dysfunctions, it recognizes that each member of the family has a latent if not an evident desire to right the wrong. Lewis himself expresses the wish. So the family itself, if it is mobilized, can heal the imbalance and fill the void. Family therapy can help. While its task is not to heal the family as an outside force, it can empower the family to take steps toward healing by modeling desirable interaction, that is, by attending to each person in turn and giving them their just due.

Obligations and Entitlements

Intergenerational family therapy recognizes a second kind of transaction that goes on in the family. It talks about obligations and entitlements. Obligations are what we owe the people who have brought us into the world and who have cared for and nurtured us as best they could. Entitlements are what other people owe us, what we deserve to get as human beings and what we should receive in light of what we have given to and been for other people.

James was eight years old when his mother died while giving birth to her fifth child. Less than a year later, James was standing outside a country schoolhouse watching his father come down the road in a horse-drawn wagon. The horses were spooked by a sudden movement in the ditch and lunged to the side. The father was thrown out of the wagon and died when he landed on the frozen Iowa ground. At that point, the family consisted of six children, four boys and two girls. The family was told that they would be separated and placed in different foster homes if they could not make it on their own. The burden fell on the eighteen-year-old boy and the sixteen-year-old girl. The family made it but not without hardship and turmoil.

Meaning and the Family

James carried the deficit of his young years into adulthood and always felt cheated out of parents, out of childhood, out of someone who would be there for him when he needed it. I imagine that emptiness and loneliness permeated the atmosphere, especially on a Sunday afternoon when the absence of a parental presence was amplified.

I think James's feeling of unfairness went beyond the absence of a parent, however traumatic that was. What happened to James said something to him about life itself: that life is basically unfair, that things that are out of control are not to be trusted, and that unfulfilled debits are a real part of our lives.

James was loaded with a sense of obligations but thought that he had few entitlements. He was heavily indebted to his older brother and sister, who served as surrogate parents. He grew up resenting authorities, especially if they were rigid and demanding as his brother was, and he identified with the weak and the needy and would try to help them whenever he could. His experience became part of the family legacy and was handed down through several succeeding generations.

James's experience of family life is an instance of how meaning is shaped and transmitted in the family. It is a product of finitude, fate, and fortune and is shaped by the response we make to them as they impinge on us. Sometimes, we are victims of overpowering forces or developments, but still we always retain an element of freedom to relate to the events as we choose. A step back from the storm helps us to gain a better perspective on it, but our tendency is to plunge ahead with the feeling that we cannot challenge or change the events that are sweeping us away. We may see the tidal wave as a dominating parent or a untimely loss or an unhelpful spouse, but the real culprit may be our own inability to act in an uncertain or an overpowering world.

Part 1: Sources of Meaning

Invisible Loyalties

With obligations and entitlements come what Barbara Krasner calls invisible loyalties, a third type of family transactions. We are indebted to those who have made significant contributions to our lives, and we remain loyal to them long after we have left home and long after we are beholden to them. We may think that we have moved beyond loyalties, but they can be called forth when someone says, unwittingly or by design, "Your family is really weird (or tight or unfriendly)." Instinctively, we come to the defense of our family and will not be pacified easily. We may even try to draw our own blood by attacking the offending person's family.

Loyalty ties are non-negotiable, that is, they cannot be treated as though they never existed. They are also non-transferable, that is, they cannot be put on another person and be satisfied in and through our relationship with the other person. Since loyalty ties often operate invisibly, they can represent obstacles to contemporary relationships. They are obligatory attachments to people who have indebted us to them, and therefore they can block our full commitment to current relationships.

As a young person, Lewis was bound to his parents, especially his mother, by the use of various maneuvers. He remembers an unforgettable instance. He was "around ten" when he did something that did not please his mother. To this day, he does not remember exactly what he said but he recalls, "My mother made it clear to me that I had failed to appreciate what she had done for me. As she packed me off to school, she told me that I didn't deserve her and that when I got home my bags would be waiting for me. I spent the day petrified that I had lost my home and my mother. Of course, that did not happen, but she heightened my resolve

Meaning and the Family

to try to please her, whatever the cost." Lewis's mother is a sad instance of a parent who calls out loyalty ties by dwelling on a child's indebtedness only to use the child to get from the child whatever the parent wants or needs.

Hopefully, Lewis's mother represents a small number of parents who take advantage of loyalty ties. Generally, loyalty ties serve a positive purpose in terms of meaning and the family. Their contribution to the family is deep and defining. For example, what my mother means to me and what I mean to her is rooted in my infancy and early years, and though that meaning has undergone remarkable, or even radical, change, my mother will always remain my mother and mean to me what mothers mean on Mother's Day, beyond the many times when she was not the ideal mother.

Invisible loyalties have a further implication for meaning and the family. When we speak of loyalties we are speaking of commitment, of a promise, spoken or assumed, to remain by another's side beyond the momentary reflex of how we feel toward each other. Commitment gives meaning staying power in relationships in which we share with special people who are tied to us in special ways and who mean special things to us. Meaning is for real, and it can serve as a stable platform on which to build in an otherwise uncertain world. In a larger sense, we are indebted and therefore committed to more than one person, and we live by invisible loyalties to each of them. This fact broadens and deepens the world of meaning in which we live and thrive.

The family is indeed a depository of great meaning, and the roots that it puts down in our early years will either nourish or starve our well-being later in life.

Chapter 5

Treasure Chests of Meaning

IN ADDITION TO RELATIONSHIPS, the self, and the family, there are many other life situations that play an important and active part in our pursuit of meaning. As a group they deserve the title of treasure chests, which means that they are valuable occurrences that serve as storehouses of meaningful events and occasions.

The list of treasure chests may be extensive, but I want to cover only a few of the major ones. I will offer a brief description of each chest, but then I invite you, the reader, to reflect on your own experience of them, since they are unique to each individual.

Special Times and Places

The small town of Bally is tucked in the green pastures of Pennsylvania, off the beaten track. Ruth and I came to the town with friends who thought we might enjoy a pasta dinner at an Italian restaurant. They were right. The setting was quaint, the owner and his staff were friendly, and the food was delicious. After dinner, our friends took us to a local creamery where we indulged in a dish of homemade ice

Treasure Chests of Meaning

cream. We enjoyed the evening so much that we have gone back on a regular basis for the last twelve years.

Our visits to Bally are filled with meaning. We have savored a variety of Italian meals, but mostly our visits are filled with causal conversation, relaxed reminiscing, and honest sharing. At the mere mention of Bally, meaningful times come to mind, and we are always eager to return to one of our favorite places.

No doubt, your life, like ours, is filled with occasions of special times and places. We could write a book about the events that fill our lives with pleasant memories. For example, I remember my college years when the whole academic community sang with passion "college of our brightest days," or I recall my days as a young parent when our children were born and grew up, or I still treasure my years of teaching when I experienced moments of great satisfaction. These special moments, and many more like them, have become an indelible part of who I am, of where I have been, and of what I have done.

Special times and places make a threefold contribution to our lives. They give us a sense of continuity, a sense of belonging, and a sense of increased fullness.

Continuity

Our daily lives often seem like a series of disconnected notes. We may be able to stand a certain degree of change and instability, but even the most flexible person among us needs to have some degree of continuity in his or her life. Places and times that are dear to us are tangible evidence of continuity, and they serve as connecting points in an otherwise disconnected world. Our place of origin, the family homestead, and the summer retreat may change in noticeable ways over the years, but their basic character and meaning remain embedded in our memories. They have an enduring and relatively stable quality that lends a sense of consistency and meaning to our lives.

Belonging

Special times and places also add a sense of belonging to our lives. We feel a part of a community that goes beyond our autonomous selves. Andras Angyal thinks that the need to go beyond the self is basic to our nature and cannot be thwarted. He puts it in this way: one of the essential marks of the individual is the tendency to "surrender himself (sic) willingly, to seek a home for himself in and to become an organic part of something that he conceives as greater than himself."[1]

When my sister Iva Lee and her husband Roger died, the family was surprised to learn that they wanted their ashes interred in the distant military cemetery at Point Loma, California. Roger had been in the armed forces, but he seldom referred to the experience. There may be a number of reasons why they choose a military cemetery, but I think that one of them was that Point Loma, and what it stood for, was special to them. It put them in touch with a larger reality than themselves. The rows of white crosses, the hallowed ground that honored those who had sacrificed for their country, and the sight of San Diego Bay below addressed and satisfied their need to be part of a world and a cause that was beyond the parameters of their individual existence.

---

1. Aden and Benner, *Counseling and the Human Predicament*, 110.

Fullness

Special times and places contribute to the fullness of life. They add a tangible and historic dimension to our lives and fill out, and give concrete form to, who we are and who we have been. More basically, they become a part of our history, our identity, our relationships, our very being. Though we may grow far beyond them, they still retain some of their importance to us. The threat of incapacitation or death often awakens in us the desire to go "home" one last time.

Our return to former times and places often reaches a point when "things have changed." Recently, my wife and I returned to our alma mater (as we had done for many years) in order to attend the college's homecoming festivities. It was a reunion year for my wife, so she had any number of friends in attendance. I was sort of an "extra." I was not a part of the celebration of seventy-five years of music at the college, so I had time on my hands. What surprised and troubled me was that I was not received as warmly as I had been in previous years. I found out that a few of my friends suffered from loss of memory, but what I felt was the emptiness of lost friendships in a time and place that was very dear to me.

Later, when I reflected on the weekend, I realized that what had happened was a natural occurrence. There comes a time, even with special places and times, when we need to let go and move on. We don't have to wipe away all traces of past friendships, but we do need to adjust our expectations of them and to realize that we too have changed. We now look to current relationships more than past ones to fill our lives (world) with meaning.

Part 1: Sources of Meaning

Nodal Events

Nodal events, or significant turning points in our lives, become storehouses of meaning. The commitment of marriage that brings together two different families and represents a link to future generations. The birth of a child that means the extension of the family and the arrival of new possibilities and new directions within the family. Anniversaries that mark the passage of time and celebrate the achievement of significant milestones. Divorce that posits a breach in the family and the loss of possibilities and commitments. And finally there is death, a stark reminder of what we should have known all along: "The Moving finger writes and having writ moves on, Nor all your piety and wit shall lure it back to cancel half a line, Nor all your tears wash out of a Word of it."[2] These nodal events, and many more like them, become depositories of meaning and shape our personal and interpersonal lives.

Brief Encounters

In addition to extended relationships, our lives are made up of what I call moments of meaning or brief encounters. The stranger we meet at a social event, the neighbor we talk to over the fence, or the person we sit next to on a plane may bring with them a glow of light in an otherwise drab world. Our mundane world is suddenly transformed into an exciting and meaningful encounter, and we are renewed by the renewal of meaning. Whether we are the person talking or the person listening, there is a person touching the life of another person, and in the process there is the rebirth and the sharing of meaning. We may not have done anything unusual to bring the moment about, and we certainly did

2. Khayyam, *The Rubaiyat*.

Treasure Chests of Meaning

not will it into being, but suddenly we are in the middle of it and we are enlivened by its benefits. Our tendency is to try to hang on to it, but that may only hasten its departure. Instead we should give ourselves to it and participate in it with our whole being.

In the Gospel of Mark, Jesus invites three disciples to follow him up a high mountain and while they are up there, Jesus is transfigured before them—"his clothes became dazzling white."[3] The disciples were in the midst of an ecstatic and moving moment, and guess what they thought of doing. Peter—impetuous Peter—said to Jesus, "It is good for us to be here; let us make three dwellings" and stay up here.

The disciples wanted to "freeze the moment," to hang on to a moment filled with wonder and meaning. Fortunately, Jesus did not agree to it, because that may have deadened the moment. Besides, Jesus and the disciples went down the mountain, and Jesus was given the opportunity to extend his ministry. He healed a boy tormented by a ruthless spirit.

Family Albums

"A picture is worth a thousand words." That is certainly true of family pictures, especially if they are organized into albums. They tell a story all their own, and give a visual and evolving picture of the family that is hard to match.

It was Jack's eightieth birthday party. The family had gathered together to celebrate the occasion. The birthday cards and packages were piled in a haphazard way, and Jack began to open the gifts. There were the usual humorous cards and a tie or two that did not match anything he had.

Jack got to a flat, rectangular package and paused to guess what it might be. The obvious guess was a book, but

---

3. Mark 9:3.

Part 1: Sources of Meaning

Jack could not imagine what kind of book would be appropriate for an eightieth birthday. As the wrapping came off the package, he caught a glimpse of himself on the front cover under the title, *JHB: His Life, Legend, and Love.* Jack flipped through a number of pages. The book was an immediate hit and remained a hit for weeks to come. It was filled with pictures of ancestors that Jack had not seen before, with pictures of his parents and siblings, of his aunts and uncles and cousins. Some of the pictures were surrounded by well wishes; others by remembrances from the past. The book brought back all kinds of memories and relationships that were an important part of Jack's life. It was a depository of great meaning, and Jack loved and cherished it.

Genealogies

Genealogies give a historical perspective on the family, and they serve as a depository of meanings from a wide variety of sources. They contain facts and fictions, objective and subjective reports, humorous and tragic accounts, cowardly and heroic deeds. They come from official records and unproven beliefs, and were passed down by reliable and not so reliable storytellers. Yet they are a valuable source of a family's history and give revealing snatches of the family, including a few family secrets that may or may not be generally known.

The more I worked with my own family history, the more I decided that I was in no position to judge which tradition was true and which one was not, unless I had solid proof to back up my decision. My task was to record all the information I had without registering my own personal opinion. Besides, I decided that the information I had, even if it contradicted itself, gave a fuller, often a more interesting picture of the family. I think that genealogies have that

Treasure Chests of Meaning

gift to give, and their gift may enhance the meanings related to the family rather than taking them away.

We are surrounded by many sources of meaning, but we need eyes to see and ears to hear; otherwise, we live in a barren world that is deprived of meaning, of sights unseen and sounds unheard. In the previous four chapters, I have tried to sensitize us to some of the "sights and sounds" that fill our lives with meaning. Actually, though, many of the meanings that are meaningful to us are often so basic to our everyday existence that we can be unaware of the vitality and richness that they give to our lives. In the morning our family, maybe like yours, gathers around the breakfast table to share the first meal of the day. The event is filled with latent meaning—what a good night's sleep means to each of us, what we mean to each other, what the day offers us and demands of us. These meanings give way to more immediate concerns, such as consuming a quick bowl of cereal and getting to work on time. The life-giving gift of relationships, family, and friendships is passed over temporarily by the need to satisfy the demands of the moment.

Meaning lives in images. Ideas and beliefs have their own power, but images linger in the mind as paradigms of meaning. The image of Santa Claus remains a symbol of goodness and gift-giving long after we see him as more myth than reality. The image of Martin Luther King Jr., standing on the steps of the Lincoln Memorial and delivering the "I Have a Dream" speech is a memorable appeal for racial equality and harmony.

Treasure chests are filled with precious jewels of times and places and pictures. And they are precious and defining depositories of meaning and memories.

Part 2

Challenges to Meaning

Chapter 6

Meaning and Suffering

WE HAVE SEEN HOW meaning becomes a part of our lives and how it helps to define who we are. It is time to discuss some of the major ways in which meaning is put to the test by life itself. We begin with the reality and role of suffering in our lives.

Suffering is a broad term referring to many different forms of human distress. Gerstenberger and Schrage identify five different sources of suffering: loss, illness, violence, fear, and failure.[1] These forms of suffering can be experienced physically, mentally, or socially and can range in intensity from mild to severe.

Job's Response to Suffering

The authors of the Book of Job in the Old Testament were wise and profound observers of life. They created a dramatic story of Job's response to suffering.[2] The story begins when Satan appeared at a meeting of "heavenly beings."

1. Gerstenberger and Schrage, *Suffering*, 2–3.
2. Job 1:8–21

51

Part 2: Challenges to Meaning

When God starts to brag about Job being "a blameless and upright man," Satan says, "Come on, God. Job is faithful to you, because you reward him richly. Take his benefits away, and Job will turn against you." God replies, "Go ahead. Test him."[3] In a short time, Job lost nearly all that he possessed. He lost his sons and daughters, all his servants, and his sheep and camels. Nevertheless, Job remained faithful and did not accuse God of wrongdoing. Satan was not satisfied. He returned to God and got permission to test Job's faith by a frontal attack on Job's body. He inflicted "loathsome sores on Job from the sole of his foot to the crown of his head." Job suffered mightily but still "did not sin with his lips." He remained reverent to God: "The Lord gave, and Lord has taken away; blessed be the name of the Lord."[4]

Job's piety is not his only response to intense suffering. He also cursed the day that he was born and consigned it to darkness and despair. "Let gloom and deep darkness claim it. Let clouds settle upon it; let the blackness of the day terrify it."[5] Job went on to complain bitterly to God, saying in effect "the intensity of [my] suffering is ample justification for the bitterness of [my] complaints."[6] Throughout his ordeal, Job insisted that he was innocent and therefore that there was no just cause or reason for his suffering.

Job's reaction sounds a bit like our own. We often feel that suffering is meaningless and not deserved, that it serves no good purpose. More pointedly, Job's story raises two questions about suffering that are profound and still relevant to us today. "If faith does not benefit us, especially in very trying moments, what does that do to our faith?" And "If life loses all meaning, and appears to be grossly

3. Job 1:6–12.
4. Job 2:7, 2:10, 1:21.
5. Job 3:5.
6. *Interpreter's Dictionary of the Bible*, II, 918.

Meaning and Suffering

unfair, what does that do to our image of God?" I have an idea of what might happen. I did not suffer as Job suffered, but it was a very trying and confusing time for me.

In the last three years, I have gone through a series (I would say an endless series) of health problems. I was hospitalized for two weeks after two months of medical trouble and spent part of the time in the intensive care unit of the hospital. Like Job, I started out believing in the graciousness of God in giving and therefore in God's right to take away. After a while I did not gain much solace from that belief. I begin to wonder why I was suffering as much as I was, and I wondered aloud where God was in all of this. As time went on my impatience grew. I identified with Job's complaints against God and in moments began to doubt God's wisdom or justice.

Unlike Job, I did not think of asking for a court in which I could present my case before God, but I held my own private and intense struggle with God. In other words, my suffering became a test of my faith and a struggle to find meaning in a fragile and uncertain world. My body, which before I took for granted, became a source of uncertainty. I did not fully understand what was going on with me, and I did not grasp the meaning of the doctor's short-term and long-term diagnoses. But it was clear to me that I was not to get out of bed without a nurse or an aid at my side, so it became a source of great meaning, and a sign of hope, when I could walk to the end of the hospital corridor with my wife and daughter and look down on a small, man-made park with a tiny stream flowing through it.

In addition to my medical condition, I experienced a shake up in what I valued and in what I aimed for. I could identify with the Preacher in Ecclesiastes, who concluded

Part 2: Challenges to Meaning

that many of our strivings are meaningless, a chasing "after wind."[7]

Before I got sick, I was involved obsessively in a manuscript that I was preparing to send to a publisher. During my illness, I lost all interest in the manuscript and did not care if it ever got published. I took a similar attitude toward many other things that were part of my world, whether they were major or minor, urgent or not. Concerns about my health became a high priority. Fortunately, our daughter, who was with us at the time, was sharp enough to keep up with the bills and to attend to other matters, including my need to take an assortment of pills on time. And in the process, I learned what was really important—that the care of loved ones is close to the heart of life's meaning.

Thankfully, there is one point where my experience differs from Job's. Job pressed for a day in court, and when he got it he got more than he asked for. Instead of listening to him, God confronted him with power and his unsearchable deeds, making Job feel small and overwhelmed. Faced with God's omnipotence and omniscience, Job bows before God and "repents in dust and ashes."[8] He grants that the meaning of human suffering is hidden in, and can remain with, the power and wisdom of God.

I have great respect for the majesty of God and continue to marvel at God's wondrous works, but thank goodness I have been given another understanding of God, and in the midst of suffering I was more in need of God's compassion than I was of God's greatness.

---

7. Eccl 2:26.
8. Job 42:6.

God's Response to Suffering

The Christian faith is bold enough—or foolish enough—to declare that God is a suffering God, a God who does not stand above our suffering but who is with us in suffering. There is a cluster of closely related beliefs about God that support this conclusion: God through Christ took on human form and therefore experienced suffering as we do. On the cross, Christ experienced firsthand the pain and humiliation of suffering and therefore can identify with us in our pain. It was through suffering that Christ released us from the consequences of our broken relationship with God. All of these beliefs about suffering and God support faith's conviction that God is not only with us in suffering but that that our suffering causes God to suffer.

I think this understanding of God has several profound things to say, and wise counsel to give, in terms of our struggle with suffering.

First, suffering is to be faced (not sought after but faced) rather than denied.

We tend to deny our suffering, to pretend that we are not suffering as much as we are. The wife of an alcoholic husband would really be unhappy if she took an honest look at her tormented life. The husband of an abrasive wife would never admit to the boys at the club that he is abused. To admit that we are suffering feels like we are undermining the fragile life of happiness that we have built up. Nevertheless, honest admission is the first step toward relief.

One day Christ said to his disciples, "We are going up to Jerusalem, and everything that is written about the Son of Man by the prophets will be accomplished."[9] Christ had a good idea of what lay ahead, but he went to Jerusalem anyway. By his example, Christ encourages us to take our

9. Luke 18:31.

Part 2: Challenges to Meaning

suffering seriously. "He invites us to acknowledge our pain and to give full recognition to our defeat or loss."[10] And if God is with us, and not against us, in suffering we can rest in the assurance that God will not forsake us but will support and sustain, even though it may not seem that way in moments of great stress.

Second, our reaction to suffering may be an encouraging example to fellow believers in the faith, especially if they are weak in the faith. With God's help, suffering becomes a means of increasing our faith, our reliance on God. Actually, suffering may drive us to God, not simply because we want to escape punishment but because we emerge with a clearer picture of our weakness and need for help. We realize that we live in a fallen world and that in our brokenness we make decisions and get into situations where suffering is the logical outcome (consequence). In other words, we see that we are part of the problem and that we cannot get out of it by our own power. Thus we are driven to God. We realize that we must put our trust in a power that stands above us, a power that is more powerful than the finiteness and the uncertainties of life. When we go to God, we find ourselves embraced by a suffering, caring presence.

Third, suffering in the name of Christ can edify, can build up the fellowship in a twofold sense. Suffering and being comforted equips us to console others with the "consolation with which we ourselves are consoled by God."[11] Having experienced God's comfort, we can enter into the afflictions of others in a much more empathic way, and in this sense we build up the fellowship by re-presenting (offering) the comfort of Christ to our wounded neighbor. Besides, in suffering we are doing in our own way what Christ has done for us, namely, we are bearing the pain and suffer-

10. Aden and Hughes, *Preaching God's Compassion*, 7.
11. 2 Cor 1:4.

Meaning and Suffering

ing of others and thus lightening their load and taking away their isolation. St. Paul says that he is "completing what is lacking in Christ's afflictions for the sake of his body, that is, the church."[12] By this phrase he does not mean that we complete, or add anything to, the saving work of Christ. Instead he means that as Christians we are united with Christ in sufferings like his and that when we endure those sufferings for the sake of the church we are carrying on his mission and work, that is, we are building up the fellowship.

However noble, the Christian understanding of suffering does not take away our suffering. It puts it in proper perspective and empowers us to go through "the darkest valley," as the Psalmist puts it in the twenty-third psalm. But the response to suffering is ours to make. In the hopelessness of a concentration camp, Frankl became aware of the toll that suffering can extract from us. In fact, out of his experience he concluded that suffering is one of the threats, if not the major threat, that can torment our existence and rob it of meaning. It was out of this experience, an experience that brought Frankl to the brink of despair, that he arrived at an empowering insight. He found that however tragic or dehumanizing the situation, we retain a freedom that cannot be taken from us—the freedom to choose how we will respond to our plight. This freedom, this capacity allows us to stand above the fray and to find meaning in life, even in suffering.

As a final word, I like Job's reaction to God more than I appreciate what Job's three friends said to him. After being wise enough to sit in silence with Job for three days, his friends began to explain to Job what his suffering meant.[13] The first friend, Eliphaz, defends God's justice and says that if Job will turn to God, God who is powerful will deliver

12. Col 1:24.
13. See *Interpreter's Dictionary of the Bible,* II, 418f.

Part 2: Challenges to Meaning

Job from adversity. The second friend, Bildad, implies that Job's children got what they deserved and suggests that if Job will return to God, he might be restored to a good life. The third friend, Zophar, maintains that God's wisdom and power are beyond human comprehension and that Job ought to change his attitude and ask God for help. All three friends were so busy defending God's justice that they did not see who was in front of them—a man in great suffering and one who stood in need of empathic and unconditional compassion, or as Nicholas Wolterstorff put it in his hour of torment, "To comfort me, you have to come close. Come sit beside me, on my mourning bench."[14]

---

14. Wolterstorff, *Lament for a Son,* 34.

Chapter 7

Meaning and Old Age

I AM NOW IN my senior years and enjoying many aspects of them. But I also experience emptiness, or the lack of meaning, in ways that I have never known before. I have lost the role and status that I once had, not only in my professional life but also in my family life. At family gatherings, my wife and I are seldom the center of attention as we once were. That is a natural development in some ways, but it means that we often feel set aside or out of it as our children deal with the world in which they live. Fortunately, they are solicitous of our health or our other concerns, but by taking over they contribute unintentionally to the emptiness of our lives.

Nancy, age 72, is experiencing changes in herself. She is less interested in being with people, and she has forgotten many events that happened in her life. She lives with the loss fairly well, and yet there is an emptiness in her life that was not there before. Now Nancy spends a lot of time going through old papers and pictures, and she gains much joy—and some sadness—by reading about past events and former relationships. What she is doing, I think, is finding meaning in life by recalling past events. She is filling the emptiness of her older years by going back, and reading about life, when it was alive with meaning.

But she is doing more than that. Her search to find meaning in a diminished world has become her purpose to live, her reason to be. She says that she is going through old papers and pictures, so that when she dies her daughter will not be left with "piles of stuff." Being considerate of her daughter is part of her mission, but living with purpose, having something to do and making some kind of contribution to life in a world that prizes busyness, is also a vital part of the picture.

It may seem like Nancy is doing the stereotypical thing of escaping the present by going back to the past. There may be some truth to this observation, but more positively she is engaged in a life-giving activity. She is addressing what it means to be human and is fulfilling that quest, not just by recalling pleasant memories of the past but by reliving unfortunate and sad events that happened back there.

Living with Change

We older adults are like most people. We seldom welcome change, especially if it comes suddenly or takes away our control of things. But our senior years are full of change, and the changes often have to do with diminishing life, rather than expanding it. We experience change in at least five areas of life.

First, there is change in our physical existence. Our bodies are not what they use to be. A look in a mirror or a look through the family album confronts us with undeniable evidence. In addition, we begin to have physical complaints one after another, and our visits to the doctor's office get more frequent and maybe more serious. One condition leads to another, and we sometimes land between a rock

Meaning and Old Age

and a hard place. A major change in our health may necessitate a change in where we live, which in turn becomes a tangible indication that the meaning of life as we know it has shifted and become more unpredictable.

Second, there is change in our vitality or energy. We move more slowly and get tired more easily. We may even require an afternoon nap, but in any case the sense of vitality that we once had gives way to reduced activity and limited energy. In our younger years, we could get things done. Now there are some things that we cannot do or even should not do.

Third, there is a change in our efficiency and productivity. Tasks take longer and sometimes it even takes longer to understand what the task is. In any case, we are not as productive as we once were and even worse people may not depend on us for what needs to be done, because we cannot do it fast enough. We are given manageable or menial tasks, and instead of being a repository of wisdom, what we know or can do is treated as outdated, if not meaningless.

When I retired I was asked to reflect on the years ahead. In response, I raised the question "Who will I be when I am no longer what I am now?" I did not realize how much I would struggle with this question. No status. No connections. No challenges. Instead, unstructured time and a diffuse identity. So I am still struggling with, "Who am I now? What do I mean to myself without the feedback of who I am to students and to other people?"

Fourth, there is change in our relationships. We may even lose relationships through death or through friends moving away, and in any case we may have less energy to maintain relationships. We may become less active and more passive. And often how people, especially our children, relate to us may change our relationship with them in noticeable or unwanted ways. While we may be envied

Part 2: Challenges to Meaning

for what seems like a leisurely life, that very fact places us outside the village square.

Five, there is a change in our social standing. We are no longer considered an authority or looked to as a source of power or strength. In fact, we may be seen as dependent—more like children than like parents. Meanwhile, we are retired in a work-oriented society and have become part of the past generation as grandparents or even great grandparents. We live in a world where what we mean to self and others and what they mean to us are not self-evident but must be reworked in some acceptable way.

Three Other Challenges

We must adjust to all these changes as they come along, not once but many times. And the changes themselves are not our greatest challenge. If we are to live with some sense of peace and satisfaction in our senior years, we must be able to do at least three other things: to accept the past, to live with the present, and to embrace what is to come.

Accept the Past

Erik Erikson, a developmental psychologist, highlights the importance of being able to accept our life as we have lived it.[1] He maintains that as our potency, performance, and adaptability decline in old age, we are confronted with the need to become what he calls a person of mature integrity. We must be content with and be able to accept the events that have shaped us and the directions that we have chosen. On the one hand, this means that we are content with,

---

1. See a summary of Erikson's point in Aden, Benner, and Ellens, *Christian Perspectives on Human Development*, 31–33.

Meaning and Old Age

and are able to accept, both the determinations that have shaped us and the self-determinations by which we have shaped ourselves. On other hand, it means that we are able to face the ambiguity of life, to acknowledge and assimilate both the triumphs and disappointments that we have experienced. We can grant that our life has been a mixture of success and failure, a nexus of health and disease. Both meanings, taken together, describe a person who has a genuine and deep-seated acceptance of life as that life has been lived and experienced.

According to Erikson, failure to achieve this sense of satisfaction means that we may struggle with feelings of bitterness and emptiness. We resent the many limitations of life and cannot acknowledge death as our imminent and final fate. For Erikson, the outcome of the struggle is determined in good part by our developmental history, but we are not locked into a predetermined end. We can take steps to rework our history, not by erasing unacceptable details but by changing our response to them.

Part of being able to accept the past involves a review of our life, a looking back on what we have done and been. Not everyone goes through this process, but many of us do, even though we may not be fully aware of it.

There is a certain art in relating to the past, in remembering what we have done and been. In actuality, there are at least three kinds of remembering, and it is the third kind of relating to the past that seems especially helpful.

First, there is a remembering that stereotypically is what the older person does. He or she talks about the past, usually in an objectified or even in a repetitious way. He or she relates to the past as something out there, something that happened a long time ago. Remembering in this sense is mostly telling a story about what happened, or supposedly happened, without really being personally involved.

Part 2: Challenges to Meaning

The self remembers the self, either to escape the present or to glorify the "good old days." In short, this kind of remembering tends to be characterized by detachment or even by shallowness and is used to serve the interests of the storyteller. As such, it is a reassurance against the desolation of old age but is not a very good way to come to terms with our past.

Second, there is a remembering at the other end of the spectrum. It is the remembering of psychoanalysis or actually of most therapeutic endeavors. It is designed to help us get in touch with the past, to recall it and to own it. It deals with experiences that have been repressed or denied, because they were unacceptable to the self. This kind of remembering is often a *long* and difficult process of overcoming defenses and resistances, so that the person's past can be comprehended and owned in its complexity and detail. It can help to clear the obstacles that are in the way of a fuller life.

The third kind of remembering is not a repetitious or objective recall of the past. It is also not a detailed remembrance of repressed material. Instead it is a personal, often a spontaneous, reliving of past relationships. It is holding someone who is dear to us in remembrance and re-experiencing shared meanings and notable events. It is getting in touch with one's world and being touched by it.

Remembering in this sense has more to do with "our life together" than it does with how we feel about this or that. It deals with the world of relationships that were. It focuses on significant events or persons while acknowledging the particular meaning that they had for us. Nicholas Wolterstorff's *Lament for a Son*[2] is an illustration of this kind of remembering. Wolterstorff lost his son to a mountain climbing accident. He reflects back on his son and on

---

2. Wolterstorff, *A Lament for a Son*. I retell his story in Aden and Hughes, *Preaching God's Compassion*, 60–62.

Meaning and Old Age

the plans and hopes he had for him "And now he's gone. That future which I embraced to myself has been destroyed. He slipped out of my arms. For twenty-five years I guarded and sustained and encouraged him to grow and become a man of his own. Then he slipped out and was smashed."[3]

Of course, Wolterstorff deals with particular feelings about his son's death, but mostly he holds his son in remembrance and relives the life he had with him and now the life that bears his absence. His remembrances serve at least three purposes: they review and relive the past; they are a tribute to his son and an acknowledgment of his importance and meaning to the family; and they recognize the absence of the son and become a foretaste of life without him.

The importance of the third kind of remembering is described in similar fashion by a former student who recalls the death of a friend and reflects on the time she spent with her friend's family as they looked through photo albums, videos, letters, and memorabilia. "We spent several days together exchanging pictures and stories, and discussing aspects of the funeral and reception. I cried buckets of tears . . . but I also laughed because I could not escape the beauty of our friendship, and the fun and momentous times we had shared."

The student's description of the role of remembering in grief can be transferred to our need to accept the past. It recalls significant events and meaningful relationships, acknowledging our disappointments and celebrating our joys. It is not an extended analysis of the past but a series of intermittent snapshots that are paradigmatic in our mind. In this sense, they are a neat summary of who we are and of what we have been. They also point to our place in the family or the community and illuminate the meaning that we had for them and they had for us. Implicitly if not explicitly,

3. Wolterstroff, *Lament for a Son*, 58.

they acknowledge where we are in life and help us to own it and to live it.

At its best, the third kind of remembering relates our life to God. It represents an opening of our life to God, a placing of our past in the hands of God. This is important, because both our impending death and our review of life raise ultimate questions. Why did I live? Why must I die? What is the meaning of it all? What happens to me after my earthly life? Most of us are unable to give a satisfying answer to these questions. We therefore look beyond ourselves for a framework, a belief system in which we can begin to get some answers to these questions. And when the answers reach the end of their explanatory power, we simply put our life in God's hands. We live by faith, believing that the triune God has sustained us in our living, has forgiven us in our failure, and has renewed us in our losses. This faith has the power to comfort us. We are assured of God's enduring love, and we can affirm our past with its disappointments and its victories as a gift that we have received and experienced.

Live the Present

We must be able to affirm the past, but also to live with a sense of fullness and meaning in the present. "One day at a time" is the watchword of Alcoholics Anonymous. It enables those who are addicted to alcohol to concentrate their efforts on the immediate situation instead of focusing on the formidable task of staying sober day after day. Living a day at a time has also become the password of the hospice movement. Hospice, an international program for the care of the dying and their families, seeks to help terminally ill patients increase the quality of life rather than being preoccupied with its length. It empowers patients to live in the present by creating an atmosphere in which they and their families can work together to make the most of life while it lasts. The program includes an honest acknowledgment of the approach of death and a discussion of its meaning for the patient and the family. The goal is to help the patient die with dignity and a sense of self-worth within the warm embrace of family members.

Psychotherapy, too, tries to empower the person to live in the present instead of being stuck in the past or escaping into the future. It is not against acknowledging the past or planning for the future, but it has found that we often cluttered up the present with unresolved issues or undue expectations. Instead of being able to give ourselves to the moment and enjoying its possibilities and meanings, we get away from life as it is and dwell in some wished-for world.

Actually, psychotherapy shows that there are at least two primary ways in which we clutter up the present. One is when unresolved issues from the past live in and distort the present, and the other is when we load the present with undue and unrealistic expectations. Sigmund Freud unearthed the first obstacle, Karen Horney the second one. We need to give brief attention to both.

The Distortion of the Present

Sigmund Freud maintained that we tend to repress unacceptable desires or impulses, that is, we tend to keep them out of consciousness.[4] The repression of desires does not strip them of their driving power. They continue to exist and to move toward some kind of satisfaction. They manifest themselves in our thoughts, words, or deeds. They come out in devious and indirect ways, expressing them-

4. See Freud, *Collected Papers*, IV, 86.

selves in our daily life as slips of the tongue, neurotic symptoms, crippling phobias, unsettling dreams, and a myriad of other forms. The upshot of this development is that the individual is tied to his or her past, that is, he or she lives in, and responds to, the present in terms of some previously unassimilated desire or experience.

This bondage to the past, this distortion of the present, can be illustrated by many examples. The hungry child's wish for ice cream is not granted, but in his sleep he dreams of falling into a large bowl of it. A spouse does not take time to mourn the loss of a partner, but when the family suffers the loss of a pet she goes into a deep and prolonged depression. A family member loses a job under circumstances that reflect on his or her competence, but instead of expressing the feelings directly, he or she flies off the handle when a friend makes a casual comment about the inadequacy of an acquaintance. The untimely reaction to present events often takes more complex forms, but the point is illustrated. Thoughts or experiences that are repressed at the time they happen can continue to exist and can distort our perception of and our reaction to present circumstances or events.

Freud's insight is directly applicable to our struggle to live in the present. Events or relationships in life that remain troubling or unassimilated may haunt our senior days and distort the way in which we see, and react to, the present moment. If we have had a series of losses earlier in life and have not come to terms with them the losses posed by the many changes that occur in our senior years may be weighed down by and even distorted by previous unassimilated losses. In a word, we may be mourning previous losses as much as we are mourning present ones.

Meaning and Old Age

The Tyranny of the "Shoulds"[5]

Karen Horney adds another perspective to our distortion of the present. She develops a concept called "the tyranny of the shoulds," which refers to insatiable inner dictates that operate on the premise "that nothing should be, or is, impossible for" us.[6] They are completely insensitive to the actual conditions under which we can find genuine fulfillment. Instead our whole life revolves around what ought to be, for we are dominated by the relentless demand that we should be different and more perfect than we really are. We are driven by what we "should be able to do, to be, to feel, to know." In this sense, the "shoulds" are qualitatively different than genuine ideals, for they are permeated by a spirit of egoism and are dominated by a spirit of coercion. Instead of urging us toward the actualization of our real selves, they destroy spontaneous growth, disturb relationships with others, and force us to live a life of insatiable demands.

Concrete examples are abundant: instead of enjoying the success of the moment, John minimizes his achievement and actually berates himself for not achieving more. Joan sticks with a demanding diet and loses a pound a week for several months, but all the while she demands more of herself and refuses to say that the diet is working. A mother devotes hours of care to her ailing child, even to the point of sacrificing her own needs, but she does not think that she is doing enough and sees the child's failure to improve as her own failure.

These are only a few instances of Horney's point. They highlight the way we bankrupt the present by measuring

---

5. Portions of the following description of Karen Horney's theory of personality are taken from my previous use of it in Aden and Hughes, *Preaching God's Compassion*, 127ff.

6. Horney, *Neurosis and Human Growth*, 68.

Part 2: Challenges to Meaning

it against the standards of what ought to be. We live in the hope that we will do better the next time and that eventually we will succeed in being and in doing the ideal. This means, in effect, that we get quagmired in guilt, which is enflamed by our unrealistic and inordinate expectations and rendered unforgivable by our unrelenting and insatiable demands. In effect, we disembowel the present. Our energies are preempted, our aspirations are skewed, our very selves are distorted or abandoned.

This whole scenario distorts our senior years. We cannot live with any sense of meaning and worth. We cannot live in the present, because it is paled by the intense inner dictates of what we think we ought to be or do. We cannot affirm life, because in fact we are engaged in a process that means the death of who we really are. We are held in the stranglehold of guilt and regret, unable to accept the forgiveness of God because we are bound by an overwhelming sense of failure and personal unworthiness. This is one of the radical ways in which our life can distort our present moment. It can shut us off from the very gift that Christ came to give us, namely, freedom from our own feverish attempts to make ourselves right and acceptable.

Embrace What Is to Come

In our senior years, the future is often uncertain. We may be in a stable situation now, but very easily it can turn into an uncertain and challenging future. We need a living faith that empowers us to trust whatever lies beyond the horizon.

To trust in God is not something that we may find easy to do when we are really tested. When things are going well, we may think that we have a strong faith. But when adversity comes, when we begin to experience some of the serious challenges of our older years, then our faith may falter. Trust

Meaning and Old Age

in God—the kind of trust that sustains us—may come at the end of a hard battle, after everything else fails.

To embrace what is to come applies not only to this life but also to what God has in store for us. We celebrate the resurrection of Jesus with its assurance that Jesus goes to prepare rooms for us. In this sense, death is not the end of our existence but the gateway to new life. We may not be anxious to get there. And yet we have the assurance that new life can come out of death, that God is not defeated by the cross.

While suffering threatens us with meaninglessness, God's presence and faithfulness in our suffering gives us hope and new meaning. Our fate matters to God and we are of infinite and supreme concern to God. It is God, then, who gives meaning to our lives and fills us with peace and purpose beyond our feverish attempts to find them. What may surprise us is the simplicity of the request. In Frankl's terms, it is to fulfill the "specific vocation or mission that is ours to do"; in Christian terms, it is to serve the neighbor in need. So simple and yet so elusive and demanding.

Chapter 8

Meaning and Death

IN THE LAND OF the Philistines there lived a giant named Goliath. He was a mighty man, equipped with the finest armor and towering over a young, naïve youth named David. The people of Israel feared Goliath and quaked at his mere presence. They tried to avoid doing battle with him at all costs.

One day David went to a stream and meticulously picked up five smooth stones. He put them in his shepherd's bag and with his sling went out to meet the giant. Goliath was insulted at the sight of young David, but David was not deterred. He took a stone from his bag, put it in his sling, and struck Goliath in the forehead. Goliath fell to the earth, defeated and immobilized.[1]

A giant dwells in our land and its name is death. Death says something very negative and discouraging about life. Because it is the end, the extinction of everything we are, death implies that life itself is ultimately meaningless. No matter what we accomplish or what we stand for, death tends to wipe us out as living creatures and thus it implies that all our striving is vain and our life serves no lasting purpose.

1. 1 Sam 17.

Meaning and Death

This scenario of discouragement is reflected in the Old Testament's struggle with the brevity of life. The Psalmist moans, "As for man [sic], his days are like grass; he flourishes like a flower of the field; for the wind passes over it, and it is gone, and its place knows it no more."[2] In Job's extended defense of his life, he echoes the thought of the Psalmist, "Man that is born of a woman is of few days and full of trouble. He comes forth like a flower, and withers; he flees like a shadow, and continues not."[3] The fleeting nature of life, like death itself, contributes to our sense of meaninglessness.

Given the dreadfulness of death, our society has been very attentive to its presence and has tried to domesticate it, actually to eliminate it, in any number of ways. We will consider three approaches to the problem. We have not been as successful as David was with Goliath, but nevertheless we keep trying.

Before we proceed any further, we need to recognize a positive side of death. Ironically, death serves or contributes to the meaning of life. By standing as a definite and immovable parameter of life, it urges us to reexamine our values and to adjust our priorities. At the mere sight of death, we may take a second look at our goals and activities and decide what is really important and valuable to us. So instead of living out our lives without much thought, we become much more selective in what we want to do and accomplish, in what is meaningful to us and what is not.

---

2. Ps 103:14–16.
3. Job 14:1–2.

Part 2: Challenges to Meaning

Scientific Attempts to Deal with Death

Science respects, but is not afraid of, Goliath. It has confronted some of the more formidable aspects of death and tried to master them.

Biological immortality is seen as a possibility someday, but even the most optimistic scientist thinks that it will be a decade or two before the goal is reached. Meanwhile, there are numerous attempts to try to make the dream come true. And in any case, there seems to be satisfaction in trying and moments of celebration when small victories are achieved.

To conquer death, we must first extend the length of our days, and that is a possibility that seems to be within our grasp. We have a chemical "reservation" that prevents cells from dying and thus allows us to live significantly longer. To achieve immortality, however, our relentless march to old age and death must be stopped. So far that is a formidable, for now an impossible, task. An article in Wikipedia, entitled "Immortality," summarizes the present causes of aging and thus the numerous obstacles that must be surmounted before the aging process is stopped. I will quote a relevant sentence from Wikipedia, but I have no authority to comment on it. "The current causes of aging in humans are cell loss (without replacement), oncogenic nuclear mutations and epimutations, cell senescence, mitochondrial mutations, lysosomal aggregates, extra cellular aggregates, random intracellular cross-linking, immune system decline, and endocrine changes."[4]

Scientists have made great advances in the diagnosis and treatment of disease in major areas of life. The study of genetics has improved the treatment of incurable diseases. The early detection of diseases has increased the chance of a cure. A better understanding of how some diseases "do

4. Wikipedia, "Immortality."

Meaning and Death

their damage" is an important aid to recovery. Vaccines that build up immunity to certain diseases prevent potentially dangerous epidemics. Drugs are constantly being developed to address particular maladies. "Breakthroughs in cell biology and telomere research are leading to treatments for cancer."[5] In many ways, then, advances in medical procedures and treatments have been remarkable, but the total elimination of all diseases remains a goal that will be reached, if ever, in the distant future. Meanwhile, the elimination of death caused by diseases escapes our grasp.

So the path to immortality remains hidden with God. If we are to escape the threat of death, we must find a different way.

A Philosophical Attempt to Deal with Death

The Greek philosopher Plato made a neat division between body and soul and posited a wide and radical division between them. The body is the material and mortal part of man, and the seat of corruption and death. It imprisons the soul during the lifetime of a person and is responsible for the pains, corruption, and sufferings that beset man. In contrast, the soul is the immortal, divine, and immutable part of man. It makes us "equal to [the] Gods" and enrobes us with the three virtues of self-control, braveness, and wisdom. Together, they combine to make justice the overarching virtue of the soul.[6]

The exact details of Plato's division of man is less important than the function it serves in addressing the threat of death. It allows us to locate death and the cause of suffering in the finite and vulnerable part of us, namely, in the

5. Ibid., 4.
6. Singer, "Immortality of the Soul," 1.

body, but it also isolates a portion of our existence from finitude and death and gives us the comforting doctrine of the immortality of the soul. This neat arrangement (solution) not only appeals to our desire to be happy and of eternal significance but it also ends our struggle with death. In fact, it takes away the apparent meaninglessness of life and breathes back into it a new status and meaning. It ascribes to humanity a power and meaning that far exceeds its ability to transcend its finitude. On a practical level, it is a great comfort against the onslaughts of death, and on an ultimate level it gives us the status of an indestructible being.

The Platonic soul may be immortal, but the threat of physical death remains. So we have a third attempt to disarm death.

A Christian Attempt to Deal with Death

The creation story in Genesis offers us a chance to cast death in a less threatening and more positive light. Since the story does not make it clear whether Adam and Eve were created mortal or immortal, it gives us space to play. We can maintain that we were created to be immortal and that our likeness to God is an indication of God's high regard for us. Or we could conclude that we were created mortal, like other animals (creatures) and then in our most charitable moments we see death as a natural and fitting culmination or completion of our finitude. The Old Testament literature approaches this thought in its concept of a good death. For the Israelites there were three conditions which, if met, make for a good death: if we live a long life, if we have children to perpetuate our name, and if we are buried in a sepulcher, we can consider ourselves blessed.

As time went on, the Israelites reflected on the idea that death was a natural end to life, and they were troubled

Meaning and Death

by the thought that God would allow them to die and go to Hades, the underworld of the dead where God is distant, if not unavailable. Their fate after death seemed inconsistent with the actions of a good and gracious God.

The Israelites then struggled with various understandings of death, including the retributive possibility the God would bless the righteous and punish unbelievers. In Daniel 12:2, the idea of some kind of resurrection makes its first and only Old Testament appearance. "Many of those who sleep in the dust of the earth shall awake, some to everlasting life and some to shame and everlasting contempt."

To New Testament believers, the death we die is not the death that God intended, but it is death after Adam and Eve, or less metaphorically, after we alienated ourselves from God and centered life in ourselves. Death then becomes at best a consequence of a broken relationship with the very Source of life and at worst a judgment and a curse. It is this death that the Christian faith addresses, specifically in its understanding of, and faith in, Christ's death and resurrection. I will use a Pauline perspective to interpret these events.

Paul believes that in and through the death and resurrection of Christ we have the power of God breaking into our lives. The power of God is the power of love, a reconciling, forgiving, and enhancing presence that deals mercifully with us. In this process, death cannot be considered apart from sin and the law, because all three are of the same piece, and all three lead to judgment and condemnation. Nevertheless, we will focus on death and consider it first from the standpoint of Christ's death and then from the standpoint Christ's resurrection.

For Paul, Christ's death was no ordinary death. It was not a death alongside other human deaths but was the supreme expression of God's desire to release us from the

Part 2: Challenges to Meaning

sting of death and from the evil powers of the present age. We are the benefactors of Christ's death by being baptized into his death and thus by sharing in his being raised from the dead. As death no longer destroys Christ, so death no longer negates us. Paul does not mean that death, sin, and the law no longer exist in the lives of believers, but that their bondage over us and their power to rule in our lives are now broken. We are free from tyranny, which does not mean for Paul that we are free to do anything we want. We are moved to live in obedience to God's rule just as before we were obedient to sin and death and disobedient to the law.

As an expression of God's love, Christ's death was a ransom for all humankind, not just for a selected few. To the unbeliever, though, his death is foolishness, not what the world would think as a way out of the powers that enslave us. Paul believes that God deliberately chose this way, so that we would not be able to boast in our own achievement but would have to rest in what the Lord has done and freely given to us.

God's gracious act of mercy and love is manifest, not only in Christ's death but also in Christ's resurrection. Jesus did not raise himself from death, but God who is sovereign and lord over life and death raised him. God was pleased with Christ's "sacrifice" and God's redeeming and recreating love resurrected Christ and opened the way to our resurrection. Paul is specific in terms of the resurrection. "What is perishable is raised imperishable, what is sown in dishonor is raised in glory, what is sown in weakness is raised in power, what is sown a physical body is raised a spiritual body."[7]

The good news is that death has been transformed. What was a sting and a curse has become a gateway to everlasting life. We grasp onto this gift and promise by faith,

7. Rom 15:42–44.

Meaning and Death

by becoming obedient to Christ and living in his imputed righteousness. For Paul being obedient is more than obeying a precept or a commandment. It is giving ourselves completely to Christ. It is belonging to him and putting our lives completely in the merciful hands of Christ's redeeming work.

Part 3

A Christian Approach to Meaning

Chapter 9

God's Plan for Us

ANY DISCUSSION OF THE meaning of life after the appearance of Rick Warren's *The Purpose-Driven Life* must take his thought into consideration. His book not only taps into a widespread concern about the purpose and meaning of life but also it lays out an approach to the subject that must be taken seriously.

Warren's basic and overarching belief is that God created us for a purpose, and that God's purpose gives meaning to our lives and defines what we should and should not do or be. In Warren's world, everything is centered in God, and all questions or concerns about life's meaning are defined and answered best, not by our own thinking, but by God's will as revealed in the Bible. For example, to the question "What should be the driving force in our lives?" Warren answers, not fear, not guilt, not the need for approval, but God's reasons for creating us.[1] Or to the question, "How should we understand what life is all about?" Warren answers, "Not from our own finite and self-centered perspective, but from the biblical understanding that life is a test, a

---

1. Warren, *The Purpose-Driven Life*, 27–35.

Part 3: A Christian Approach to Meaning

trust, and a temporary assignment."[2] Or again, to the question "What should we live for?" Warren's answer is, "Not for ourselves but for the glory of God."[3]

If Warren is right our primary task, if not our only task, is to align ourselves with what God intends or wants. For Warren, that means five things: First, we are to please God by loving, trusting, and obeying God. Second, we are to be an active part of God's family by being a regular and close member of the fellowship. Third, we are to become like Christ by letting Christ live through us. Fourth, we are to give back to life by serving God. Five, we are to fulfill our mission in the world by abandoning our own agenda and accepting God's agenda for our lives.

In the process of dealing with these five items, Warren covers every aspect of a Christian's life, including worship, church membership, fellowship, discipleship, service, and mission. He is specific about the details and expectations of each aspect and clarifies, implicitly if not explicitly, how each contributes to the meaning of life (to a Christian's life). He has no doubt about God's role in each instance or about God's will or wishes in each case. He avoids the terms "should" or "should not," but a deterministic mandate seems to be just beneath the surface of what he says. For example, in discussing how we are "shaped to serve God," Warren says, "[God] carefully mixed the DNA cocktail that created you . . . Not only did God shape you before your birth, [but] he planned every day of your life to support his shaping process."[4]

If we go along with Warren's theological stance, we are left with the question, "What is there to discuss?" God has arranged (pre-arranged) everything and the answers

2. Ibid., 41–52.
3. Ibid., 53–59.
4. Ibid., 235.

God's Plan for Us

are found in God or in the Bible. If our life runs counter to God, we are simply "off the track" or rebellious, and we need to change our ways or our thinking.

I do not think that Warren intends to come out with a pre-determined world, but he certainly seems to stand in danger of it, maybe because he wants to instill purpose in people whose lives are empty or have lost direction. It would be nice and reassuring to think that God has worked out all the details related to our purpose and meaning, but I don't think that God wants us to live in a world where everything is decided and we are puppets of predetermination. In any case, Warren becomes so busy laying out the practical implications of this thought for the church that he does not clarify other aspects of God's relationship with us. Furthermore, as previous chapters have shown there is a human side to the pursuit of meaning that needs extended consideration.

Warren's great contribution to our discussion is to remind us that in any consideration of meaning, especially if it deals with a broad question about the meaning of life, we get to a point where we need to turn to a theological/religious perspective on the subject. We have looked at Warren's approach to the topic. I want to present another approach.

Chapter 10

God's Gift of Meaning in an Uncertain World

Have you ever felt the judgment of God, ever felt that God was holding you accountable? Adam and Eve in the Book of Genesis did. They heard the sound of God walking in the garden, and they hid. When God caught up with them, he laid a judgment on both of them. To the man he said, "Cursed is the ground because of you. In toil you shall eat of it all the days of your life." To the woman he said, "I will greatly increase your pangs in childbearing, in pain you shall bring forth children."[1]

You may not have felt the judgment of God as acutely as Adam and Eve did, but if we go with the Pauline/Augustinian analysis of our plight, all of us are alienated from God and live in the emptiness and void of God's absence. There is no redeeming purpose and meaning in that.

The Christian faith deals with this whole situation in its understanding of God's grace and forgiveness. We are forgiven by God by putting our faith in Christ, not in ourselves. As I see it, that is only a part of God's love—a very

1. Gen 3:16–17.

God's Gift of Meaning in an Uncertain World

important part but nevertheless only a part. In our alienation from God, we need more than forgiveness. We need a rebirth, a restored sense of meaning and purpose. I think the Christian faith offers a profound and positive understanding of our meaning and significance in God's world

A Threefold Affirmation

The Christian faith maintains that God relates to us in a threefold way—as Creator, Redeemer, and Sanctifier. In each case God affirms us and gives meaning to our lives.

First, God the Creator affirms us by giving us life. God not only brings us into existence but surrounds us with everything that is necessary to nourish, sustain, and protect us throughout life. Actually, God is an extravagant God who gives us far more than we need or can comprehend. We could be created to survive as simple organisms but with the Psalmist we can say, "I am fearfully and wonderfully made."[2] A few basics would sustain and nourish us, but God gives us a world that supplies us with food and clothing, home and shelter, sun and clouds, light and darkness. God endows us with an imagination to see beyond present horizons and a mind that can probe the mysteries of the universe. With these abundant blessings, God entrusts us with purpose and responsibility. We are "to tend to the earth" and to exercise just "dominion over every living thing."[3]

God's providential care gives real meaning to our lives. It means that we are no accident of creation, but that we are at the very heart of God's concern. We are underwritten by God's care and live in the presence of God with a certain sense of security and significance. Our preferred status in

2. Ps 139:14.
3. Gen 1:26.

Part 3: A Christian Approach to Meaning

the ranks of God's creatures means that when we die it is not a simple matter of an unidentified member of the species dying but the loss of a living organism, the loss of a unique and irreplaceable creature who meant something special to those who knew and loved him or her.

Second, God the Redeemer affirms us by forgiving us. We were created to live in close union with God, but we turned from God and made ourselves the source and center of existence. Our alienation from God was not just a transgression of a commandment, but a rebellion against God and a refusal to let God be God in our lives. Our rebellion enslaved us, and we could not free ourselves from the tyranny of alienation and wrongdoing.

God did not forsake us. He reached out to bring us back into fellowship by sending Jesus into our brokenness to pay the price of our disobedience. If by faith we grasp unto Christ's work, we are treated as if we bear the righteousness of Christ instead of suffering the condemnation of our rebellion.

What an affirmation of us. "While we still were sinners Christ died for us. While we were enemies, we were reconciled to God through the death of his Son."[4]

God's affirmation of us adds great meaning to our lives. It is the meaning of a God who loves us and cares for us, not a God who prefabricates and uses us. It means that our life and meaning are not built on our own goodness or efforts, but on the unmerited gift of being accepted even while we are unacceptable and unworthy.

Third, God the Sanctifier affirms us by empowering and renewing us. Given our alienation from God, we must have a healing power at work in our lives and in the world in order to survive. We cannot redeem or recreate ourselves. Like an alcoholic, we get caught in situations where there

---

4. Rom 6:8–10.

seems to be no way out. At such times we despair of being changed, and by our frantic and egoistic efforts we only dig ourselves into deeper trouble.

God is not content to let us continue on the path of destruction, but God works quietly and constantly to renew our life and to help us go in the right direction. The Holy Spirit as the power of God brings hope and renewal. It calls, enlightens, and sanctifies us, though its work in our lives is never instant or complete. It has its peaks and valleys, or as theologians say, we always remain both sinner and saint. Nevertheless, it blesses us with the possibility of rebirth and empowers us in moments of discouragement.

God's threefold affirmation of us requires something of us. We need to acknowledge God's presence in our lives and be aware that meaning in God's world comes not only in the form of divine promise but also in the form of concrete and personal blessings, like a granddaughter's recognition of how much we have contributed to her life or like a spouse's gratitude for sixty years of companionship. In addition to God's affirmation of us, the Christian faith lays down a threefold path to a meaningful life.

Three Landmarks

1. We find meaning in life by dying to ourselves. This does not mean that we negate ourselves but that we stop making ourselves the center of meaning. As we have noted several times, we are to discover meaning in the world in which we live. A self-created meaning is no meaning at all. It is only a fantasy of our own self-importance. We are wonderfully made but that does not mean that we can find meaning in ourselves alone. And in any ultimate sense, only God gives lasting and eternal meaning to our lives.

Part 3: A Christian Approach to Meaning

> Reinhold Niebuhr, an influential American theologian in World War II times, points the self beyond itself by maintaining that life or meaning must be grounded in an ultimate reality. He puts it in pithy sentences, "The self that stands outside itself and the world cannot find the meaning of life in itself or the world. Ultimately, the meaning of existence can only be found in God, since we can transcend and see through every meaning or scheme that we ourselves might create."[5]
>
> Of course, we can ascribe lasting and absolute importance to our finite creations, but in the end they only prove to be sad instances of egoistic self-assertion and become further evidence that we must transcend ourselves in order genuinely to fulfill ourselves.

2. We find meaning in life by serving others, by being there for other people in their hour of need. Our mandate from God is not to build ourselves up but to build up the fellowship of believers. It is in giving that we receive, it is in emptying ourselves that we are filled. It is in feeding others that we are fed.

    This paradoxical truth carries a certain biblical warrant to it, especially in St. Paul's thought where being obedient to the Word means meeting the needs of the needy. Nancy also represents empirical evidence to support this mandate. Earlier we noted that in her older years, Nancy lost a life filled with meaning. She puts meaning back into her life by spending time with papers and stories from former times. She gives this activity a certain priority—until someone needs her help. Then she drops whatever she is doing to assist the person in need. Her life gains renewed meaning by serving

---

5. Niebuhr, *The Nature and Destiny of Man*, vol. 1, 14.

others. For her, it is not just a matter of experiencing a sense of satisfaction, but more important she gains a reason to be, a purpose in life's greater scheme of things.

3. We find meaning in life by anchoring our life in the life of Christ, by trusting in his redemptive power to heal our brokenness with God. Besides, Christ puts everything in proper perspective, most of all the self-centered idea that we will find meaning in life by trying to earn it. Our good deeds, however good, are also tainted with self-concern, and thus they are never a perfect fulfillment of God's law. On the contrary, we must live by God's undeserved gift of forgiveness, and when we do our life gains new meaning, even as we are empowered to pursue a life that is genuinely more meaningful and fulfilling.

Our search for meaning has led us to ultimate concerns. What do we mean to God? How do we experience meaning in God's world? For me the Christian understanding of our human situation is a profound and life-giving answer. It transforms the threat of death into the promise of eternal life. It shifts our attempt to find meaning in an uncertain world into the blessed assurance that we are children of God.

Bibliography

Aden, LeRoy, David G. Benner, and J. Harold Ellens, *Christian Perspectives on Human Development*. Grand Rapids: Baker, 1992.

Aden, LeRoy, and David Benner. *Counseling and the Human Predicament: A Study of Sin, Guilt, and Forgiveness*. Grand Rapids: Baker, 1989.

Aden, LeRoy, and Robert G. Hughes. *Preaching God's Compassion: Comforting Those Who Suffer*. Minneapolis: Fortress, 2002.

Angyal, Andras. "A Theoretical Model for Personality Studies." *Journal of Personality*, vol. 20 (September 1951) 131–42.

Becker, Ernest. *The Denial of Death*. New York: Free Press, 1973.

Boeree, C. George. "Viktor Frankl 1915–1997." 2006. Online: http://webspace.ship.edu/cgboer/frank.html.

Boszormenyi-Nagy, Ivan, and Barbara Krasner. *Between Give and Take: A Clinical Guide to Contextual Therapy*. New York: Brunner/Mazel, 1986.

Buber, Martin. *I and Thou*. New York: Scribner Classics, 2000.

Buttrick, George Arthur, ed. *Interpreter's Dictionary of the Bible: An Illustrated Encyclopedia*, vol. 2. Nashville: Abingdon, 1962.

Erikson, Erik H. *Identity and the Life Cycle*. New York: Norton, 1980.

Erikson, Erik H. *Childhood and Society*. 2nd edition. New York: Norton, 1963.

Frankl, Viktor E. *Man's Search for Meaning: An Introduction to Logotherapy*. Boston: Beacon, 1959.

———. *The Will to Meaning: Foundations and Applications*. New York: Meridian, 1970.

Freud, Sigmund. *Collected Papers*, IV. Edited by Ernest Jones. London: The Hogarth Press and the Institute of Pyscho-analysis, 1959.

Gerstenberger, Erhard S., and Wolfgang Schrage. *Suffering*. Translated by John Steely. Nashville: Abingdon, 1977.

Bibliography

Horney, Karen. *Neurosis and Human Growth: The Struggle toward Self-Realization*. New York: Norton, 1950.

Hunter, Rodney J., gen. ed. *Dictionary of Pastoral Care and Counseling*. Nashville: Abingdon, 1990.

Khayyam, Omar. *Rubaiyat*. Online: Library@Cornell.edu/coldey/Mideast/okhym.htm.

———. "Rubaiyat of Omar Khayyam." Online: http://en.wikipedia.org/wiki/Rubaiyat_of_Omar_Khayyam.

Mitchell, Kenneth and Herbert Anderson, *All Our Losses, All Our Griefs: Resources for Pastoral Care*. Philadelphia: Westminster, 1983.

Niebuhr, Reinhold. *The Nature and Destiny of Man,* vol. 1. New York: Scribner's, 1941.

———. *The Self and the Dramas of History*. New York: Scribner's, 1955.

Shakespeare, William. *The Tragedy of Hamlet*. Boston: Heath, 1917.

Singer, Isibore. "Immortality of the Soul." Online: www.jewishencyclopedia.com/articles8092-immortality-of-the-soul.

"Tiger Woods." Online: http://wikipedia.org/wikw/Tiger__Woods.

Veira, Meredith. "Happy at Home." *Good Housekeeping*, September, 2011. Interview by *Good Housekeeping* Editor Rosemary Ellis. Online: www.goodhousekeeping.com/celebrity interviews and quotes.

Warren, Rick. *The Purpose-Driven Life: What on Earth Am I Here For?* Grand Rapids: Zondervan, 2002.

Wikipedia. "Immortality." Online: http://en.wikipedia.org/wiki/Immorality.

Wolterstorff, Nicholas. *Lament for a Son*. Grand Rapids: Eerdman's, 1987.

Woods, Tiger. "About Tiger Woods." Online: http//web.tigerwoods.com/aboutTiger/bio.

An Adult Ministry Study Guide

Session 1: Our Search for Meaning

Finding Meaning in an Uncertain World [hereafter referred to as "the book"] is designed to aid those who read and discuss its chapters in their own search for meaning. It attempts to lead participants to places where meaning can be found and guides them through obstacles that may impede that search.

It is the conviction of the author of this Study Guide that meaning emerges most effectively in a small group setting where as few as three or four or as many as eight to ten people come together to share their thoughts and to reflect on their understanding of the book. This assumes that the group members will read each chapter in advance of the class and will come together prepared to discuss questions and comments. (This expectation should be made clear at the outset of the class and may need to be reinforced regularly.)

The book's basic orientation (below) may be affixed to wall boards in the area where the discussion occurs or, in slide form, be projected on a wall.

Finding Meaning in an Uncertain World

> All of us have a desire to live with purpose and to find meaning in life.
>
> But the uncertain, unpredictable world (sickness, broken relationships, other losses) challenges us and makes this search ongoing.
>
> We question, "What is the meaning of my life?"
>
> God gives us the ability to stand above difficulty and discover what provides meaning.
>
> But we tend to seek for meaning in persons and things that do not satisfy. (Romans 7:15)
>
> We often feel empty and sad. (Psalm 42)
>
> We may blame God. (See Psalm 13:1–2)
>
> But God is with us in this search for meaning. We are God's chosen people, and this reality is our chief source of meaning and purpose. (See 1 Peter 2:9–10)

The study guide follows the sequence of the book, covering the book in ten sessions. However, the sessions can be increased or decreased depending upon the needs or wishes of the group. Personal interaction should take priority over the check-list approach. The group may choose to skip a particular topic or chapter, or conversely, the group may add a session and invite an "outside expert" to assist going deeper into a particularly difficult topic.

A helpful preparation chapter for the leader is pp. 25–30 in Wangerin, Mourning into Dancing, a book found in many church libraries.

The theologian Paul Tillich, in his classic book The Courage to Be, identifies loss of a spiritual center as the basic cause of meaninglessness.

An Adult Ministry Study Guide

Chapter 1 Meaning And Meaninglessness

In the book, LeRoy Aden uses the passage from Ecclesiastes 2:1–11 to highlight the meaninglessness of many "pleasures" we 21st century people tend to pursue. We in America tend to empty life of absolute values and to give priority to relative or flawed values.

In America, the search for "happiness" often replaces the search for "meaning." We tend to equate happiness with pleasure, or the sum of pleasure over pain in a given period of time. Such pleasures are often reduced to economic gains, what we have and what we can get.

"He who has a why to live can bear with almost any how." Frankl's story and his writings highlight the struggle to find meaning in and through suffering.

In 2 Corinthians particularly St. Paul struggles with finding meaning in suffering. In chapter 11 he chronicles his many sufferings and goes on in chapter 12 to focus on a so-called "thorn in the flesh." "Three times I appealed to the Lord about this, that it would leave me, but he said to me 'My grace is sufficient for you, for power is made perfect in weakness.'" (12:8–9) When suffering for Christ's sake, Paul finds strength in weakness, meaning and purpose in suffering.

Following Paul, Lutherans espouse a "theology of the cross" that finds meaning in and through suffering. Christ models this "suffering servant," not a king of glory but a servant who gave his life for us. God is often found in our failures, not our successes, in the darkness rather than in the light. The cross of Jesus is the world's NO but God's YES.

In his Christmas message to the English people in the darkest year of World War II, George VI related:

> "I said to the man who stood at the gate of the year, Give me a light that I may tread safely into

Finding Meaning in an Uncertain World

> the unknown. And he replied, Go out into the darkness and put your hand into the hand of God. That shall be to you better than light and safer than a known way."

Discussion[1]

1. Chapter one implies that our lives move between meaning and meaninglessness, between fullness and emptiness. As a nation, when have we been surprised by dark clouds moving in a menacing way across bright and sunny skies? In what way has the American dream yielded to feelings of emptiness, shallowness, lost direction, or boredom in your life?

2. After a careful study of our American way of life, Frankl concluded that we live in a milieu of meaninglessness because we have divested life of everything that gives meaning to it. In what ways do you agree with his assessment? How do you think we handle the threat of meaninglessness (4–5)? (Harry Chapin's song entitled "Vacancy" may be used to "prime the pump.")

3. In the Book of Genesis the first creation story begins, "*In the beginning when God created the heavens and the earth, the earth was a formless void and darkness covered the face of the deep . . . .*" (Gen. 1:1–2). But it also goes on to relate that God brought order and life where there had been chaos and nothingness, "*and God saw that it was good*" (1:10, 18, 21, 25). What

---

1. ALOA is grateful to Dr. LeRoy Aden, the book's author, for suggesting many of the questions for discussion. As leaders of the study become more familiar with the participants, their interests and their concerns, other questions may suggest themselves. Numerical references in parenthesis refer to pages in the book.

An Adult Ministry Study Guide

parallels do you see between the creation story and the polarity between meaning and meaninglessness?

4. The Guidelines to Meaning (5–7), drawn from Victor Frankl's encounter with meaninglessness in Nazi prison camps, are intended to be practical guides for our lives. Which of these can you embrace? Any disagreements?

Part 1 Sources of Meaning

Chapter 2 Meaning And Relationships

When the book turns to sources of meaning, it turns first to relationships. The Bible (Genesis 1 and 2) also begins with relationships and deals with them in a priority order:

- Relationship of God to the world
- Relationship of God to humans (creation in the image of God)
- Relationship of humans to the world (stewardship)
- Relationship of human to human

The conclusion of this ancient narrative portrays a creation marked by wholeness and concord: "And God saw everything that he had made, and, behold, it was very good." The disorders and fractured relationships that occur in Genesis 3 and following are traceable to human sin.

The initial paragraph in the chapter deserves emphasis: "We must discover our own meaning, that is, what life means to us and what we mean to ourselves and others." (11) There is no common meaning for every human being. Given a mix of talents and experiences, differing relationships, and various life contexts, clearly we need to discover our own meaning.

Finding Meaning in an Uncertain World

Humans do require affirmation of some type, although it may be a new thought for some that even negative interactions provide a backhanded sort of affirmation (13). On the positive side, not only do we need recognition and respect as human beings, but it is a recognized human desire to be special to someone or some other persons.

The Tiger Woods example is helpful to underscore the role of 1) special gifts, 2) hard work, and 3) continuing effort in the search for meaning. Woods may be a further example of how disrupted relationships result in loss and the grief that results from loss (20–21). However, facing the reality of loss and working through the resulting stages of grief can lead to the restoration of hope and new life (21–23).

In the Disruption of Meaning section (19–21), the book suggests a variety of disruptions that function as "little deaths" including empty nesting, retirement, and the death of those close to us (e.g. spouse). Grieving involves letting go of former relationships and building new ones.

The restoration of a right relationship with God (a gift of God that the Bible terms "grace") is central to finding meaning and purpose in life, even amid uncertain human relationships. The book deals with this reality in other chapters and concludes with this affirmation in Chapter 10.

Discussion

1. Why are relationships so important in the birth of meaning? What do you think of Erik Erikson's claim about the importance of being affirmed as a person by someone who is important to us? (12–14)

2. What relationships have been especially important to you in terms of validating your existence as a person of worth and value (12–13)?

An Adult Ministry Study Guide

3. How do you respond to people who seem to dismiss you or act as if you do not exist? How do you feel when this occurs? What helpful behaviors have you found in dealing with these situations?

4. Can you identify biblical, historical, or current public figures such as Tiger Woods (17–18) who model some of his life characteristics in the search for meaning and who, unfortunately, also suffer from disrupted relationships and a loss of meaning? How have they worked through grief in moving toward restoration of hope and new life?

Chapter 3 Meaning And The Self

Psalm 42:5 may be a place to begin (or conclude) the discussion of meaning and the self. This psalmist admits to emptiness and a search for meaning, finally affirming hope in the God relationship.

> *Why are you cast down, O my soul,*
> *And why are you disquieted within me?*
> *Hope in God; for I shall again praise him,*
> *My help and my God*

The book asks what role the self plays in the search for a meaningful life. The Meredith Vieira narrative reveals the challenge of discovering who we are "at the core." The danger of defining ourselves by our jobs and other human values (e.g. wealth, family, status) mutes or confuses the more basic issue of who we really are. When we value ourselves in this way, loss of a job, financial reversal, severed relationships, retirement all feel like failure of the self.

The book carefully distinguishes being "centered on the self" from being a "centered person," an "integrated whole" (28). Note Jesus' response to the mother of the sons of Zebedee who asked for special places for the sons at Jesus right and left hands:

"Whoever wishes to be great among you must be your servant, and whoever wishes to be first among you must be your slave, just as the Son of Man came not to be served but to serve, and to give his life a ransom for many." (Matthew 20:26–28)

In chapter 4:11–16 of Ephesians, Paul explores the issue of meaning by urging followers to "build up the body of Christ." A centered person is not out to defend or build up a personal ego. Rather, such a person is freed to reach out in love and service to others without looking for recognition or reward.

Again, the centered person is not created to serve some specific and predetermined purpose of a controlling creator or, selfishly, to "actualize the self." Rather, guided by God's Holy Spirit we are freed to search for meaning in the constellation of our lives, work, relationships, our faith commitments, and available opportunities to serve.

Discussion

1. In the book, the self is the second source of meaning or, more precisely, the self is an arbitrator of meaning that determines who we are and who we are to become. Have you paused to get a sense of which you are—your "self," the part of you that you identify as "I" or "me"? Describe your sense of who you are.

2. Reflect on some of the things you judge as especially meaningful and others you judge to be relatively unimportant. Do your findings surprise you? In reflection, do you sense that some of your choices ought to be questioned or rethought? Will you share one?

An Adult Ministry Study Guide

3. Recall the story of Meredith Vieira (25) and imagine what inner workings gave her the wisdom and courage to act as she did. What qualities in Vieira either match or suggest some of your own gifts (e.g. keen intuition, sharp mind, determined will) which can and should be used to make decisions?

4. What does it look like to honor the humanity of another person?

Chapter 4 Meaning and the Family

Chapter 4 explores the centrality of the family in the search for meaning. "Our family of origin gives us the first, and maybe the most enduring, impression that we have of life. It is the crucible in which we form our understanding of the world and in which we begin to clarify what we mean to self and others" (32).

The Balance between Give and Receive

This section develops the effects, positive and negative, of what the book terms "relational justice" (33ff). In families, some kind of equality must be developed between what we give to others and what we receive from them. As in the case of Lewis (33–35), if this does not occur, if we feel cheated of proper attention and respect, the deficit experience in one relationship may be worked out negatively in others over the course of a lifetime.

The Old Testament/Hebrew Scriptures have prominent examples of dysfunctional families and abuses of relational justice. While Genesis 1 and 2 proclaim God's good creation, by Genesis 3 sin appears, and by Genesis 4 human-to-human relationships are affected negatively. The story of sin and brokenness continues as Cain kills his own brother over an argument that began at the altar of God. Hostility of one human to one another poisons families.

The discussion leader may use Genesis 27 as illustrative of such hostility. This chapter chronicles the favoritism of Isaac for his oldest son Esau (common in that culture) and the conspiracy of wife Rebekah and son Jacob to cheat Esau of his father's blessing. Esau's anger at this treachery led him to plot the murder of his brother and led to a fissure in the family.

Obligations and Entitlements

In the book, "obligations" are defined as what we "owe" to those who brought us into the world and cared for us. "Entitlements" are what other people owe us, what we deserve to get in light of "what we have given to and been for other people" (36). In the story of James (36–37), negative feelings regarding obligations and a deficit of entitlements marred his life.

Once again, the book of Genesis (chapters 37–50) provides a saga (the Joseph stories) that exemplifies how family dysfunction works itself out in a negative way. Jacob favored one of his youngest sons, Joseph, "more than any other of his children, because he was the son of his old age" (37:3) and made for Joseph a so-called "coat of many colors." For this, and because of Joseph's own dreams of preeminence in the family, his brother's resented him. The saga played itself out with Joseph's sale into slavery and his rise to prominence in Egypt. The good news in the story is God's use of this situation to bring the family to Egypt, thus saving their lives and keeping the family line and God's promise of a blessing through the family intact.

An Adult Ministry Study Guide

Invisible Loyalties

The book returns to the story of Lewis (38–39) to highlight how loyalty to family can function in both positive and negative ways. It may be insightful for the discussion group to explore the church as a "family" and sometimes a dysfunctional one. In his first letter to the church at Corinth, Paul laments the divisions in the congregation. Repeatedly he refers to them as "brothers and sisters" (with him part of the body of Christ—chapter 12). Especially in chapter 1 (see verses 10–17), but also in chapter 11, Paul laments the divisions ("factions") in the congregation caused by visible and invisible loyalties and proclaims vigorously the unity of the family in and through baptism.

While the church is sometimes caricatured as a bunch of "goody goodies," the Bible is clear that Christians are (using a Lutheran phrase) "simul justus et peccator" (at once justified and sinners, "one in the Spirit and one in the Lord" but also a divided and often dysfunctional family).

(While it may not be wise to discuss current problems in your congregation, most group members will have experienced cliques, factions, and hidden loyalties in other churches or organizations that were destructive of meaning. In this context it would be well to stress the baptismal unity of Christ's own family, while recognizing the reality that sin persists in the lives of the redeemed.)

Discussion

1. The impact of the family is the third source of meaning, and its impact can be positive and enduring. What positive values and gifts have you received from your core and extended families. Are there core or extended family members who were, for you, exemplars

Finding Meaning in an Uncertain World

or mentors in some valuable aspect of life?

2. Conversely, the experience of family for many persons may be ambivalent, disheartening, or even destructive. Discuss the balance between giving and getting (33), obligations and entitlements (36) and the effect of an imbalance in dysfunctional families. (See the definitions of obligations and entitlements on page 36).

3. Have you previously considered the idea (or experienced the reality) that congregations can be and often are dysfunctional families? Read 1 Corinthians 1:10–17. What is the apostle Paul's concern and message in this opening portion of the letter?

Chapter 5 Treasure Chests Of Meaning

The book identifies treasure chests as "valuable occurrences that serve as storehouses of meaningful events and occasions" (40).

Special times and places contribute to our lives, giving . . .

- A sense of continuity
- A sense of belonging
- A sense of increased fullness

Construct a Lifeline

A common way to get at the categories of meaning listed above is to create a lifeline. The leader may suggest this as a project for a small discussion group.

A useful resource for beginning personal lifelines is Remembering Your Story: Creating Your Own Spiritual Autobiography, by Richard L. Morgan (Upper Room Books,

An Adult Ministry Study Guide

Nashville, TN). The four paragraphs that follow summarize key sections of Morgan's book. In handout form, they will assist members to get started during the week prior to this session of the class.

1. Beginning with the year of your birth, break up your life into seven year periods beginning with the year of your birth and concluding at the present. Use a large ring (loose leaf) notebook with tab dividers to separate and label the sections. Initially devote one page to each period, and when a section page fills, add another. It may help to create memory anchors by listing the homes, town or city, and dates of residence in each seven year period.

2. Create a memory flow by noting on the bottom of the page (in telegraphic style) memories associated with these places, happy and sad. Indicate which dwellings hold special memories and which are turning points in your story (e.g. downsized, out of work for 8 months, marriage, first child born, life work begun, back surgery).

3. Use appropriate markers to designate and help to locate positive/joyful events (e.g. arrow up) and negative/painful events (arrow down), suggesting what we often call life's "ups and downs."

4. Identify "grace moments"—when God seemed present and active in your story. Reflect about those moments (e.g. significant persons involved, your feelings, consequences, how God fit into the situation). Also, identify times when you needed God most (e.g. felt confused, abandoned, wanted to praise God).

How does this project connect to deepening life's meaning for older persons?

- In every person's life there are key moments and

events that alter life's course. Looking back at these nodal points, we can see that our response to these events helped to define who we were as persons.

- For older persons, looking back is more than nostalgia. Reprising the past reminds us how we have changed and grown and how we can continue to respond to the future.
- Passing on the story of our lives is a wonderful heritage for our children and grandchildren and is a way to hand down values and traditions of family and faith.

As Frederick Buechner has said in Telling Secrets, "Maybe nothing is more important than that we keep track . . . of those stories of who we are and where we have come from and the people we have met along the way because it is precisely through these stories in all their particularity . . . that God is revealed to each of us most powerfully and personally" (3).

This chapter invites members of the group to get acquainted, or reacquainted, with their particular depositories, to hold in remembrance a few of the important meanings that are recorded, and to share (as they feel moved to do) with the discussion group. It may be comfortable to bring a picture of a former dwelling (e.g. family homestead) to class, pass it around, and share one key event/meaning related to that dwelling.

Discussion

1. Is there a particular family celebration or tradition filled with meaning that you can picture and relate to the group?
2. Is there a special individual in your history (e.g. family

An Adult Ministry Study Guide

member, friend, congregational member, business associate) who influenced your life in a special way? Do you have a picture (e.g. photograph or verbal description) to share?

3. Family histories and genealogies serve as depositories of meaning. Are you willing to share a family record or significant piece of a family tree?

Part 2 Challenges To Meaning

Chapter 6 Meaning And Suffering

The book identifies suffering as the first of three challenges to meaning. Assuming that most members of the discussion group have read the chapter in advance, it may be well to ask them to identify key points in the book's discussion of this monumental challenge to faith. Then discuss each and identify Biblical corroboration for each. The list below will assist the leader

1. God is a suffering God, who in Christ has suffered death on the cross. Each one of the four gospels is an extended passion narrative that climaxes in the death and resurrection of Jesus.

2. God does not will or send suffering and death. Luke 13:1–5

3. Suffering is not the direct result of a person's sins. John 9:1–12.

4. God does not stand above us but is with us in suffering. See Romans 8:31–38.

5. Suffering is to be faced rather than denied. Mark 8:27–35.

6. Suffering can build up the fellowship by equipping us

Finding Meaning in an Uncertain World

to witness to others and strengthen them in their sufferings. 2 Corinthians 1:3–7.

7. These key points do not constitute complete answers to suffering. See the Job story and the sections where the "comforters" (his three friends) attempt rational answers. Job needed their listening and their compassion, not their "answers."

The challenge in dealing with this major theological and life issue is its many facets and its lack of "answers." But that should not dissuade us from engaging the issue. *"In this lifetime we will never fathom some of the mysteries of human existence. But the quest, in spite of the struggling it brings, is itself part of the process of healing and wholeness."* [2]

Discussion

1. Victor Frankl considered chronic or constant suffering a major challenge to meaning, as it was in his own life, but Frankl also discovered that we have the power to choose how we are going to relate to it (57). Have you experienced consequences and challenges as the result of a major loss in your family? How were the effects of this handled by key family members?

2. Jesus by his example indicates that we should face our suffering and not deny its reality and seriousness (55). What might this have to do with spiritual growth?

3. Job cursed the day he was born and complained bitterly to God, yet he remained faithful to God and did not turn against him. How do you suppose God relates to this forked reaction? Why?

---

2. *Making sense out of sorrow: A Journey of Faith*, Foster McCurley and Alan Weitzman (Trinity Press International, 1995).

An Adult Ministry Study Guide

4. In the Gospel of Mark, a father whose son has been tormented by an unclean spirit comes to Jesus for help. When Jesus suggests that healing is a matter of faith, the father cries out, "I believe. Help my unbelief." (Mark 9:24). What is the father asking? Have you experienced this dilemma?

Chapter 7 Meaning And Old Age

The discussion leader will notice that this chapter is longer than many others in the book and, should the group wish to engage the material in depth, the chapter may require more than one week to discuss fully. At least three reactions from older adult groups may be anticipated:

1. While admitting the reality of many of the issues and "losses" seniors face or may face, some readers will experience this chapter of the book as obsessively gloomy and may wish to hurry past the material.

2. A second reaction from some will be to challenge the heavy stress on change and loss as negative, testifying instead to their own celebration of God's gift of life and health beyond age 65 or 70, a retirement free of many of the stresses of child-raising and working years, and fresh opportunities to find meaning and serve in life's second half.

3. Others will wonder "how old is old?" in a world where mortality limits are being pushed well beyond the 80's for both women and men. It may be more helpful for them to put aside chronological age and consider that older adults will be in a variety of life situations and connections, states of health and mobility, with different spiritual and emotional backgrounds. Some will be active and involved, perhaps still working part

time, making new friends, traveling and enjoying life. Others will have begun to experience physical decline, life narrowing, but are still involved and coping well with physical and other life changes. Still other older adults will be restricted physically and perhaps emotionally, have difficulty driving, and be less able to travel or get around and keep up with younger children and grandchildren.

Facing Reality

Old age is not for cowards!" If you've heard that complaint, it was probably from seniors who are suffering, with losses in life "piling up." Particularly when people feel overwhelmed and a bit "sorry for themselves," the decibel level of complaints increases.

Change and loss are part of life from beginning to end. Later losses are prefigured in the sadness of a vacation's final day or saying good-bye to a spouse when leaving for a week working "on the road." Serious losses occur when a friend moves to another state, a daughter goes off to college, or a son accepts a new position far from home. Finally, the chapter both details and suggests critical losses including forced retirement, loss of position at work, and marginalization in the family. These losses prefigure the ultimate losses of the death of loved ones and premonitions of one's own death.

Years ago John Updike captured this feeling of impending loss in Rabbit at Rest, Updike's final novel, about the ex-basketball star Harry "Rabbit" Angstrom. Struggling with brooding anxiety evoked in part by age and

An Adult Ministry Study Guide

declining health,[3] Rabbit becomes painfully aware of his own mortality.

Standing amid the tan, excited post-Christmas crowd at the Southwest Florida Regional Airport, Rabbit Angstrom has a funny sudden feeling that what he has come to meet, what's floating in unseen about to land, is not his son Nelson, daughter-in-law Pru and their two children but something more ominous and intimately his: his own death, shaped vaguely like an airplane. The sensation chills him, above and beyond the terminal air-conditioning.[4]

The temptation is to close the book on the author's chapter 7, but that would be a mistake. Closing the book, putting it away for another day, simply thinking pleasant thoughts would be "denial," which in the long run never works. Mental health depends, in part, upon a person's ability to face life as it is, without lying, without self-deception, with integrity. Our Christian faith helps us to make sense of life, to deal with difficult experiences daily while living in hope.

Living In Hope

Health, then, includes both reality and hope. Health is being able to face the contradictions of the world without giving in to despair. Hope is variously defined.

On a human level, there are some reassuring things to say about hope and meaningful older age. Longevity studies have shown that retirees regularly report being happier than younger and many middle adults. Job stresses, stresses as children become rebellious teens, financial pressures

---

3. Aden and Hughes, *Preaching God's Compassion* (Fortress Press, 2002), pp. 84ff.

4. John Updike, *Rabbit at Rest* (Fawcett Columbine, 1990), p. 1.

with college costs tend to pile on for many middle adults. But somewhere in the 50's the trend reverses and people report feeling better about themselves and their lives. Working longer as health allows, saving faithfully for retirement, exercising daily are critical steps. As one magazine put it, "Keeping active physically and staying socially engaged" is a smart move for engendering hope in older age.[5]

Psychologically, hope involves a rediscovery of meaning. David K. Switzer defines hope as "the possibility and openness toward the meaningfulness of the future which keeps faith alive and active in the present."[6]

For Christians, hope can be summed up in the words "God" and "Jesus." In particular, hope is linked to the gracious action of God seen in the life, death, and resurrection of Jesus the Christ. As Saint Paul testified in his letter to the church at Rome:

"Therefore, since we are justified by faith, we have peace with God through our Lord Jesus Christ, through whom we have obtained access to this grace in which we stand, and we boast in our hope of sharing the glory of God. And not only that, but we also boast in our sufferings, knowing that suffering produces endurance, and endurance produces character, and character produces hope, and hope does not disappoint us, because God's love has been poured into our hearts through the Holy Spirit that has been given to us." Romans 5:1–5

In this passage, hope is focused both in the future ("our hope of sharing the glory of God") and in the present (hope that gives meaning to suffering). In a fellowship of suffering, believers walk with other believers, singing songs of hope and consolation.

---

5. Money, November 2014, p. 68
6. David K. Switzer, *The Dynamics of Grief* (Abingdon), p. 205.

An Adult Ministry Study Guide

A classic passage for discussion and reflection is the post-Easter story of Jesus' disciples and the great draft of fishes (John 21:1–19). Frustration, failure, and hopelessness are not the final word for them. After a fruitless night of labor, trusting in Jesus' word of promise led to an overflowing gift from God. And . . . the once disheartened disciples have a new sense of direction, "Feed my sheep." The narrative development of the text suggests a way to deal with loss:

- Face suffering, don't deny it.
- Rely on God; don't try to handle it alone.
- Having been comforted, console others. (2 Cor. 1:4)

Discussion

1. The book lists five ways we experience change in our "golden years." Review these five points (60–62) and be prepared to discuss which one of the five has been most difficult for you. Which one have you adopted to most easily?

2. The book suggests that old age is a time of diminished life, a time when our lives contract rather than expand. Can you identify ways in which you have learned to cope with these changes? Are there instances where life has expanded in a positive way?

3. The book makes a distinction between three types of remembering (63–65). The third type, a recounting of the past so that meanings of important human relationships come back to life, is a positive reliving. Share about ways in which you have engaged in this positive reliving. Have any of the "treasure chests of meaning" in chapter 5 (41–47) been useful in this recounting?

Chapter 8 Meaning And Death

In this chapter, the book uses the David and Goliath story to introduce death as the "giant" that challenges meaning because it is "the end of everything." The author than introduces and dismisses several attempts to deal with death's ultimate threat:

- Science attempts to conquer death by extending the length of our days. Admittedly, science has made encouraging strides, more than doubling life spans over the past century through advances in both treatments and medical procedures. However, longer life has not opened a path to immortality. This is not a biblical view.

- Admittedly, the Bible does use the term "soul," but in most cases it is a synonym for the "whole person." The New Testament view is that at death, the whole person dies (physical body) and rests in Christ until the resurrection of the renewed person (a spiritual body). See 1 Cor. 15:42–44, not Romans 15 as stated incorrectly on page 78.

- After his death on the cross, Jesus was raised by God to new life, and by our baptism into the risen Christ we share in his resurrection. For we who are believers, while the whole person dies, death finally has no power over us (Rom. 6:3–11).

Part 3 A Christian Approach to Meaning

Chapter 9 God's Plan for Us

Prior to the start of class, it may be a useful exercise to request everyone in the group to write a few sentences on the

An Adult Ministry Study Guide

subject, "God's plan for us." Don't require signatures. The intent is not to embarrass. You may not wish to collect the sheets; getting the class thinking is the primary purpose of the exercise. But whether you read the responses or not, do expect a broad range of ideas in an increasingly secular America.

- Expect a blank sheet of paper or two. God's plan is not a subject most Lutherans think about very often, so mild confusion or even bewilderment can be expected.

- If a young person or two are in the group, sociologist Christian Smith would warn us to expect something vague and vapid, such as, "God exists, and he wants us to be nice to each other, and to be happy and successful." Many of today's youth (and more than a few adults) have been "catechized by the culture," despite having endured a year or two of Lutheran instruction.

- At the other end of the spectrum, you may find a Rick Warren (in disguise, of course) who believes that "God planned every day of our lives to support his shaping purpose" (Book summary, p. 84). For such a person, everything that happens, the good and the bad, is part of God's plan for us. Push that far enough, and you will find folks who believe that the car that struck the child, the flood that washed the house downstream, and the infection that became an epidemic were all "God's will." At funerals expect to hear similar attempts to simplify the complex.

- Or, ask about God's plan and you may find some version of the theory that the good are rewarded and the evil punished. That version does not pass either the reality test or the Biblical test. Fact is, the good do suffer and wicked people do flourish. Fact is, Jesus healed

Finding Meaning in an Uncertain World

the sick, fed the hungry, and forgave the sinful. Even the biblical Job did not believe that his sin caused his world to cave in around him.

So . . . what are we to believe about God's plan for us?

Lutherans do believe that God created us for a purpose, "and that God's purpose gives meaning to our lives and defines what we should or should not do or be" (Book's summation of the main thrust of Rick Warren's The Purpose-Driven Life).

First, the Bible teaches that we humans were made to be the image of God in the world, granted dignity, and made responsible to God for all other creatures. Second, the Bible tells us that, though special, we human beings are mortal. Third, though moral and undeserving, we are loved by God now and forever.

"The love of God accounts for the reason God made us. The same love assures God's

> presence with us, even in our worst times. And the love that created us and sustains us does not disappear at death; it creates us anew."[7]

Discussion

1. Death is one battle we won't win, but the victory has already been won for us. What does this statement mean to you? What comfort does it give?

2. The Greek philosopher Plato has maintained that a part of us—the soul—stands over against the mortal part of us—the body—and that therefore a part of us is immortal and continues to live when the body

---

7. *Making Sense out of Sorrow: A Journey of Faith*, Foster McCurley and Alan Weitzman (Trinity Press International, 1995), p. 76.

An Adult Ministry Study Guide

dies. The Christian faith, on the other hand, gives full weight to death ("no part of us survives death") but it also believes in the resurrection ("as Christ was raised from the dead, we too will be raised—changed, but whole beings"). 1 Corinthians 15: 35–57. What is comforting and what is disturbing about both views?

3. How does our society avoid the reality of death? Does our society prepare us for death? How and how not? Does the church prepare us for death? How and how not?[8]

Chapter 10 God's Gift of Meaning in an Uncertain World

It may be helpful to conclude the search for meaning with a strong affirmation. The search for meaning is not a journey we take alone. God is with us on this pilgrimage. Despite the sin that persists in the lives of the redeemed, we remain God's people, and this reality is our chief source of meaning and purpose. See 1 Peter 2:9–10

"God encounters us as we are on the road, in the midst of the journey. God meets us as we go about the ordinary or extraordinary tasks of our lives: seeking a mate, looking for a job, fleeing from danger, seeking escape from a difficult situation or relationship, searching for identity—all these might describe what Jacob was doing when he was encountered by God."[9]

---

8. Examining the liturgy for Ash Wednesday, with its imposition of ashes, may be instructive ("Remember that you are dust, and to dust you shall return.")

9. Frank R. VanDevelder, *The Biblical Journey of Faith* (Fortress Press, 1988), p. 32.

Finding Meaning in an Uncertain World

The book employs the threefold affirmation of God as Creator, Redeemer, and Sanctifier to suggest the many ways that God continues to encounter us on the road, "in the midst of the journey."

As Creator, God is not simply a "past tense" deity, part of our own and the world's beginnings, but God continues to create and sustain in innumerable ways. Some who believe in God envision a sort of "watchmaker God," one who set the universe spinning and wandered off to engage a more interesting project. No! As a teacher of mine regularly reminded my seminary class, "If God ever ceased to create, the world as we know it would disappear into nothingness."

As Redeemer, God did not abandon us and our fellow creatures to our rebellion and sin. "While we were still sinners, Christ died for us." But more than that. While baptism washes us clean and links us to the death and resurrection of Christ forever, the truth is that we constantly lose sight of God's will for our lives and fall back again into sin. A "past tense" deity might abandon us to our own devices, but God continues to search us out and through the Holy Spirit moves us to seek forgiveness and pardon.

As Sanctifier, God is a healing power in our lives, affirming and renewing us, strengthening our faith in the midst of doubt, giving us courage for the daily struggles. "The Holy Spirit as the power of God brings hope and renewal" (89).

Discussion

The book suggest three "landmarks"—significant guides on the journey toward meaning.

1. The book suggests that we find meaning in life "by dying to ourselves." What does that mean to you? Give a positive example. Are there negative examples or

An Adult Ministry Study Guide

misunderstandings of dying to the self?

2. The book suggests that we find meaning in life "by serving others." What does that mean to you? What positive examples occur to you? Are there negative examples or misunderstandings of what it means to serve others?

3. The book suggests that we find meaning in life by "anchoring our lives in the life of Christ." Once again, cite positive examples that may occur to you? As well, are there possible misunderstandings that occur to you?

This study guide is dedicated to my friend and co-author LeRoy H. Aden, in thankful remembrance of our joint teaching endeavors and family friendships as faculty colleagues at Lutheran Theological Seminary, Philadelphia during the final quarter of the 20th century.

Robert G. Hughes